A Longman Cultural Edition

KING LEAR

Edited by

Claire McEachern

University of California, Los Angeles

PEARSON
Longman

New York San Francisco Boston
London Toronto Sydney Tokyo Singapore Madrid
Mexico City Munich Paris Cape Town Hong Kong Montreal

Vice President and Editor-in-Chief: Joseph P. Terry
Development Editor: Barbara Santoro
Executive Marketing Manager: Ann Stypuloski
Production Coordinator: Shafiena Ghani
Project Coordination, Text Design, and Electronic Page Makeup: Dianne Hall
Cover Designer/Manager: John Callahan
Cover Illustration: Sir John Gilbert, *Cordelia in the Court of King Lear,*
  courtesy of Getty Images, Inc.
Manufacturing Buyer: Roy L. Pickering
Printer and Binder: R R Donnelley and Sons Company / Harrisonburg
Cover Printer: Coral Graphics Services, Inc.

Cover Illustration: *Cordelia in the Court of King Lear,* 1873 by Sir John Gilbert.
Courtesy of Getty Images, Inc.

Library of Congress Cataloging-in-Publication Data

Shakespeare, William, 1564–1616.
    [King Lear]
    King Lear / edited by Claire McEachern.
        p. cm. — (A Longman cultural edition)
    Includes bibliographical references (p. 261–264)
    ISBN 0-321-10722-5 (softcover)
        1. Lear, King (Legendary character)—Drama. 2. Inheritance and succession—
Drama. 3. Fathers and daughters—Drama. 4. Kings and rulers—Drama. 5. Aging
parents—Drama. 6. Britons—Drama. I. McEachern, Claire Elizabeth, 1963–
II. Title. III. Series.

PR2819.A2M36 2005
822.3'3—dc22
                                                                    2004053363

Please visit our website at http://www.ablongman.com

ISBN: 0-321-10722-5

    5 6 7 8 9 10—DOH—07 06

Contents

"Good" and "Evil"   200

Early Readings and Rewritings   220

List of Illustrations

About Longman Cultural Editions

Reading always seems to vibrate with the transformation of the day—now, yesterday, and centuries ago, when the presses first put printed language into wide circulation. Correspondingly, literary culture has always been a matter of change: of new practices confronting established traditions; of texts transforming under the pressure of new techniques of reading and new perspectives of understanding; of canons shifting and expanding; of informing traditions getting reviewed and renewed, recast and reformed by emerging cultural interests and concerns; of culture, too, as a variable "text"—a reading. Inspired by the innovative *Longman Anthology of British Literature,* Longman Cultural Editions respond creatively to the changes, past and recent, by presenting key texts in contexts that illuminate the lively intersections of literature, tradition, and culture. A principal work is made more interesting by materials that place it in relation to its past, present, and future, enabling us to see how it may be reworking traditional debates and practices, how it appears amid the conversations and controversies of its own historical moment, how it gains new significances in subsequent eras of reading and reaction. Readers new to the work will discover attractive paths for exploration, while those more experienced will encounter fresh perspectives and provocative juxtapositions.

Longman Cultural Editions serve not only several kinds of readers but also (appropriately) their several contexts, from various courses of study to independent adventure. Handsomely produced and affordably priced, our volumes offer appealing companions to *The Longman Anthology of British Literature,* in some cases enriching and expanding units originally developed for the *Anthology*, and in other cases presenting this wealth for the first time. The logic and composition of the contexts vary across the series. The constants are the complete text of an important literary work, reliably edited, headed by an inviting introduction, and supplemented by helpful annotation; a table of dates to track its composition, publication, and public reception in relation to biographical, cultural, and historical events; and a guide for further inquiry and study. With these common measures and uncommon assets, Longman Cultural Editions encourage your literary pleasures with resources for lively reflection and adventurous inquiry.

Susan J. Wolfson
General Editor
Professor of English
Princeton University

About This Edition

To put *King Lear* in its place and time requires an even greater measure of "impertinence" (to borrow nineteenth-century critic William Hazlitt's term) than for most of Shakespeare's plays. This play, so cosmic in its desolation, resists attempts at historical specificity. Shakespeare sets the action in a mythical British past and embeds within it visions of an apocalyptic future. The geography of the play's Britain is hallucinatory, and the events and persons represented seem at once too near (families in crisis) and too far (old kingdoms at war) from our own experience. No other of Shakespeare's works dedicates itself so thoroughly to dismantling, as so much mere finery, the apparatus of social and political custom in order to focus on the "poor, bared, fork'd animal" that is a human being. Even for readers inclined to regard an essential human identity as a cultural fiction, the phrasing of human actions in terms of nearly animal loyalties and antipathies in *King Lear* can make the attempt to summon early modern historical and cultural contexts seem an awkward rationalization, curiously beside the point.

Nonetheless, an encounter with these contexts can give us a framework for the play's most troubling questions. *King Lear* is a play haunted by enigmas. Why does Cordelia refuse to flatter her father? Why does her reply anger him so much? Why does he choose to divide his kingdom? Why does Gloucester believe that his legitimate son (not even his bastard) would plot against him, and why does this same son believe that his father believes this? Why, later on, doesn't "legitimate" Edgar reveal his disguised identity as "Poor Tom" to his blinded father? Why, and when, does King Lear go mad? The questions go on, and the elusive answers have generated rich interpretations and debates. In assembling a selection of sources, analogues, and other resonant texts, I have not sought to tame these enigmas; nor do I mean to insist on the play's exclusive early modern location. The questions of and about *King Lear* have remained pressing ones precisely because our own moment, some four hundred years later, shares so much with Shakespeare's. The goal of this edition is to clarify the questions that we want to ask of this play and that it asks of us.

The contextual materials in this edition of *King Lear* approach this mutual interrogation by framing issues that can seem at once too familiar (and thus be taken for granted) and at the same time impossibly remote. The issues are principally thematic: the representation of the social world, the character types, and the ethical climate of the play. A sampling of Shakespeare's narrative sources sheds light on his construction of both plot and character. The next section presents materials on the early modern state, both theoretical (definitions of kingship) and local (James I's arguments for the identification of king and father and island geography). Then follows a set of texts that help define the early modern household: the relations between parents and children, masters and servants, kings and fools; the nature of filial love; the role of property in affect and loyalty. *King Lear* is notorious for its portrait of ethical and metaphysical complexity. The section on "good" and "evil" presents the various models of human nature and divine presence that were available to Shakespeare. All these materials have been selected from early modern editions, with glosses to assist understanding. I have kept original spellings in the documents of the "contexts" sections, with the exception of i/j and u/v, which have been modernized.

It can be a revelation to readers accustomed to Shakespeare's monumental status in our own culture that his plays draw on texts that are not only multiple but also mutually contradictory. *King Lear* is perhaps the most complicated of his plays in this respect. This edition is fortunate to be able to offer the reader a text, glosses, and collation prepared by David Bevington—"collation" because King Lear has come down to us in two principal versions, a "quarto" publication and a later "folio" publication, with some differences so significant that a few editors have designated two distinct plays. The contextual unit on "The Texts of *King Lear*" sketches some of the principal decisions made in producing a text.

Literature is produced in communities bounded by time and place, not only their original communities (in this case, that of the early seventeenth century) but also the subsequent ones in which it is read and (in this instance) performed. The selection of responses gathered in "Early Readings and Rewritings" points to some of the ways in which the meanings of *King Lear* have been reinvented over time, at least through the nineteenth century. For readers who wish to explore further, the "Further Reading" section lists some of the most influential approaches to the play. Readers in search of an extensive performance history of this play will not find it in this edition, but the "Further Reading" guide lists places where such history can be found.

My organization of this edition of *King Lear* has accumulated debts that I am happy to acknowledge. R. A. Foakes has been, as ever, a generous and skeptical guide, and Debora Shuger was insistent on the presence of forgiveness in the Contexts section. The Longman team has been a great source of assistance, especially Susan Wolfson, Anne Brunell, Barbara Santoro, Dianne Hall, and Chrysta Meadowbrooke. The Huntington Library provided both material help and generous permissions in the securing of illustrations; the Tate Gallery kindly provided the image on p. 133 and permission to use it; and we were granted permission to use the cover image courtesy of Getty Images, Inc.

Claire McEachern
University of California, Los Angeles

Introduction

Literature, Sir Philip Sidney wrote, is often expected to repair the imperfections of real life, to offer a "golden world" in solace for the inadequacies of our own lived experience. *King Lear*, however, is a play that asks us to confront and bear faults that cannot be undone. Shakespeare opens the play with an adulterer's jocular "blushing" acknowledgment of a bastard son. This same son goes on to provoke much of the play's suffering, implicitly rooted in the adulterous lapse of his father, Gloucester, too late to recall or repair. And whereas this father's trouble may be that he has one son too many, King Lear's stems from the fact that he has no son at all, only three daughters. This predicament is not so expressly owed to paternal error (merely stubborn fate), but it requires that Lear decide how to best bestow his island kingdom upon three daughters, all of whom have inherited his fatal willfulness. Lear's method of division unleashes a chain of catastrophes of which his own rage is undoubtedly the greatest catalyst. It is a rage whose objects—obstinate children, the loss of authority, and mortality itself—are as immovable as they are legitimately provoking. Fathers and we their audience are forced to come to terms (or admit that we cannot do so) with things that cannot be helped: the flaws of human character, the deforming effects of political power on human bonds, and perhaps most important, the irreparable losses exacted on us by time.

Our sense of being overtaken by a momentum we cannot control (moving us toward death, among other things) is built into the very opening lines of the play, in which so much seems determined before the fact of our arrival, conveying the sense of our arriving, epic-like, in the middle of things long in train. The division of a kingdom is at issue—surely an unorthodox and momentous event, even for those of us with only a passing knowledge of kingdoms. Yet two lords discuss it as something that is both a foregone and an unremarkable conclusion. It is nonetheless one also recently modified. At one point Albany, husband of Lear's eldest daughter, had been "more affected" (that is, favored) by the king, "but now" he is valued equally with Cornwall, his counterpart at the other end of the kingdom: "it appears not which of the dukes he values most" (1.1.1–5)

The moments that follow increase our sense that the ground is shifting underfoot. In the midst of what by any measure ought to be a fairly rhetorical distribution of power and a ritual performance of daughterly love, the strange cavils of Cordelia, the king's youngest child, provoke yet another change of course "upon the gad" (1.2.26). Rather than a relatively stable tripartite division, the kingdom will be divided into only two "equal moieties," a distribution promising "likely wars . . . twixt the Dukes" (2.1.10–11). To throw good rule after bad mathematics, Lear resigns his "power, / Preeminence and all the large effects / That troop with majesty," retaining only "The name and all th'addition to a king"—whatever *that* means (1.1.127–133). The change can be explained only (if at all) by reference to what Kent diagnoses as "hideous rashness" (1.1.149), an emotion that overruns not just statecraft but the truth of love.

With the action barely afoot, then, we find ourselves sorting through the debris of an explosion whose fuse appears to have been lit long ago. It is no consolation to know, at least according to his daughter Goneril, that Lear's behavior exhibits "the imperfections of long-ingraffed condition" (1.1.294–295). By definition, volatility is not a quality to which one becomes accustomed. To compound the sense of our being overtaken by events whose course cannot be diverted, Shakespeare creates characters whose infirmities are underscored by association. He gives us not one but two fathers unwise in the loves of their offspring and intemperate in their judgments and actions. Both Lear's and Gloucester's stories have precedents in different sources, but it is Shakespeare's combination into one tale that creates the sense of paternal error not as idiosyncratic but as systemic, something that cannot be argued with. Both Lear and Gloucester are hasty, paranoid, and irresponsible, qualities that "the infirmity of . . . age" (1.1.291) does not apparently improve.

The pressure these types exert on our imagination is increased by the way they seem to shed the anchoring specificities of time and place, so that fatherly tyranny seems not just epidemic to the society depicted—an aristocratic one, in a quasi-mythical British past—but universally recognizable and common to our own. The play ricochets between the poles of folklore and family romance, once upon a time and right now, so that while we might wish to contain or frame its events as the property of larger-than-life mythic personages (ancient British royalty with large inheritances), we inevitably find ourselves explaining it in terms closer to home: the complicated bonds between parents and children, made more so by the transfer of powers between generations; sibling rivalry; material covetousness. In the folklore plot, we identify with the good daughter. In the more perennial story, children of an aging and demanding parent might feel (to their own chagrin) some fleeting sympathy with Goneril and Regan, or feel at least what it is to hear, again and again, that Cordelia was her father's favorite. Shakespeare dares to say it: a parent can like one child better than his others, and children know this and feel the pain and resentment of the preference.

In addition to making us feel like we must run to keep pace with events long in motion, *King Lear* also requires of us a flexibility of sympathy despite the strain of grappling with an overpowering and flammable personality type. When the play opens, the conventions of genre and culture that urge our identification with title characters and authority figures are challenged by the sheer outrageousness of Lear's treatment of Cordelia and Kent. Lear's subsequent tantrum at Goneril's house further strains our sympathy. Gloucester's ready willingness to believe, second-hand, the tale of Edgar's resentment suggests a home truth in the "oppression of aged tyranny" (1.2.48). Both fathers display a shocking, almost willed ignorance of love and identity, an ignorance that is not just exasperating but also dangerous to those around them.

Yet even as these two fathers are insufferable, they in turn are made to suffer, and this exerts a steady, subtle pull on our regard for them. With Lear, it is not only the loyalty of Kent and the fool, or his connections to them and the "naked wretch" Poor Tom, that urge our own care for Lear but also the pain and shame with which he acknowledges his mistakes, nearly as soon as he commits them: "O Lear, Lear, Lear! / Beat at this gate that let thy folly in / And thy dear judgment out!" (1.4.254–256). His is an unstinting, if wincing, self-knowledge that belies the claim that "he hath ever but slenderly known himself" (1.1.291–292). Its dignity and bravery make more terrible his incipient madness. His plea for the compassion due to old age as something not only necessary but also inevitable, however socially discomfiting, points out that his elder daughters' condescension—"being weak, seem so" (2.4.198)—apparently presupposes themselves exempt from the condition. (Only those whose own death is comfortably distant can commend a gentle voyage into that good night.) One need not be an apologist for power structures to see in Lear "A father, and a gracious agèd man / Whose reverence even the head-lugged bear would lick" (4.2.42–43); common decency and a modicum of empathy would suffice.

If Gloucester is less prescient, the savagery of his blinding (one of the most horrifying events on the Shakespearean stage) surely overwhelms whatever errors he commits. It is a shocking hyperbole of our aggravation with him, which stops us short in the desire for his comeuppance. Both of these men are more sinned against than sinning, and they never claimed themselves to be sinless in the first place—which is more than we can say for their children (even Cordelia's initial righteousness, her verbal prudery, can grate). The greatest factor in our eventual common cause with these two sinners is that any firm alliance with those who would punish them is unthinkable. (Part of the play's severity is that it offers us no intermediate position.) Whatever these fathers' faults, they do not deserve what happens to them.

If anything links the play's villains and heroes, it is the suspect conviction that faults should or can be redressed. *King Lear* makes us examine tidy notions of justice, the idea that actions warrant payment, that people *deserve* something, that goodness is rewarded and evil punished, that good and evil are purely distinct. What does such deserving mean, and how do people calculate the balance between acts and their rewards? Who, indeed, are we to do so? The play's "good" characters are most outspoken on this subject, usually in reference to a supernatural apportioning agent, albeit a reticent one. Albany: "If that the heavens do not their visible spirits / Send quickly down to tame these vile offences, / It will come,

Humanity must perforce prey on itself, / Like monsters of the deep" (4.2.47–51). Lear: "O heavens! / If you do love old men, . . . / Make it your cause. Send down, and take my part!"(2.4.186–189). The most sanctimonious of these appeals to a partisan heaven is Edgar: "The gods are just, and of our pleasant vices / Make instruments to plague us. / The dark and vicious place where thee he got / Cost him his eyes" (5.3.170–173).

If *King Lear* whets our appetite for just rewards, the play also repeatedly frustrates it. The ethical and dramatic satisfactions promised by Edgar's final charade of an unknown knight enacting divine vengeance on Edmund via trial by combat are terribly fleeting. They prove as irrelevant to the final tally as his earlier "trifling" with his blinded father does to the end of curing Gloucester of despair. (Might it not have been kinder to grant Gloucester's desire "to see thee in my touch" (4.1.23)?) Edgar's play-acting in effect ultimately hinders poetic justice, occupying time that could have saved Cordelia. The good are not rewarded in *King Lear*, or not nearly enough, and the punishment of the bad is a sorry consolation for the suffering they inflict. Moreover, the good can behave badly, and the bad have some good points, if not good causes.

Shakespeare gives a similar treatment to other human institutions. The play solicits skepticism toward power structures: power corrupts, absolute power corrupts absolutely; property is theft; and so on. But what isn't so familiar is that the greatest demystifier of "the great image of authority" is no subaltern rebel but King Lear himself: "Thou rascal beadle, hold thy bloody hand! / Why dost thou lash that whore? Strip thine own back; / Thou hotly lusts to use her in that kind / For which thou whipp'st her" (4.6.155–158).

Shakespeare fans a desire to escape, reform, or "throw off" as "lendings" the fictions that both organize community and breed its tensions: law, property, marriage, hierarchy. But the play simultaneously inculcates a tugging knowledge that there are no alternatives to these flawed systems. Lear's refuge on the stormy heath seems the polar opposite of the court world and his family struggles; yet he finds himself in the company of others and stages a trial, reinventing the social form even in the wilderness. Gloucester gives his purse to the beggar, believing he relinquishes his claim to privilege: "So distribution should undo excess / And each man have enough" (4.1.68–69). The irony is that the money goes to the person who would have rightfully inherited it, and no such revolution takes place. His bastard son Edmund claims a rebel's exemption from "the plague of custom" (1.2.3), but he really wants in, not out: "Legitimate Edgar, I must have your land" (1.2.16). Legitimate children, for all their privileges and social acceptance, may be as horrible as those conceived in the "lusty stealth of nature" (1.2.11).

Despite the great suffering these characters both inflict and endure, at the end of the play Shakespeare makes it clear that the larger social systems that sustain suffering are still in place. It is either Albany or Edgar (depending on your text) who speaks the conventional farewell of two couplets. The particular speaker seems inconsequential in that it doesn't really matter who presides over the resumption of social rhythms.

However, human goodness is not absent from the play. Lear does love Cordelia, and she him, and they both die knowing this. For this we are grateful. The "milk-livered" (4.2.51) Albany's uncharacteristically sardonic knowledge of Goneril—"You are not worth the dust which the rude wind / Blows in your face" (4.2.31–32)—is gratifying. Kent's loyalty to his perverse lord encourages our affection, as does the fool's refusal to go lightly on his master (a king who can suffer a fool lightly is still a king). Other balms include the tenderness and ferocity of Cornwall's servants (in the quarto), the gentility of Gloucester's tenant, and the other unnamed souls quietly insistent in their performance of a compassion that goes beyond duty. Above all, we feel Lear's goodness and greatness. What most torments him is not the knowledge that he is abused but that he has abused: a "sovereign shame so elbows him" (4.3.43). Contrition does not begin to describe it. Finally and fiercely, even at the end of a journey that would have defeated most of us midway, he has some fight left in him.

But none of these virtues is enough—organized enough, timely enough, canny enough, lucky enough—to prevent disaster. These are not virtue's talents.

The poet John Keats thought *King Lear* to be Shakespeare's greatest work, and he is not alone. The play has qualified for that accolade not only by the gravity of its genre (while there is such a thing as great comedy, comedies rarely achieve "greatness") but also from the uncompromising maturity of its accomplishments. A long-standing narrative of Shakespeare's career tends to describe a progress of comedy succeeded by history, tragedy, and romance, with a caesura of mood and form in 1603, with the transition from Elizabeth I to James I. But Shakespeare wrote tragedy from the beginning of his theater career in the 1590s. Like his early comedies, Shakespeare's early tragedies bear marks of classical influence, in particular in their dependence on the formal model of Seneca's revenge plays (a model of justice that it would take *Hamlet* to interrogate). Roughly fifteen years and an astonishing twenty-eight plays after his first play arrived, *King Lear*—a play that exposes as bankrupt the calibrations of justice—appears. If the tragedy is not the culmination of Shakespeare's accomplishment (he kept writing, after all), many earlier roads do lead to *Lear*. *Hamlet* (c. 1599–1601) explores tensions between generations and a disgust at sexuality; *Othello* (c. 1603–1604) is driven by another hero who fails to know love. The progenitors are not just these other tragedies (and we should note that early modern categories of genre were more fluid than our own). Intergenerational tension is the springboard of comedy, and the ironies of political change, as well as the intersection of families and politics, are the province of the English history play.

Yet for all these precedents, *King Lear* is extraordinary. The language is intense and extravagant, even for Shakespearean tragedy; its range goes from the tender ("Come, let's away to prison . . ." (5.3.8) to the excruciating ("I am bound / Upon a wheel of fire that mine own tears / Do scald like molten lead"(4.7.47–49)). There is a dark turn to Shakespeare's writing that comes at the dawn of the new century. *King Lear* has much in common with "problem plays" such as *Measure of Measure* or *Troilus and Cressida*, a sense of society and sexes as diseased. *All's Well That Ends Well* supplies a harbinger of the mutually predatory tie between the generations.

The bitterness of such a turn coincides with and contrasts with events in Shakespeare's professional trajectory. In the 1590s he arrived and thrived on a competitive London theater scene in which the traditional vagabond status of players was receding before an increasingly professional trade and theatrical practice. Actor-sharers had permanent performance spaces rather than inn yards, established and increasing repertoires, and aristocratic patrons to license their activities and protect them from city authorities less enthusiastic about the presence of theater. By 1594, Shakespeare was a member of the Lord Chamberlain's Men, a company that would eventually become one of two with a monopoly to perform. By 1599, the Lord Chamberlain's Men were sharers in the Globe Theater property, and with the accession of King James I to the English throne in 1603, Shakespeare's company became the King's Men (and, as of 1608, lessors of a second indoor venue at Black-friar's Hall). The first recorded performance of *King Lear* occurred at court on December 26, 1606, during the holiday festivities. While the institutional identity of this theater is notoriously complex—illegal yet licensed by the monarch himself—it is a measure of either Shakespeare's continuing aesthetic audacity or his professional confidence that his most scathing indictment of human institutions coincided with the apex of his professional and poetic power.

Table of Dates

1558   Elizabeth I, a Protestant, ascends to the English throne after the death of her Catholic half-sister Mary Tudor.

1561   A translation of Jean Calvin's *Institutes of the Christian Religion* is published.

1562   *Gorboduc* (a play on the division of Britain and the perils of succession) is published.

1563   *Second Tome of Homilies* is printed.

1564   Shakespeare is born at Stratford-on-Avon.

1574   John Higgins's *Mirror for Magistrates* is published.

1577   Raphael Holinshed's *Chronicles* is published (including William Harrison's *An Historical Description of the Iland of Britaine*).

1581   Charles Merbury's *A Brief Discourse of Royal Monarchie, as of the Best Common Weale* is published.

1582   Shakespeare marries Anne Hathaway in December.

1583   In May, Shakespeare's daughter Susanna is born in Stratford–on-Avon (baptized on May 26).

        Sir Thomas Smith's *De Republica Anglorum* is published.

1585   Shakespeare's twins Hamnet and Judith are born (baptized on February 2).

1589   Jane Anger's *Her Protection for Women* is published.

1590   Sir Philip Sidney's *The Countesse of Pembrokes Arcadia* is published.

The second edition of Sackville and Norton's *Gorbuduc* is published.

1592   Shakespeare (the "upstart crow") receives his first mention in print as an actor and playwright in a pamphlet by rival playwright and author Robert Greene.

1593   The preface and first three books of Richard Hooker's *Of the Laws of Ecclesiastical Polity* are published.

1594   The position of Shakespeare as a member in Lord Chamberlain's acting company is first recorded in this year.

For the first time, a play by Shakespeare (*Titus Andronicus*) is published.

The first records of a performance of a play called "Kinge Leare" (April 6) by the Queen's and Sussex's men appear in this year.

1598   For the first time, Shakespeare's plays are published with his name on the title page: *Loves Labor's Lost* (Q1); *Richard II* (Q2); *Richard III* (Q3). ("Q" refers to a quarto-formatted book.)

King James VI of Scotland publishes *The True Law of Free Monarchies*.

1599   The Globe playhouse opens in London; Shakespeare becomes a shareholder. The principal clown in Lord Chamberlain's troupe, Will Kempe, leaves and is replaced by Robert Armin (who will play Lear's fool).

1600   Robert Armin publishes *Foole upon Foole*.

1603   Queen Elizabeth I dies, and James VI of Scotland ascends to the English throne. James becomes the patron of Shakespeare's acting company, now named the King's Men.

Samuel Harsnett's *A Declaration of Egregious Popish Impostures* is published.

John Florio's translation of Michel de Montaigne's *Essays* is published in England.

1604   James gives his first speech to Parliament, including a proposal to unite England and Scotland under British rule.

1605   An anonymous play, *King Leir*, is published.

A series of lunar and solar eclipses is visible in England.

The Gunpowder Plot of some Catholic rebels to blow up Parliament and kill the king fails (November 5).

1606   The first recorded performance of *King Lear* occurs at Whitehall Palace before James I (December 26).

1607   *King Lear* is entered in the Stationer's Register (November 26).

1608   A quarto version of *King Lear* is published.

A syndicate of King's Men actors leases an indoor theater, Blackfriar's Hall.

1616   Shakespeare dies in Stratford-on-Avon (April 23).

1619   An (unauthorized?) publication of the second quarto of *King Lear* (dated 1608) appears.

1623   The first Folio edition of Shakespeare's collected works is published. (A folio, with larger pages than a quarto, is a handsome, expensive production.)

King Lear

by William Shakespeare

King Lear

ভ্ূ২

Dramatis Personae

KING LEAR
GONERIL,
REGAN,   } *Lear's daughters*
CORDELIA,
DUKE OF ALBANY, *Goneril's husband*
DUKE OF CORNWALL, *Regan's husband*
KING OF FRANCE, *Cordelia's suitor and husband*
DUKE OF BURGUNDY, *suitor to Cordelia*

EARL OF KENT, *later disguised as Caius*
EARL OF GLOUCESTER
EDGAR, *Gloucester's son and heir, later disguised as poor Tom*
EDMUND, *Gloucester's bastard son*

OSWALD, *Goneril's steward*
A KNIGHT *serving King Lear*
Lear's FOOL
CURAN, *in Gloucester's household*
GENTLEMEN
Three SERVANTS
OLD MAN, *a tenant of Gloucester*
Three MESSENGERS
A GENTLEMAN *attending Cordelia as a Doctor*
Two CAPTAINS
HERALD

Knights, Gentlemen, Attendants, Servants, Officers,
   Soldiers, Trumpeters

SCENE: *Britain*

ACT 1
SCENE 1

Location: King Lear's palace

Enter Kent, Gloucester, and Edmund

KENT   I thought the King had more affected° the Duke of
Albany° than Cornwall.

GLOUCESTER   It did always seem so to us; but now in the division of the kingdom it appears not which of the dukes he
values most, for equalities are so weighed that curiosity in   5
neither can make choice of either's moiety.°

KENT   Is not this your son, my lord?

GLOUCESTER   His breeding,° sir, hath been at my charge.° I have so
often blushed to acknowledge him that now I am brazed° to't.

KENT   I cannot conceive° you.   10

GLOUCESTER   Sir, this young fellow's mother could; whereupon
she grew round-wombed and had indeed, sir, a son for her
cradle ere she had a husband for her bed. Do you smell a
fault?°

KENT   I cannot wish the fault undone, the issue° of it being so   15
proper.°

GLOUCESTER   But I have a son, sir, by order of law,° some year°
elder than this, who yet is no dearer in my account.° Though
this knave° came something° saucily to the world before he
was sent for, yet was his mother fair, there was good sport at   20
his making, and the whoreson° must be acknowledged.—Do
you know this noble gentleman, Edmund?

EDMUND   No, my lord.

GLOUCESTER   My lord of Kent. Remember him hereafter as my
honorable friend.   25

---

1 affected favored   **2 Albany** Scotland   **5–6 equalities . . . moiety** the shares balance so equally that close scrutiny cannot find advantage in either's portion
8 breeding raising, care | **charge** expense   **9 brazed** hardened   **10 conceive** un-
derstand (but Gloucester puns in the sense of "become pregnant")   **14 fault** (1) sin
(2) loss of scent by the hounds | **issue** (1) result (2) offspring   **16 proper** (1) excel-
lent (2) handsome   **17 by order of law** legitimate | **some year** about a year
18 account estimation   **19 knave** young fellow (not said disapprovingly, though the
word is ironic) | **something** somewhat   **21 whoreson** low fellow; suggesting bas-
tardy, but (like *knave* above) used with affectionate condescension

EDMUND   My services° to Your Lordship.

KENT   I must love you, and sue° to know you better.

EDMUND   Sir, I shall study deserving.°

GLOUCESTER   He hath been out° nine years, and away he shall
again. The King is coming.   30

> *Sennet.° Enter [one bearing a coronet, then]°*
> *King Lear, Cornwall, Albany, Goneril,*
> *Regan, Cordelia, and attendants*

LEAR   Attend° the lords of France and Burgundy, Gloucester.

GLOUCESTER   I shall, my liege.   *Exit*

LEAR   Meantime we° shall express our° darker purpose.°
Give me the map there. [*He takes a map*]
                          Know that we have divided
In three our kingdom; and 'tis our fast° intent   35
To shake all cares and business from our age,
Conferring them on younger strengths while we
Unburdened crawl toward death. Our son of Cornwall,
And you, our no less loving son of Albany,
We have this hour a constant will to publish°   40
Our daughters' several° dowers, that future strife
May be prevented now. The princes, France and Burgundy,
Great rivals in our youngest daughter's love,
Long in our court have made their amorous sojourn
And here are to be answered. Tell me, my daughters—   45
Since now we will divest us both of rule,
Interest of° territory, cares of state—
Which of you shall we say doth love us most,
That we our largest bounty may extend
Where nature doth with merit challenge?° Goneril,   50
Our eldest born, speak first.

---

26 **services** duty   27 **sue** petition, beg   28 **study deserving** strive to be worthy (of
your esteem)   29 **out** abroad, absent   30.1 *sennet* trumpet signal heralding a pro-
cession | **one . . . then** (this direction is from the Quarto; the *coronet* is perhaps
intended for Cordelia or her betrothed; a coronet signifies nobility below the rank
of king)   31 **attend** wait upon, usher ceremoniously   33 **we, our** (the royal plural;
also in lines 37–44, etc.) | **darker purpose** undeclared intention   35 **fast** firm
40 **constant . . . publish** firm resolve to proclaim   41 **several** individual
47 **interest of** right or title to, possession of   50 **where . . . challenge** where both
natural affection and merit claim our bounty as its due

GONERIL

Sir, I love you more than words can wield the matter,
Dearer than eyesight, space, and liberty,°
Beyond what can be valued, rich or rare,
No less than life, with grace, health, beauty, honor; 55
As much as child e'er loved, or father found;°
A love that makes breath poor and speech unable.°
Beyond all manner of so much I love you.

CORDELIA [*aside*]

What shall Cordelia speak? Love and be silent.

LEAR [*indicating on map*]

Of all these bounds, even from this line to this, 60
With shadowy° forests and with champains riched,°
With plenteous rivers and wide-skirted meads,°
We make thee lady. To thine and Albany's issue
Be this perpetual.—What says our second daughter,
Our dearest Regan, wife of Cornwall? Speak. 65

REGAN   I am made of that self mettle° as my sister,
And prize me at her worth.° In my true heart
I find she names my very deed of love;°
Only she comes too short, that° I profess
Myself an enemy to all other joys 70
Which the most precious square of sense possesses,°
And find I am alone felicitate°
In your dear Highness' love.

CORDELIA [*aside*]   Then poor Cordelia!
And yet not so, since I am sure my love's
More ponderous° than my tongue. 75

LEAR   To thee and thine hereditary ever
Remain this ample third of our fair kingdom,
No less in space, validity,° and pleasure°

---

53 **space, and liberty** possession of land, and freedom of action   56 **found** found
himself to be loved   57 **breath . . . unable** utterance impoverished and speech inad-
equate   61 **shadowy** shady | **champains riched** fertile plains   62 **plenteous . . .
meads** abundant rivers bordered with wide meadows   66 **that self mettle** that same
spirited temperament   67 **prize . . . worth** value myself as her equal (in love for
you) (*prize* suggests "price")   68 **names . . . love** describes my love in action
69 **that** in that   71 **which . . . possesses** which the most delicately sensitive part of
my nature can enjoy   72 **felicitate** made happy   75 **ponderous** weighty   78 **validity**
value | **pleasure** pleasing features

Than that conferred on Goneril.—Now, our joy,
Although our last and least,° to whose young love   80
The vines° of France and milk° of Burgundy
Strive to be interessed,° what can you say to draw°
A third more opulent than your sisters'? Speak.
CORDELIA   Nothing, my lord.
LEAR   Nothing?   85
CORDELIA   Nothing.
LEAR   Nothing will come of nothing. Speak again.
CORDELIA   Unhappy that I am, I cannot heave
   My heart into my mouth. I love Your Majesty
   According to my bond,° no more nor less.   90
LEAR   How, how, Cordelia? Mend your speech a little,
   Lest you may mar your fortunes.
CORDELIA   Good my lord,
   You have begot me, bred me, loved me. I
   Return those duties back as are right fit,°
   Obey you, love you, and most honor you.   95
   Why have my sisters husbands if they say
   They love you all?° Haply,° when I shall wed,
   That lord whose hand must take my plight° shall carry
   Half my love with him, half my care and duty.
   Sure I shall never marry like my sisters,   100
   To love my father all.
LEAR   But goes thy heart with this?
CORDELIA   Ay, my good lord.
LEAR   So young, and so untender?
CORDELIA   So young, my lord, and true.
LEAR   Let it be so! Thy truth then be thy dower!   105
   For, by the sacred radiance of the sun,
   The mysteries° of Hecate° and the night,
   By all the operation° of the orbs°
   From whom° we do exist and cease to be,

---

80 **least** youngest   81 **vines** vineyards | **milk** pastures (?)   82 **be interessed** be
affiliated, establish a claim, be admitted as to a privilege | **draw** win   90 **bond**
filial obligation   94 **right fit** proper and fitting   97 **all** exclusively, and with all of
themselves | **haply** perhaps; with luck   98 **plight** pledge in marriage   107 **mysteries**
secret rites | **Hecate** goddess of witchcraft and the moon   108 **operation** influence
| **orbs** planets and stars   109 **from whom** under whose influence

Here I disclaim all my paternal care, 110
Propinquity, and property of blood,°
And as a stranger to my heart and me
Hold thee from this° forever. The barbarous Scythian,°
Or he that makes his generation messes°
To gorge his appetite, shall to my bosom 115
Be as well neighbored,° pitied, and relieved
As thou my sometime° daughter.
KENT   Good my liege—
LEAR   Peace, Kent!
Come not between the dragon and his wrath.
I loved her most, and thought to set my rest° 120
On her kind nursery.° [*To Cordelia*]
                          Hence, and avoid° my sight!—
So be my grave my peace, as° here I give
Her father's heart from her. Call France. Who stirs?°
Call Burgundy.   [*Exit one*]
                          Cornwall and Albany,
With my two daughters' dowers digest° the third. 125
Let pride, which she calls plainness, marry her.°
I do invest you jointly with my power,
Preeminence, and all the large effects°
That troop with° majesty. Ourself° by monthly course,
With reservation° of an hundred knights 130
By you to be sustained, shall our abode
Make with you by due turns. Only we shall retain
The name and all th'addition° to a king.
The sway,° revenue, execution of the rest,
Belovèd sons, be yours, which to confirm, 135

---

111 propinquity . . . blood close kinship, and rights and duties entailed in blood ties **113 this** this time forth | **Scythian** (Scythians were famous in antiquity for savagery) **114 makes . . . messes** makes meals of his children or parents **116 neighbored** helped in a neighborly way **117 sometime** former **120 set my rest** rely wholly (a phrase from a game of cards, meaning "to stake all") **121 nursery** nursing, care | **avoid** get out of **122 so . . . peace, as** as I hope to rest peacefully in my grave **123 who stirs?** jump to it; don't just stand there **125 digest** assimilate, incorporate **126 let . . . her** let pride, which she calls plain speaking, be her dowry and get her a husband **128 effects** outward shows **129 troop with** accompany, serve | **ourself** (the royal "we") **130 with reservation of** reserving to myself the right to be attended by **133 th'addition** the honors and prerogatives **134 sway** sovereign authority

This coronet° part between you.

KENT   Royal Lear,
  Whom I have ever honored as my king,
  Loved as my father, as my master followed,
  As my great patron thought on in my prayers—

LEAR   The bow is bent and drawn. Make from° the shaft.   140

KENT   Let it fall° rather, though the fork° invade
  The region of my heart. Be Kent unmannerly
  When Lear is mad. What wouldst thou do, old man?
  Think'st thou that duty shall have dread to speak
  When power to flattery bows?   145
  To plainness honor's bound°
  When majesty falls to folly. Reserve thy state,°
  And in thy best consideration check°
  This hideous rashness. Answer my life my judgment,°
  Thy youngest daughter does not love thee least,   150
  Nor are those emptyhearted whose low sounds
  Reverb no hollowness.°

LEAR   Kent, on thy life, no more.

KENT   My life I never held but as a pawn
  To wage° against thine enemies, nor fear to lose it,
  Thy safety being motive.°

LEAR   Out of my sight!   155

KENT   See better, Lear, and let me still remain
  The true° blank of thine eye.

LEAR   Now, by Apollo—

KENT   Now, by Apollo, King,
  Thou swear'st thy gods in vain.   160

LEAR   Oh, vassal!° Miscreant!°

                                [Laying his hand on his sword]

136 coronet (perhaps Lear gestures toward this coronet that was to have symbolized Cordelia's dowry and marriage, hands it to his sons-in-law, or actually attempts to divide it)   **140 make from** get out of the way of   **141 fall** strike | **fork** barbed head of an arrow   **146 to . . . bound** loyalty demands frankness   **147 reserve thy state** retain your royal authority   **148 and . . . check** and with wise deliberation restrain   **149 answer . . . judgment** I wager my life on my judgment that   **152 reverb no hollowness** do not reverberate like a hollow drum, insincerely   **153–4 my . . . wage** I never regarded my life other than as a pledge to hazard in warfare   **155 motive** that which prompts me to act   **157 the true . . . eye** the means to enable you to see better (*blank* means "the white center of the target," or "the true direct aim," as in "point-blank," traveling in a straight line)   **161 vassal** wretch | **miscreant** (literally, infidel, heretic; hence, villain, rascal)

ALBANY, CORNWALL   Dear sir, forbear.

KENT   Kill thy physician, and the fee bestow
    Upon the foul disease. Revoke thy gift,
    Or whilst I can vent clamor from my throat   165
    I'll tell thee thou dost evil.

LEAR   Hear me, recreant,° on thine allegiance hear me!
    That° thou hast sought to make us break our vows,
    Which we durst never yet, and with strained° pride
    To come betwixt our sentence and our power,°   170
    Which nor our nature nor our place° can bear,
    Our potency made good,° take thy reward.
    Five days we do allot thee for provision
    To shield thee from disasters of the world,
    And on the sixth to turn thy hated back   175
    Upon our kingdom. If on the tenth day following
    Thy banished trunk° be found in our dominions,
    The moment is thy death. Away! By Jupiter,
    This shall not be revoked.

KENT   Fare thee well, King. Sith° thus thou wilt appear,   180
    Freedom lives hence and banishment is here.
    [*To Cordelia*] The gods to their dear shelter take thee, maid,
    That justly think'st and hast most rightly said!
    [*To Regan and Goneril*] And your large speeches may your
       deeds approve,°
    That good effects may spring from words of love.   185
    Thus Kent, O princes, bids you all adieu.
    He'll shape his old course° in a country new.   *Exit*

> *Flourish.° Enter Gloucester, with*
> *France and Burgundy; attendants*

GLOUCESTER   Here's France and Burgundy, my noble lord.

LEAR   My lord of Burgundy,
    We first address° toward you, who with this king   190

---

167 recreant traitor   **168 that** in that, since   **169 strained** excessive   **170 to . . .
power** to block my power to command and judge   **171 which . . . place** which
neither my temperament nor my office as king   **172 our . . . good** my power
enacted, demonstrated   **177 trunk** body   **180 sith** since   **184 your . . . approve**
may your deeds confirm your speeches with their vast claims   **187 shape . . . course**
follow his traditional plainspoken ways   **187.1** *flourish* trumpet fanfare used for
the entrance or exit of important persons   **190 address** address myself

Hath rivaled° for our daughter. What in the least°
Will you require in present dower with her
Or cease your quest of love?

BURGUNDY   Most royal Majesty,
I crave no more than hath Your Highness offered,
Nor will you tender° less.

LEAR   Right noble Burgundy,   195
When she was dear to us we did hold her so,°
But now her price is fallen. Sir, there she stands.
If aught within that little-seeming substance,°
Or all of it, with our displeasure pieced,°
And nothing more, may fitly like° Your Grace,   200
She's there, and she is yours.

BURGUNDY   I know no answer.

LEAR   Will you, with those infirmities she owes,°
Unfriended, new-adopted to our hate,
Dowered with our curse and strangered° with our oath,
Take her, or leave her?

BURGUNDY   Pardon me, royal sir.   205
Election makes not up in such conditions.°

LEAR   Then leave her, sir, for by the power that made me,
I tell you° all her wealth. [*To France*] For° you, great King,
I would not from your love make such a stray°
To° match you where I hate; therefore beseech° you   210
T'avert your liking° a more worthier way
Than on a wretch whom Nature is ashamed
Almost t'acknowledge hers.

FRANCE   This is most strange,
That she whom even but now was your best object,
The argument° of your praise, balm of your age,   215
The best, the dearest, should in this trice° of time
Commit a thing so monstrous to° dismantle

---

191 **rivaled** competed | **in the least** at the lowest   195 **tender** offer   196 **so** *dear*, beloved and valued at a high price   198 **little-seeming substance** one who seems substantial but whose substance is, in fact, little, or one who refuses to flatter   199 **pieced** added, joined   200 **like** please   202 **owes** owns   204 **strangered** disowned   206 **election . . . conditions** no choice is possible under such conditions   208 **tell you** (1) inform you of (2) enumerate for you | **for** as for   209 **make such a stray** stray so far   210 **to** as to | **beseech** I beseech   211 **t'avert your liking** to turn your affections   215 **argument** theme   216 **trice** moment   217 **to** as to

So many folds of favor. Sure her offense
Must be of such unnatural degree
That monsters it,° or your forevouched affection   220
Fall into taint,° which to believe of her
Must be a faith that reason without miracle
Should never plant in me.

CORDELIA   I yet beseech Your Majesty—
If for I want° that glib and oily art   225
To speak and purpose not,° since what I well intend
I'll do't before I speak—that you make known
It is no vicious blot, murder, or foulness,°
No unchaste action or dishonored step
That hath deprived me of your grace and favor,   230
But even for want of that for which° I am richer:
A still-soliciting° eye and such a tongue
That I am glad I have not, though not to have it
Hath lost me in your liking.

LEAR   Better thou
Hadst not been born than not t'have pleased me better.   235

FRANCE   Is it but this? A tardiness in nature
Which often leaves the history° unspoke
That it intends to do?—My lord of Burgundy,
What say you to the lady? Love's not love
When it is mingled with regards that stands   240
Aloof from th'entire point.° Will you have her?
She is herself a dowry.

BURGUNDY [to Lear]   Royal King,
Give but that portion which yourself proposed,
And here I take Cordelia by the hand,
Duchess of Burgundy.   245

LEAR   Nothing. I have sworn. I am firm.

BURGUNDY [to Cordelia]
I am sorry, then, you have so lost a father
That you must lose a husband.

CORDELIA   Peace be with Burgundy!

220 monsters it makes it monstrous   220–21 or . . . taint or else the affection for
her you have hitherto affirmed must fall into suspicion   225 for I want because I
lack   226 purpose not not intend to do what I say   228 foulness immorality
231 for which for lack of which   232 still-soliciting ever begging   237 history
tale, narrative   240–41 regards . . . point irrelevant considerations

Since that respects of fortune° are his love,
I shall not be his wife.   250
FRANCE   Fairest Cordelia, that art most rich being poor,
  Most choice, forsaken, and most loved, despised,
  Thee and thy virtues here I seize upon,
  Be it lawful° I take up what's cast away.

                               [*He takes her hand*]

  Gods, gods! 'Tis strange that from their cold'st neglect°   255
  My love should kindle to inflamed respect.°—
  Thy dowerless daughter, King, thrown to my chance,°
  Is queen of us, of ours, and our fair France.
  Not all the dukes of wat'rish° Burgundy
  Can buy this unprized° precious maid of me.—   260
  Bid them farewell, Cordelia, though unkind.°
  Thou losest here,° a better where° to find.
LEAR   Thou hast her, France. Let her be thine, for we
  Have no such daughter, nor shall ever see
  That face of hers again. Therefore begone   265
  Without our grace, our love, our benison.°
  Come, noble Burgundy.

                     Flourish. Exeunt [*all but France,*
                        Goneril, Regan, and Cordelia]

FRANCE   Bid farewell to your sisters.
CORDELIA   Ye jewels of our father, with washed° eyes
  Cordelia leaves you. I know you what you are,   270
  And like a sister° am most loath to call
  Your faults as they are named.° Love well our father.
  To your professèd bosoms° I commit him.
  But yet, alas, stood I within his grace,
  I would prefer° him to a better place.   275
  So, farewell to you both.

---

249 since . . . fortune since concern for wealth and position   **254 be it lawful** if it be lawful that   **255 from . . . neglect** out of the cold neglect of the gods   **256 inflamed respect** ardent regard   **257 chance** lot   **259 wat'rish** (1) well-watered with rivers (2) feeble, watery   **260 unprized** not appreciated (with perhaps a sense also of "priceless")   **261 though unkind** though they have behaved unnaturally   **262 here** this place | **where** place elsewhere   **266 benison** blessing   **269 washed** tear-washed   **271 like a sister** because I am your sister   **272 as . . . named** by their true names   **273 professèd bosoms** publicly avowed love   **275 prefer** advance, recommend

REGAN Prescribe not us our duty.

GONERIL   Let your study
Be to content your lord, who hath received you
At Fortune's alms.° You have obedience scanted,
And well are worth the want that you have wanted.°   280

CORDELIA Time shall unfold what plighted cunning hides;
Who covers faults, at last shame them derides.°
Well may you prosper!

FRANCE   Come, my fair Cordelia.

Exeunt France and Cordelia

GONERIL Sister, it is not little I have to say of what most nearly
appertains to us both. I think our father will hence tonight.   285

REGAN That's most certain, and with you; next month with us.

GONERIL You see how full of changes his age is; the observation we have made of it hath not been little. He always loved
our sister most, and with what poor judgment he hath now
cast her off appears too grossly.°   290

REGAN 'Tis the infirmity of his age. Yet he hath ever but slenderly known himself.

GONERIL The best and soundest of his time hath been but rash.°
Then must we look from his age to receive not alone the imperfections of long-ingraffed condition,° but therewithal°   295
the unruly waywardness that in firm and choleric years bring
with them.

REGAN Such unconstant starts° are we like° to have from him
as this of Kent's banishment.

GONERIL There is further compliment° of leave-taking between   300
France and him. Pray you, let us hit° together. If our father
carry authority with such disposition as he bears, this last
surrender of his will but offend us.°

---

279 **at . . . alms** as a pittance or dole from Fortune   280 **and well . . . wanted** and well
deserve to be without the dowry and the parental affection that you have both lacked
and flouted   281–2 **time . . . derides** Time will bring to light what cunning attempts to
conceal as if in the folds of a cloak; those who hide their faults may do so for a while,
but in time they will be shamed and derided   290 **grossly** obviously   293 **the best . . .
rash** even in the prime of his life, he was stormy and unpredictable   295 **long-ingraffed
condition** long-implanted habit | **therewithal** added thereto   298 **unconstant starts**
impulsive outbursts | **like** likely   300 **compliment** ceremony   301 **hit** agree   301–3
if . . . offend us if our father continues to boss us around with his accustomed imperi-
ousness, this most recent display of willfulness will do us nothing but harm

REGAN We shall further think of it.

GONERIL We must do something, and i'th' heat.°　　　　　305

Exeunt

❖

ACT 1
SCENE 2

Location: The Earl of Gloucester's house

Enter Bastard [Edmund, with a letter]

EDMUND Thou, Nature,° art my goddess; to thy law
　　My services are bound. Wherefore should I
　　Stand in the plague of custom° and permit
　　The curiosity of nations° to deprive me,
　　For that° I am some twelve or fourteen moonshines°　　　5
　　Lag of° a brother? Why bastard? Wherefore base?
　　When my dimensions° are as well compact,°
　　My mind as generous,° and my shape as true,
　　As honest° madam's issue? Why brand they us
　　With base? With baseness? Bastardy? Base, base?　　　10
　　Who in the lusty stealth of nature take
　　More composition and fierce quality°
　　Than doth within a dull, stale, tirèd bed
　　Go to th' creating a whole tribe of fops°
　　Got° 'tween asleep and wake? Well, then,　　　　　15
　　Legitimate Edgar, I must have your land.
　　Our father's love is to the bastard Edmund
　　As to th' legitimate. Fine word, "legitimate"!
　　Well, my legitimate, if this letter speed°
　　And my invention thrive,° Edmund the base　　　20

---

305 i'th' heat while the iron is hot

1 Nature the sanction that governs the material world through mechanistic amoral forces **3 stand . . . custom** submit to the vexatious injustice of convention **4 the curiosity of nations** arbitrary social gradations **5 for that** because | **moonshines** months **6 lag of** lagging behind **7 dimensions** proportions | **compact** knit together, fitted **8 generous** noble, refined **9 honest** chaste **11–12 who . . . quality** whose begetting in the sexual act both requires and engenders a fuller mixture and more energetic force **14 fops** fools **15 got** begotten **19 speed** succeed, prosper **20 invention thrive** scheme prosper

Shall top th' legitimate. I grow, I prosper.
Now, gods, stand up for bastards!

Enter Gloucester

GLOUCESTER
Kent banished thus? And France in choler parted?
And the King gone tonight?° Prescribed° his power,
Confined to exhibition?° All this done   25
Upon the gad?° Edmund, how now? What news?
EDMUND   So please your Lordship, none.

[*Putting up the letter*]

GLOUCESTER   Why so earnestly seek you to put up that letter?
EDMUND   I know no news, my lord.
GLOUCESTER   What paper were you reading?   30
EDMUND   Nothing, my lord.
GLOUCESTER   No? What needed then that terrible dispatch° of it
into your pocket? The quality of nothing hath not such need
to hide itself. Let's see. Come, if it be nothing I shall not
need spectacles.   35
EDMUND   I beseech you, sir, pardon me. It is a letter from my
brother, that I have not all o'erread; and for° so much as I
have perused, I find it not fit for your o'erlooking.°
GLOUCESTER   Give me the letter, sir.
EDMUND   I shall offend either to detain or give it. The contents,   40
as in part I understand them, are to blame.°
GLOUCESTER   Let's see, let's see.

[*Edmund gives the letter*]

EDMUND   I hope for my brother's justification he wrote this but
as an essay or taste° of my virtue.
GLOUCESTER [*reads*]   "This policy and reverence of° age makes   45
the world bitter to the best of our times,° keeps our fortunes
from us till our oldness cannot relish them. I begin to find an
idle and fond° bondage in the oppression of aged tyranny,

---

24 tonight last night | **prescribed** limited   **25 exhibition** an allowance, pension
26 upon the gad suddenly, as if pricked by a gad or spur   **32 terrible dispatch** fearful
quick disposal   **37 for** as for   **38 o'erlooking** perusal   **41 to blame** (the Folio
reading, "too blame," "too blameworthy to be shown," may be correct)   **44 essay
or taste** assay, test   **45 policy and reverence of** policy of reverencing   **46 the best . . .
times** the best years of our lives, our youth   **48 idle and fond** useless and foolish

who sways° not as it hath power but as it is suffered.° Come
to me, that of this I may speak more. If our father would 50
sleep till I waked him, you should enjoy half his revenue forever and live the beloved of your brother, Edgar."
    Hum! Conspiracy! "Sleep till I waked him, you should
enjoy half his revenue." My son Edgar! Had he a hand to
write this? A heart and brain to breed it in? When came you 55
to this?° Who brought it?

EDMUND   It was not brought me, my lord; there's the cunning
    of it. I found it thrown in at the casement° of my closet.°

GLOUCESTER   You know the character° to be your brother's?

EDMUND   If the matter° were good, my lord, I durst swear it were 60
    his; but in respect of that° I would fain° think it were not.

GLOUCESTER   It is his.

EDMUND   It is his hand, my lord, but I hope his heart is not in
    the contents.

GLOUCESTER   Has he never before sounded you in this business? 65

EDMUND   Never, my lord. But I have heard him oft maintain it
    to be fit° that, sons at perfect age° and fathers declined,° the
    father should be as ward to the son, and the son manage his
    revenue.

GLOUCESTER   Oh, villain, villain!° His very opinion in the letter! 70
    Abhorred° villain! Unnatural, detested,° brutish villain!
    Worse than brutish! Go, sirrah,° seek him. I'll apprehend
    him. Abominable villain! Where is he?

EDMUND   I do not well know, my lord. If it shall please you to
    suspend your indignation against my brother till you can de- 75
    rive from him better testimony of his intent, you should run
    a certain course;° where,° if you violently proceed against
    him, mistaking his purpose, it would make a great gap in
    your own honor and shake in pieces the heart of his obedi-
    ence. I dare pawn down° my life for him that he hath writ 80

---

49 who sways which rules | **suffered** permitted   **56 to this** upon this (letter)
58 casement window | **closet** private room   **59 character** handwriting   **60 matter**
contents   **61 in . . . that** considering what the contents are | **fain** gladly
67 fit fitting, appropriate | **perfect age** full maturity | **declined** having become
feeble   **70 villain** vile wretch, diabolical schemer   **71 abhorred** abhorrent | **detested**
hated and hateful   **72 sirrah** (form of address used to inferiors or children)
76–7 run a certain course proceed with safety and certainty | **where** whereas
80 pawn down stake

this to feel° my affection to Your Honor, and to no other
pretense of danger.°

GLOUCESTER Think you so?

EDMUND If Your Honor judge it meet,° I will place you where
you shall hear us confer of this, and by an auricular assur-   85
ance have your satisfaction,° and that without any further
delay than this very evening.

GLOUCESTER He cannot be such a monster—

EDMUND Nor is not, sure.

GLOUCESTER To his father, that so tenderly and entirely loves   90
him. Heaven and earth! Edmund, seek him out; wind me
into him,° I pray you. Frame° the business after your own
wisdom.° I would unstate myself to be in a due resolution.°

EDMUND I will seek him, sir, presently,° convey° the business
as I shall find means, and acquaint you withal.°   95

GLOUCESTER These late° eclipses in the sun and moon portend
no good to us. Though the wisdom of nature° can reason it
thus and thus, yet nature finds itself scourged by the sequent
effects.° Love cools, friendship falls off, brothers divide; in
cities, mutinies; in countries, discord; in palaces, treason;   100
and the bond cracked twixt son and father. This villain of
mine comes under the prediction; there's son against father.
The King falls from bias of nature;° there's father against
child. We have seen the best of our time. Machinations, hollowness, treachery, and all ruinous disorders follow us dis-   105
quietly to our graves. Find out this villain, Edmund; it shall
lose thee nothing.° Do it carefully. And the noble and true-
hearted Kent banished! His offense, honesty! 'Tis strange.

Exit

EDMUND This is the excellent foppery° of the world, that
when we are sick in fortune—often the surfeits of our own   110

---

81 feel feel out   **82 pretense of danger** dangerous purpose   **84 meet** fitting, proper
85–6 by an . . . satisfaction satisfy yourself as to the truth by what you hear
91–2 wind me into him insinuate yourself into his confidence (*me* is used colloqui-
ally)   **92 frame** arrange   **92–3 after your own wisdom** as you think best   **93 I
would . . . resolution** I would give up my wealth and rank to know the truth, have
my doubts resolved   **94 presently** immediately | **convey** manage   **95 withal**
therewith   **96 late** recent   **97 the wisdom of nature** natural science   **98–9 sequent
effects** devastating consequences   **103 bias of nature** natural inclination   **107 lose
thee nothing** earn you a reward   **109 foppery** foolishness   **110–11 surfeits . . .
behavior** consequences of our own overindulgence

behavior—we make guilty of our disasters the sun, the
moon, and stars, as if we were villains on° necessity, fools by
heavenly compulsion, knaves, thieves, and treachers° by
spherical predominance,° drunkards, liars, and adulterers by
an enforced obedience of planetary influence, and all that   115
we are evil in, by a divine° thrusting on. An admirable eva-
sion of whoremaster man, to lay his goatish° disposition on
the charge° of a star! My father compounded with my
mother under the Dragon's tail° and my nativity was under
Ursa Major,° so that it follows I am rough and lecherous.   120
Fut,° I should have been that° I am, had the maidenliest star
in the firmament twinkled on my bastardizing. Edgar—

Enter Edgar

and pat° he comes like the catastrophe° of the old comedy.
My cue is villainous melancholy, with a sigh like Tom o'
Bedlam.°—Oh, these eclipses do portend these divisions!°   125
Fa, sol, la, mi.

EDGAR   How now, brother Edmund, what serious contemplation are you in?

EDMUND   I am thinking, brother, of a prediction I read this
other day,° what should follow these eclipses.   130

EDGAR   Do you busy yourself with that?

EDMUND   I promise° you, the effects he writes of succeed unhappily,° as of unnaturalness between the child and the parent, death, dearth, dissolutions of ancient amities, divisions
in state, menaces and maledictions against king and nobles,   135

---

112 **on** by   113 **treachers** traitors   114 **spherical predominance** astrological
determinism, because a certain planet was ascendant at the hour of our birth
116 **divine** supernatural   117 **goatish** lecherous   117–18 **on the charge** to the
responsibility   118–19 **compounded . . . Dragon's tail** had sex with my mother
under the constellation Draco (not one of the regular signs of the zodiac), or under
the descending point at which the moon's orbit intersects with the ecliptic or
apparent orbit of the sun (when an eclipse might occur)   119–20 **Ursa Major** the
big bear or dipper—not one of the regular signs of the zodiac   121 **fut** 'Sfoot, by
Christ's foot | **that** what   123 **pat** on cue | **catastrophe** conclusion, resolution (of
a play)   124–25 **Tom o' Bedlam** a lunatic patient of Bethlehem Hospital in London
turned out to beg for his bread   125 **divisions** social and family conflicts (but with
a musical sense also of florid variations on a theme, thus prompting Edmund's
singing)   129–30 **this other day** the other day   132 **promise** assure   132–33 **succeed**
unhappily follow unluckily

needless diffidences,° banishment of friends, dissipation of
cohorts,° nuptial breaches, and I know not what.

EDGAR   How long have you been a sectary astronomical?°

EDMUND   Come, come, when saw you my father last?

EDGAR   The night gone by.   140

EDMUND   Spake you with him?

EDGAR   Ay, two hours together.

EDMUND   Parted you in good terms? Found you no displeasure
in him by word nor countenance?°

EDGAR   None at all.   145

EDMUND   Bethink yourself wherein you may have offended
him, and at my entreaty forbear his presence° until some little time hath qualified° the heat of his displeasure, which at
this instant so rageth in him that with the mischief of your
person° it would scarcely allay.°   150

EDGAR   Some villain hath done me wrong.

EDMUND   That's my fear. I pray you, have a continent for-
bearance° till the speed of his rage goes slower; and, as I say,
retire with me to my lodging, from whence I will fitly° bring
you to hear my lord° speak. Pray ye, go! There's my key. [*He* 155
gives a key] If you do stir abroad, go armed.

EDGAR   Armed, brother?

EDMUND   Brother, I advise you to the best. I am no honest man
if there be any good meaning° toward you. I have told you
what I have seen and heard, but faintly,° nothing like the im- 160
age and horror° of it. Pray you, away.

EDGAR   Shall I hear from you anon?

EDMUND   I do serve you in this business.   *Exit [Edgar]*
A credulous father and a brother noble,
Whose nature is so far from doing harms   165
That he suspects none; on whose foolish honesty
My practices° ride easy. I see the business.°

136 **needless diffidences** groundless distrust of others   136–37 **dissipation of cohorts**
breaking up of military companies, large-scale desertions   138 **sectary astronomical**
believer in astrology   144 **countenance** demeanor   147 **forbear his presence** avoid
meeting him   148 **qualified** moderated   149–50 **with . . . person** with the harmful
effect of your presence; or, even if there were injury done to you   150 **allay** be
allayed   152–53 **have . . . forbearance** keep a wary distance   154 **fitly** at a fit time
155 **my lord** our father   159 **meaning** intention   160 **but faintly** only with a faint
impression   160–61 **image and horror** horrid reality   167 **practices** plots | **the
business** how my plots should proceed

Let me, if not by birth, have lands by wit.°
All with me's meet° that I can fashion fit.°

Exit

❖

ACT 1
SCENE 3

Location: The Duke of Albany's palace

Enter Goneril, and [Oswald, her] steward

GONERIL   Did my father strike my gentleman for chiding of his
fool?

OSWALD   Ay, madam.

GONERIL   By day and night he wrongs me! Every hour
He flashes into one gross crime° or other   5
That sets us all at odds. I'll not endure it.
His knights grow riotous, and himself upbraids us
On every trifle. When he returns from hunting
I will not speak with him. Say I am sick.
If you come slack° of former services   10
You shall do well; the fault of it I'll answer.°

[Horns within]

OSWALD   He's coming, madam. I hear him.

GONERIL   Put on what weary negligence you please,
You and your fellows. I'd have it come to question.°
If he distaste° it, let him to my sister,   15
Whose mind and mine, I know, in that are one,
Not to be overruled. Idle° old man,
That still would manage those authorities°
That he hath given away! Now, by my life,
Old fools are babes again, and must be used   20
With checks as flatteries, when they are seen abused.°
Remember what I have said.

---

168 **wit** cleverness   169 **meet** justifiable | **fit** to my purpose

5 **crime** offense   10 **come slack** fall short   11 **answer** be answerable for   14 **come to question** be made an issue   15 **distaste** dislike   17 **idle** foolish   18 **manage those authorities** exercise those prerogatives   21 **with . . . abused** with rebukes in place of flattering attentiveness, when such flattery is seen to be taken advantage of

OSWALD Well, madam.

GONERIL And let his knights have colder looks among you.
What grows of it, no matter. Advise your fellows so.   25
I would breed from hence occasions,° and I shall,
That I may speak.° I'll write straight° to my sister
To hold my very course. Prepare for dinner.

Exeunt

❖

ACT 1
SCENE 4

Location: The Duke of Albany's palace still.
The sense of time is virtually continuous

Enter Kent [disguised]

KENT If but as well° I other accents borrow
That can my speech diffuse,° my good intent
May carry through itself to that full issue
For which I razed my likeness.° Now, banished Kent,
If thou canst serve where thou dost stand condemned,   5
So may it come° thy master, whom thou lov'st,
Shall find thee full of labors.

Horns within. Enter Lear,
[Knights,] and attendants

LEAR Let me not stay° a jot for dinner. Go get it ready.
[Exit an Attendant°]
[To Kent] How now, what art thou?

KENT A man, sir.   10

LEAR What dost thou profess?° What wouldst thou with us?

---

26 occasions opportunities for taking offense **27 speak** speak bluntly | **straight** immediately

1 as well as well as I have disguised myself by means of costume **2 diffuse** render confused or indistinct **3–4 may . . . likeness** may achieve the desired result for which I scraped off my beard and erased my outward appearance **6 come** come to pass that **8 stay** wait **8.1 *attendant*** (this attendant may be a knight; certainly the one who speaks at line 46 is a knight) **11 what . . . profess?** what is your special calling? (but Kent puns in his answer on *profess* meaning to "claim")

KENT   I do profess to be no less than I seem: to serve him truly
that will put me in trust, to love him that is honest,° to con-
verse° with him that is wise and says little, to fear judgment,°
to fight when I cannot choose,° and to eat no fish.°   15

LEAR   What art thou?

KENT   A very honest-hearted fellow, and as poor as the King.

LEAR   If thou be'st as poor for a subject as he's for a king,
thou'rt poor enough. What wouldst thou?

KENT   Service.   20

LEAR   Who wouldst thou serve?

KENT   You.

LEAR   Dost thou know me, fellow?

KENT   No, sir, but you have that in your countenance° which I
would fain call master.   25

LEAR   What's that?

KENT   Authority.

LEAR   What services canst do?

KENT   I can keep honest counsel,° ride, run, mar a curious° tale
in telling it, and deliver a plain message bluntly. That which   30
ordinary men are fit for I am qualified in, and the best of me
is diligence.

LEAR   How old art thou?

KENT   Not so young, sir, to love° a woman for singing, nor so
old to dote on her for anything. I have years on my back   35
forty-eight.

LEAR   Follow me; thou shalt serve me. If I like thee no worse
after dinner, I will not part from thee yet.—Dinner, ho, dinner! Where's my knave, my fool? Go you and call my fool
hither.   [*Exit one*]   40

Enter steward [*Oswald*]

You! You, sirrah, where's my daughter?

OSWALD   So please you—   *Exit*

LEAR   What says the fellow there? Call the clodpoll° back.

                                                        [*Exit a Knight*]

---

13 **honest** honorable   13–14 **converse** associate   14 **judgment** God's judgment
15 **choose** choose but to fight | **eat no fish** eat a manly diet (?), be a good Protestant (?)
24 **countenance** face and bearing   29 **keep honest counsel** respect confidences |
curious ornate, elaborate   34 **to love** as to love   43 **clodpoll** blockhead

Where's my fool, ho? I think the world's asleep.

[Enter Knight]

How now? Where's that mongrel?   45
KNIGHT   He says, my lord, your daughter is not well.
LEAR   Why came not the slave back to me when I called him?
KNIGHT   Sir, he answered me in the roundest° manner, he
would not.
LEAR   He would not?   50
KNIGHT   My lord, I know not what the matter is, but to my
judgment Your Highness is not entertained° with that cere-
monious affection as you were wont. There's a great abate-
ment of kindness appears as well in the general dependents°
as in the Duke himself also and your daughter.   55
LEAR   Ha? Say'st thou so?
KNIGHT   I beseech you, pardon me, my lord, if I be mistaken,
for my duty cannot be silent when I think Your Highness
wronged.
LEAR   Thou but rememberest° me of mine own conception.° I   60
have perceived a most faint° neglect of late, which I have
rather blamed as mine own jealous curiosity° than as a very
pretense° and purpose of unkindness. I will look further into't. But where's my fool? I have not seen him this° two days.
KNIGHT   Since my young lady's going into France, sir, the Fool 65
hath much pined away.
LEAR   No more of that. I have noted it well. Go you and tell
my daughter I would speak with her. *[Exit one]* Go you call
hither my fool.   *Exit one*

Enter steward [Oswald]

Oh, you, sir, you, come you hither, sir. Who am I, sir?   70
OSWALD   My lady's father.
LEAR   "My lady's father"? My lord's knave! You whoreson
dog, you slave, you cur!
OSWALD   I am none of these, my lord, I beseech your pardon.

---

48 roundest bluntest   **52 entertained** treated   **54 general dependents** servants
generally   **60 rememberest** remind │ **conception** idea, thought   **61 faint** halfhearted
62 jealous curiosity overscrupulous regard for matters of etiquette   **62–63 very
pretense** true intention   **64 this** these

LEAR   Do you bandy looks° with me, you rascal?   75

                                 [*He strikes Oswald*]

OSWALD   I'll not be strucken,° my lord.

KENT   Nor tripped neither, you base football° player.

                          [*He trips up Oswald's heels*]

LEAR   I thank thee, fellow. Thou serv'st me, and I'll love thee.

KENT   Come, sir, arise, away! I'll teach you differences.° Away,
away! If you will measure your lubber's length again,° tarry;   80
but away! Go to.° Have you wisdom?° So.

                               [*He pushes Oswald out*]

LEAR   Now, my friendly knave, I thank thee. There's earnest of°
thy service.   [*He gives Kent money*]

                                  Enter Fool

FOOL   Let me hire him too. Here's my coxcomb.°

                          [*Offering Kent his cap*]

LEAR   How now, my pretty knave, how dost thou?   85

FOOL [*to Kent*]   Sirrah, you were best° take my coxcomb.

KENT   Why Fool?

FOOL   Why? For taking one's part that's out of favor. Nay, an
thou canst not smile as the wind sits, thou'lt catch cold
shortly.° There, take my coxcomb. Why, this fellow has ban-   90
ished° two on 's° daughters and did the third a blessing°
against his will. If thou follow him, thou must needs wear
my coxcomb.—How now, nuncle?° Would I had two cox-
combs and two daughters.

LEAR   Why, my boy?   95

FOOL   If I gave them all my living,° I'd keep my coxcombs° myself. There's mine; beg another of thy daughters.°

---

75 **bandy looks** exchange glances (in such a way as to imply that Oswald and Lear
are social equals)   76 **strucken** struck   77 **football** (a raucous street game played
by the lower classes)   79 **differences** distinctions in rank   80 **if . . . again** i.e., if you
want to be laid out flat again, you clumsy ox   81 **go to** (an expression of impatience or
anger) | **have you wisdom?** wise up   82 **earnest of** a first payment for   84 **coxcomb**
fool's cap, crested with a red comb   86 **you were best** you had better   88–90 **an . . .
shortly** if you can't play along with those in power, you'll find yourself out in the
cold   90–91 **banished** (paradoxically, by giving Goneril and Regan his kingdom,
Lear has lost them, given them power over him) | **on 's** of his   91 **blessing** bestowing
Cordelia on France and saving her from the curse of insolent prosperity   93 **nuncle**
(contraction of "mine uncle," the Fool's way of addressing Lear)   96 **living** property
| **keep my coxcombs** (as proof of my folly)   97 **beg . . . daughters** beg for the coxcomb
that you deserve for dealing with your daughters as you did

LEAR   Take heed, sirrah—the whip.

FOOL   Truth's a dog must to kennel. He must be whipped out,
when the Lady Brach° may stand by th' fire and stink.   100

LEAR   A pestilent gall° to me!

FOOL   Sirrah, I'll teach thee a speech.

LEAR   Do.

FOOL   Mark it, nuncle:

> Have more than thou showest,°   105
> Speak less than thou knowest,
> Lend less than thou owest,°
> Ride more than thou goest,°
> Learn° more than thou trowest,°
> Set less than thou throwest;°   110
> Leave thy drink and thy whore,
> And keep in-a-door,°
> And thou shalt have more
> Than two tens to a score.°

KENT   This is nothing, Fool.   115

FOOL   Then 'tis like the breath of an unfee'd lawyer;° you gave
me nothing for't. Can you make no use of nothing, nuncle?

LEAR   Why, no, boy. Nothing can be made out of nothing.

FOOL [*to Kent*]   Prithee, tell him; so much the rent of his land
comes to.° He will not believe a fool.   120

LEAR   A bitter fool!

FOOL   Dost know the difference, my boy, between a bitter° fool
and a sweet one?

LEAR   No, lad. Teach me.

FOOL   That lord that counseled thee   125
        To give away thy land,
        Come place him here by me;

---

100 Brach bitch hound (here likened to Goneril and Regan, who have been given favored places despite their reeking of dishonest flattery) **101 gall** irritation, bitterness—literally, a painful swelling, or bile (Lear is stung by the Fool's gibe because it is so true) **105 have . . . showest** don't display your wealth ostentatiously **107 owest** own **108 goest** on foot (travel unostentatiously on horseback, not afoot) **109 learn** listen to | **trowest** believe **110 set . . . throwest** don't stake everything on a single throw **112 in-a-door** indoors, at home **113–14 and . . . score** and you will do better than break even (since a *score* equals two tens, or twenty) **116 'tis . . . lawyer** it is free—and useless—advice (lawyers, being proverbially mercenary, would not give good advice unless paid well) **119–20 so . . . to** (because Lear has given away his land, he can collect no rent) **121 bitter** satirical

Do thou for him stand.°
The sweet and bitter fool
  Will presently° appear: 130
The one in motley° here,
  The other found out there.°

LEAR Dost thou call me fool, boy?

FOOL All thy other titles thou hast given away; that
thou wast born with.   135

KENT This is not altogether fool, my lord.

FOOL No, faith, lords and great men will not let me;° if I had a
monopoly out,° they would have part on't.° And ladies too,
they will not let me have all the fool to myself; they'll be
snatching.° Nuncle, give me an egg and I'll give thee two 140
crowns.

LEAR What two crowns shall they be?

FOOL Why, after I have cut the egg i'th' middle and eat up the
meat,° the two crowns of the egg. When thou clovest thy
crown i'th' middle and gav'st away both parts, thou bor'st 145
thine ass on thy back o'er the dirt.° Thou hadst little wit in
thy bald crown when thou gav'st thy golden one away. If I
speak like myself in this, let him be whipped that first finds
it so.°   [*Sings*]

  "Fools had ne'er less grace in a year,   150
    For wise men are grown foppish
  And know not how their wits to wear,
    Their manners are so apish."°

LEAR When were you wont to be so full of songs, sirrah?

---

128 Do . . . stand take his place **130 presently** immediately **131 motley** the
parti-colored dress of the professional fool (the Fool identifies himself as the sweet
fool, Lear as the bitter fool who counseled himself to give away his kingdom)
132 found out there discovered there (the Fool points at Lear) **137 no . . . let me**
great persons at court will not let me monopolize folly; I am not *altogether fool* in
the sense of being "all the fool there is" **138 a monopoly out** a corner on the
market (the granting of monopolies was a common abuse under King James and
Queen Elizabeth) **|** **on't** of it **140 snatching** seizing their share (including sexual
pleasure) **143–44 and eat . . . meat** and have eaten the edible part **145–46 bor'st . . .
dirt** bore the ass instead of letting the ass bear you **147–49 if . . . so** if I speak like
a fool in saying this, let the first person to discover the truth of this be whipped
(since in this corrupt world those who speak truth are punished for doing so)
150–53 "Fools . . . apish" "Fools have never been so out of favor, for wise men
foppishly trade places with the fools and no longer know how to show off their wit
to advantage, they have grown so foolish in their manners"

FOOL   I have used° it, nuncle, e'er since thou mad'st thy 155
    daughters thy mothers; for when thou gav'st them the rod
    and putt'st down thine own breeches,   [*Sings*]
        "Then they for sudden joy did weep,
          And I for sorrow sung,
        That such a king should play bo-peep°   160
          And go the fools among."
    Prithee, nuncle, keep a schoolmaster that can teach
    thy fool to lie. I would fain learn to lie.

LEAR   An° you lie, sirrah, we'll have you whipped.

FOOL   I marvel what kin thou and thy daughters are. They'll 165
    have me whipped for speaking true, thou'lt have me
    whipped for lying, and sometimes I am whipped for holding
    my peace. I had rather be any kind o' thing than a fool. And
    yet I would not be thee, nuncle. Thou hast pared thy wit o'
    both sides and left nothing i'th' middle. Here comes one o' 170
    th' parings.

                                      Enter Goneril

LEAR   How now, daughter? What makes that frontlet on?°
    You are too much of late i'th' frown.

FOOL   Thou wast a pretty fellow when thou hadst no need to
    care for her frowning; now thou art an O without a figure.° 175
    I am better than thou art now; I am a fool, thou art nothing.
    [*To Goneril*] Yes, forsooth, I will hold my tongue; so your
    face bids me, though you say nothing.
        Mum, mum,
        He that keeps nor crust nor crumb,   180
        Weary of all, shall want° some.
    [*Pointing to Lear*] That's a shelled peascod.°

GONERIL   Not only, sir, this your all-licensed° fool,
    But other of your insolent retinue
    Do hourly carp° and quarrel, breaking forth   185

---

155 **used** practiced   160 **bo-peep** (a child's game)   164 **an** if   172 **what . . . on?**
What is that frown doing on your forehead?   175 **O without a figure** zero, cipher of
no value unless preceded by a digit   180–81 **he . . . some** that person who, having
grown weary of his possessions, gives all away, will find himself in need of part of
what is gone   181 **want** lack   182 **shelled peascod** shelled pea pod, empty of its
contents   183 **all-licensed** allowed to speak or act as he pleases   185 **carp** find fault

In rank° and not-to-be-endurèd riots. Sir,
I had thought by making this well known unto you
To have found a safe° redress, but now grow fearful,
By what yourself too late° have spoke and done,
That you protect this course and put it on°   190
By your allowance;° which if you should, the fault
Would not scape censure, nor the redresses sleep
Which in the tender of a wholesome weal
Might in their working do you that offense,
Which else were shame, that then necessity   195
Will call discreet proceeding.°

FOOL   For you know, nuncle,
          "The hedge sparrow fed the cuckoo° so long
          That it had it° head bit off by it young."°
So, out went the candle, and we were left darkling.°   200

LEAR [*to Goneril*] Are you our daughter?

GONERIL   I would you would make use of your good wisdom,
Whereof I know you are fraught,° and put away
These dispositions° which of late transport you
From what you rightly are.   205

FOOL   May not an ass know when the cart draws the horse?°
Whoop, Jug!° I love thee.

LEAR   Does any here know me? This is not Lear.
Does Lear walk thus, speak thus? Where are his eyes?
Either his notion° weakens, or his discernings   210
Are lethargied°—Ha! Waking?° 'Tis not so.
Who is it that can tell me who I am?

FOOL   Lear's shadow.

LEAR   I would learn that;° for, by the marks of sovereignty,°

---

186 rank gross, excessive **188 safe** certain **189 too late** all too recently **190 put it on** encourage it **191 allowance** approval **192–96 nor . . . proceeding** nor would the punishments lie dormant which, out of care for the common welfare, might prove unpleasant to you—proceedings that the stern necessity of the times will regard as prudent even if under normal circumstances they might seem shameful **198 cuckoo** a bird that lays its eggs in other birds' nests **199 it** its | **it young** the young cuckoo (a cautionary fable about ungrateful children) **200 darkling** in the dark **203 fraught** freighted, provided **204 dispositions** inclinations, moods **206 may . . . horse?** may not even a fool see that matters are backwards when a daughter lectures her father? **207 Jug** Joan (the origin of this phrase is uncertain) **210 notion** intellectual power **210–11 or his . . . lethargied** or his faculties are asleep **211 waking?** am I really awake? **214 that** who I am | **marks of sovereignty** outward and visible evidence of being king

Knowledge, and reason, I should be false persuaded   215
    I had daughters.°
FOOL   Which° they will make an obedient father.
LEAR   Your name, fair gentlewoman?
GONERIL   This admiration,° sir, is much o'th' savor
    Of other° your new pranks. I do beseech you   220
    To understand my purposes aright.
    As you are old and reverend, should° be wise.
    Here do you keep a hundred knights and squires,
    Men so disordered, so debauched and bold°
    That this our court, infected with their manners,   225
    Shows° like a riotous inn. Epicurism° and lust
    Makes it more like a tavern or a brothel
    Than a graced° palace. The shame itself doth speak
    For instant remedy. Be then desired,°
    By her that else will take the thing she begs,   230
    A little to disquantity your train,°
    And the remainders that shall still depend°
    To be such men as may besort° your age,
    Which know themselves and you.°
LEAR   Darkness and devils!
    Saddle my horses! Call my train° together!   [*Exit one*]   235
    Degenerate bastard, I'll not trouble thee.
    Yet have I left a daughter.
GONERIL   You strike my people, and your disordered rabble
    Make servants of their betters.

                                  Enter Albany

LEAR   Woe, that° too late repents!—Oh, sir, are you come?   240
    Is it your will? Speak, sir.—Prepare my horses.   [*Exit one*]
    Ingratitude, thou marble-hearted fiend,

215–16 I should . . . daughters all these outward signs of sanity and status would seem to suggest (falsely) that I am the king who had obedient daughters **217 which** whom **219 admiration** (guise of) wonderment **220 other** other of **222 should** you should **224 men . . . bold** men so disorderly, so depraved and impudent **226 shows** appears | **Epicurism** excess, hedonism **228 graced** dignified **229 desired** requested **231 disquantity your train** diminish the number of your attendants **232 the remainders . . . depend** those who remain to attend you **233 besort** befit **234 which . . . you** servants who have proper self-knowledge and an awareness of how they should serve you **235 train** retinue **240 woe, that** woe to the person who

More hideous when thou show'st thee in a child
Than the sea monster!

ALBANY   Pray, sir, be patient.   245

LEAR [*to Goneril*]   Detested kite,° thou liest!
My train are men of choice and rarest parts,°
That all particulars of duty know
And in the most exact regard° support
The worships of their name.° Oh, most small fault,   250
How ugly didst thou in Cordelia show!
Which, like an engine, wrenched my frame of nature
From the fixed place,° drew from my heart all love,
And added to the gall.° Oh, Lear, Lear, Lear!
Beat at this gate [*striking his head*] that let thy folly in   255
And thy dear° judgment out!—Go, go, my people.

                                          [*Exeunt some*]

ALBANY   My lord, I am guiltless as I am ignorant
Of what hath moved you.

LEAR   It may be so, my lord.—
Hear, Nature, hear! Dear goddess, hear!
Suspend thy purpose if thou didst intend   260
To make this creature fruitful!
Into her womb convey sterility;
Dry up in her the organs of increase,
And from her derogate° body never spring
A babe to honor her! If she must teem,°   265
Create her child of spleen,° that it may live
And be a thwart disnatured° torment to her!
Let it stamp wrinkles in her brow of youth,
With cadent° tears fret° channels in her cheeks,
Turn all her mother's pains and benefits°   270
To laughter and contempt, that she may feel

---

246 **kite** bird of prey   247 **parts** qualities   249 **in . . . regard** with close attention to detail   249–50 **and . . . name** and with utter scrupulousness may uphold the honor of their reputation   252–53 **which . . . place** which, like a powerful mechanical contrivance, wrenched my natural affection away from where it belonged   254 **gall** bitterness   256 **dear** precious   264 **derogate** debased   265 **teem** produce offspring   266 **spleen** violent ill nature   267 **thwart disnatured** obstinate, perverse, and unnatural, unfilial   269 **cadent** cascading | **fret** wear away   270 **benefits** pleasures of motherhood

How sharper than a serpent's tooth it is
To have a thankless child! Away, away!
            Exit [with Kent and the rest of Lear's followers]
ALBANY   Now, gods that we adore, whereof comes this?
GONERIL   Never afflict yourself to know° more of it,   275
    But let his disposition° have that scope
    As° dotage gives it.

                                   Enter Lear

LEAR   What, fifty of my followers at a clap?
    Within a fortnight?
ALBANY   What's the matter, sir?
LEAR   I'll tell thee. *[To Goneril]* Life and death! I am ashamed   280
    That thou hast power to shake my manhood thus,
    That these hot tears, which break from me perforce,
    Should make thee worth them.° Blasts and fogs° upon thee!
    Th'untented° woundings of a father's curse
    Pierce every sense about thee! Old fond° eyes,   285
    Beweep° this cause again, I'll pluck ye out
    And cast you, with the waters that you loose,°
    To temper clay.° Yea, is't come to this?
    Ha! Let it be so. I have another daughter,
    Who, I am sure, is kind and comfortable.°   290
    When she shall hear this of thee, with her nails
    She'll flay thy wolvish visage. Thou shalt find
    That I'll resume the shape° which thou dost think
    I have cast off forever.   *Exit*
GONERIL *[to Albany]*   Do you mark that?°
ALBANY   I cannot be so partial, Goneril,   295
    To° the great love I bear you—

---

275 **never . . . know** don't distress yourself by seeking to know   276 **disposition** humor, mood   277 **as** that   283 **should . . . them** should seem to suggest that you are worth a king's tears | **blasts and fogs** infectious blights and disease-bearing fogs 284 **untented** too deep to be probed and cleansed   285 **fond** foolish   286 **beweep** if you weep for   287 **loose** let loose (in tears)   288 **to temper clay** to mix with earth (Lear threatens to cast both his eyes and their tears to the ground)   290 **comfortable** comforting   293 **the shape** the kingship   294 **do . . . that?** did you hear his threat to resume royal power?   296 **to** because of

GONERIL Pray you, content.—What, Oswald, ho!
[*To the Fool*] You, sir, more knave than fool, after your
  master.
FOOL
  Nuncle Lear, nuncle Lear! Tarry, take the Fool with thee.°
          A fox, when one has caught her,   300
          And such a daughter
          Should sure to the slaughter,°
          If my cap would buy a halter.°
          So the Fool follows after.   *Exit*
GONERIL
  This man hath had good counsel.° A hundred knights?   305
  'Tis politic° and safe to let him keep
  At point° a hundred knights—yes, that on every dream,°
  Each buzz,° each fancy, each complaint, dislike,
  He may enguard° his dotage with their powers
  And hold our lives in mercy.°—Oswald, I say!   310
ALBANY Well, you may fear too far.°
GONERIL Safer than trust too far.
  Let me still take away° the harms I fear,
  Not fear still to be taken.° I know his heart.
  What he hath uttered I have writ my sister.   315
  If she sustain him and his hundred knights
  When I have showed th'unfitness—

                              Enter steward [*Oswald*]

                              How now, Oswald?
  What, have you writ that letter to my sister?
OSWALD Ay, madam.
GONERIL Take you some company and away to horse.   320
  Inform her full of my particular fear,
  And thereto add such reasons of your own

---

299 take . . . thee (1) take me with you (2) take the name "fool" with you (a stock phrase of taunting farewell) **302 should sure** should certainly be sent **303 halter** (1) rope for leading an animal (2) hangman's noose **305 this . . . counsel** (said sarcastically) **306 politic** prudent (said ironically) **307 at point** armed and ready I **dream** imagined wrong **308 buzz** idle rumor **309 enguard** protect **310 in mercy** at his mercy **311 fear too far** overestimate the danger **313 still take away** always remove **314 not . . . taken** rather than dwell continually in the fear of being taken prisoner by such harms

As may compact° it more. Get you gone,
And hasten your return.   [*Exit Oswald*]
                    No, no, my lord,
This milky gentleness and course° of yours   325
Though I condemn not, yet, under pardon,°
You're much more attasked° for want of wisdom
Than praised for harmful mildness.°
ALBANY   How far your eyes may pierce° I cannot tell.
Striving to better, oft we mar what's well.   330
GONERIL   Nay, then—
ALBANY   Well, well, th'event.°

                              Exeunt

❖

ACT 1
SCENE 5

Location: Before Albany's palace

Enter Lear, Kent [disguised as Caius], and Fool

LEAR [*giving a letter to Kent*]   Go you before to Gloucester°
with these letters.° Acquaint my daughter no further with
anything you know than comes from her demand° out of°
the letter. If your diligence be not speedy, I shall be there
afore you.   5
KENT   I will not sleep, my lord, till I have delivered your letter.
                                        Exit
FOOL   If a man's brains were in 's heels, were't not in danger
of kibes?°
LEAR   Ay, boy.
FOOL   Then, I prithee, be merry. Thy wit shall not go slipshod.°   10

323 **compact** confirm   325 **milky . . . course** effeminate and gentle way   326 **under
pardon** if you'll excuse my saying so   327 **attasked** taken to task for, blamed
328 **harmful mildness** mildness that causes harm   329 **pierce** see into matters
332 **th'event** time will tell

1 **Gloucester** the place in Gloucestershire   2 **these letters** this letter   3 **demand**
inquiry | **out of** prompted by   7–8 **were't . . . kibes?** wouldn't his brains be in
danger of that common affliction of the heel called chilblains?   10 **thy wit . . . slipshod**
your brains would have no need for slippers to avoid chafing the chilblains, since
you have no brains (anyone who journeys to Regan in hopes of kind treatment is
utterly brainless)

LEAR   Ha, ha, ha!

FOOL   Shalt° see thy other daughter will use thee kindly,° for though she's as like this as a crab's like an apple, yet I can tell what I can tell.

LEAR   What canst tell, boy?   15

FOOL   She will taste as like this as a crab° does to a crab. Thou canst tell why one's nose stands i'th' middle on 's° face?

LEAR   No.

FOOL   Why, to keep one's eyes of either side 's° nose, that what a man cannot smell out he may spy into.   20

LEAR   I did her° wrong.

FOOL   Canst tell how an oyster makes his shell?

LEAR   No.

FOOL   Nor I neither. But I can tell why a snail has a house.

LEAR   Why?   25

FOOL   Why, to put 's head in, not to give it away to his daughters and leave his horns without a case.°

LEAR   I will forget my nature.° So kind a father!—Be my horses ready?

FOOL   Thy asses are gone about 'em.° The reason why the   30 seven stars° are no more than seven is a pretty reason.

LEAR   Because they are not eight.

FOOL   Yes, indeed. Thou wouldst make a good fool.

LEAR   To take't again perforce!° Monster ingratitude!

FOOL   If thou wert my fool, nuncle, I'd have thee beaten for be-   35 ing old before thy time.

LEAR   How's that?

FOOL   Thou shouldst not have been old till thou hadst been wise.

---

12 shalt thou shalt | kindly (1) with filial kindness (2) according to her own nature
16 crab crab apple   17 on 's of his   19 of either side 's on either side of his   21 her
Cordelia   26–27 why, to . . . case the snail's head and horns are unendangered with
its *case* or shell; Lear, conversely, has given away his crown to his daughters, leaving
his brows unadorned and vulnerable (with a suggestion too of the cuckold's horned
head, as though Lear's victimization had a sexual dimension)   28 nature natural
affection (compare line 12 and note)   30 thy . . . 'em your servants (who labor like
asses in your service) have gone about readying the horses   31 seven stars Pleiades
34 to take't . . . perforce! to think that Goneril would forcibly take back again the
privileges guaranteed to me! (or perhaps Lear is meditating an armed restoration of
his monarchy)

LEAR   Oh, let me not be mad, not mad, sweet heaven!   40
Keep me in temper;° I would not be mad!

[Enter Gentleman]

How now, are the horses ready?
GENTLEMAN   Ready, my lord.
LEAR   Come, boy.   *[Exeunt Lear and Gentleman]*
FOOL   She that's a maid now, and laughs at my departure,   45
Shall not be a maid long, unless things° be cut shorter.°

Exit

❖

ACT 2
SCENE 1

Location: The Earl of Gloucester's house

Enter Bastard [Edmund] and Curan, severally°

EDMUND   Save° thee, Curan.
CURAN   And you, sir. I have been with your father and given
him notice that the Duke of Cornwall and Regan his
duchess will be here with him this night.
EDMUND   How comes that?   5
CURAN   Nay, I know not. You have heard of the news
abroad°—I mean the whispered ones,° for they are yet but
ear-kissing arguments?°
EDMUND   Not I. Pray you, what are they?
CURAN   Have you heard of no likely wars toward° twixt the   10
Dukes of Cornwall and Albany?
EDMUND   Not a word.
CURAN   You may do, then, in time. Fare you well, sir.

Exit

---

41 temper mental equilibrium   **46 things** penises | **cut shorter** (a bawdy joke
addressed to the audience)

0.1 severally separately   **1 save** God save   **7 abroad** going the rounds | **ones**
the news, regarded as plural   **8 ear-kissing arguments** lightly whispered topics
10 toward impending

EDMUND   The Duke be here tonight? The better! Best!°
This weaves itself perforce into my business.   15
My father hath set guard to take my brother,
And I have one thing, of a queasy question,°
Which I must act. Briefness and fortune,° work!—
Brother, a word. Descend. Brother, I say!

Enter Edgar

My father watches. Oh, sir, fly this place!   20
Intelligence is given where you are hid.
You have now the good advantage of the night.
Have you not spoken 'gainst the Duke of Cornwall?
He's coming hither, now, i'th' night, i'th' haste,°
And Regan with him. Have you nothing said   25
Upon his party° 'gainst the Duke of Albany?
Advise yourself.°
EDGAR   I am sure on't,° not a word.
EDMUND   I hear my father coming. Pardon me;
In cunning I must draw my sword upon you.
Draw. Seem to defend yourself. Now, quit you° well.—   30
                                                [They draw]
Yield! Come before my father!—Light, ho, here!—
Fly, brother.—Torches, torches!—So, farewell.°
                                                Exit Edgar
Some blood drawn on me would beget opinion
Of my more fierce endeavor.° I have seen drunkards
Do more than this in sport.
[He wounds himself in the arm] Father, father!   35
Stop, stop! No help?

Enter Gloucester, and servants with torches

---

14 **the better! best!** so much the better; in fact, the best that could happen!
17 **queasy question** matter not for queasy stomachs   18 **briefness and fortune**
expeditious dispatch and good luck   24 **i'th' haste** in great haste   26 **upon his
party** recklessly on Cornwall's behalf (? it would be dangerous to speak on either
side)   27 **advise yourself** consider your situation │ **on't** of it   30 **quit you** defend,
acquit yourself   31–32 **yield . . . farewell** (Edmund speaks loudly as though trying to
arrest Edgar, calls for others to help, and privately bids Edgar to flee)   33–34 **beget . . .
endeavor** create an impression of my having fought fiercely

GLOUCESTER　　　　　　　　Now, Edmund, where's the villain?

EDMUND　Here stood he in the dark, his sharp sword out,
　Mumbling of wicked charms, conjuring the moon
　To stand 's° auspicious mistress.

GLOUCESTER　　　　　　　　But where is he?

EDMUND　Look, sir, I bleed.

GLOUCESTER　　　　　　　　Where is the villain, Edmund?　　40

EDMUND　Fled this way, sir. When by no means he could—

GLOUCESTER　Pursue him, ho! Go after.

　　　　　　　　　　　[*Exeunt some servants*]
　　　　　　　　　　　By no means what?

EDMUND　Persuade me to the murder of Your Lordship,
　But that° I told him the revenging gods
　'Gainst parricides did all the thunder bend,°　　45
　Spoke with how manifold and strong a bond
　The child was bound to th' father; sir, in fine,°
　Seeing how loathly opposite° I stood
　To his unnatural purpose, in fell motion°
　With his preparèd° sword he charges home°　　50
　My unprovided° body, latched° mine arm;
　And when he saw my best alarumed° spirits,
　Bold in the quarrel's right,° roused to th'encounter,
　Or whether ghasted° by the noise I made,
　Full suddenly he fled.

GLOUCESTER　　　　　　　　Let him fly far.°　　55
　Not in this land shall he remain uncaught;
　And found—dispatch.° The noble Duke my master,
　My worthy arch and patron,° comes tonight.
　By his authority I will proclaim it
　That he which finds him shall deserve our thanks,　　60
　Bringing the murderous coward to the stake;°
　He that conceals him, death.

---

39 **stand 's** stand his, act as his　44 **that** when　45 **bend** aim　47 **in fine** in conclusion　48 **loathly opposite** loathingly opposed　49 **fell motion** deadly thrust　50 **preparèd** unsheathed and ready | **home** to the very heart　51 **unprovided** unprotected | **latched** nicked, lanced　52 **best alarumed** thoroughly aroused to action, as by a trumpet　53 **quarrel's right** justice of the cause　54 **ghasted** frightened　55 **let him fly far** any fleeing, no matter how far, will be in vain　57 **dispatch** that will be the end for him　58 **arch and patron** chief patron　61 **to the stake** to reckoning

EDMUND   When I dissuaded him from his intent
　　And found him pight° to do it, with curst° speech
　　I threatened to discover° him. He replied,　　　　　　　　65
　　"Thou unpossessing° bastard, dost thou think,
　　If I would stand against thee, would the reposal°
　　Of any trust, virtue, or worth in thee
　　Make thy words faithed?° No. What° I should deny—
　　As this I would, ay, though thou didst produce　　　　70
　　My very character°—I'd turn° it all
　　To thy suggestion,° plot, and damnèd practice;°
　　And thou must make a dullard of the world
　　If they not thought the profits of my death
　　Were very pregnant and potential spirits　　　　　　　75
　　To make thee seek it."°
GLOUCESTER　　　　　　　　Oh, strange and fastened° villain!
　　Would he deny his letter, said he?
　　I never got° him.　　　　　　　　　　　*Tucket° within*
　　Hark, the Duke's trumpets! I know not why he comes.
　　All ports° I'll bar; the villain shall not scape.　　　80
　　The Duke must grant me that. Besides, his picture°
　　I will send far and near, that all the kingdom
　　May have due note of him; and of my land,
　　Loyal and natural° boy, I'll work the means
　　To make thee capable.°　　　　　　　　　　　　85

　　　　　Enter Cornwall, Regan, and attendants

CORNWALL　　How now, my noble friend? Since I came hither,
　　Which I can call but now, I have heard strange news.
REGAN   If it be true, all vengeance comes too short
　　Which can pursue th'offender. How dost, my lord?

---

64 pight determined | **curst** angry　**65 discover** expose　**66 unpossessing** unable
to inherit, beggarly　**67 reposal** placing　**69 faithed** believed　**what** that which,
whatever　**71 character** written testimony, handwriting | **turn** attribute　**72 sug-
gestion** instigation | **practice** scheming　**73–76 and . . . seek it** and you must think
everyone slow-witted indeed not to suppose that they would see how the profits to
be gained by my death would be fertile and potent tempters to make you seek my
death　**76 strange and fastened** unnatural and hardened　**78 got** begot | **s.d.**
tucket series of notes on the trumpet, here indicating Cornwall's arrival　**80 ports**
seaports, or gateways　**81 picture** description　**84 natural** (1) prompted by natural
feelings of loyalty and affection (2) bastard　**85 capable** legally able to become the
inheritor

GLOUCESTER   Oh madam, my old heart is cracked, it's cracked!   90
REGAN   What, did my father's godson seek your life?
        He whom my father named? Your Edgar?
GLOUCESTER   Oh, lady, lady, shame would have it hid!
REGAN   Was he not companion with the riotous knights
    That tended upon my father?   95
GLOUCESTER   I know not, madam. 'Tis too bad, too bad.
EDMUND   Yes, madam, he was of that consort.°
REGAN   No marvel, then, though° he were ill affected.°
    'Tis they have put him on° the old man's death,
    To have th'expense and spoil° of his revenues.   100
    I have this present evening from my sister
    Been well informed of them, and with such cautions
    That if they come to sojourn at my house
    I'll not be there.
CORNWALL   Nor I, assure thee, Regan.
    Edmund, I hear that you have shown your father   105
    A childlike° office.
EDMUND   It was my duty, sir.
GLOUCESTER *[to Cornwall]*
    He did bewray his practice,° and received
    This hurt you see striving to apprehend° him.
CORNWALL   Is he pursued?
GLOUCESTER   Ay, my good lord.
CORNWALL   If he be taken, he shall never more   110
    Be feared of doing harm. Make your own purpose,
    How in my strength you please.° For° you, Edmund,
    Whose virtue and obedience doth this instant
    So much commend itself, you shall be ours.
    Natures of such deep trust we shall much need;   115
    You we first seize on.
EDMUND   I shall serve you, sir,
    Truly, however else.°
GLOUCESTER   For him I thank Your Grace.

---

97 **consort** crew   98 **though** if | **ill affected** ill-disposed, disloyal   99 **put him on** incited him to   100 **th'expense and spoil** the squandering   106 **childlike** filial   107 **bewray his practice** expose his (Edgar's) plot   108 **apprehend** arrest   111–12 **make . . . please** go about achieving your purpose, making free use of my authority and resources   112 **for** as for   117 **however else** above all else

CORNWALL   You know not why we came to visit you—
REGAN   —Thus out of season, threading dark-eyed night: 120
Occasions, noble Gloucester, of some poise,°
Wherein we must have use of your advice.
Our father he hath writ, so hath our sister,
Of differences,° which° I least thought it fit
To answer from our home.° The several messengers   125
From hence attend dispatch.° Our good old friend,
Lay comforts to your bosom, and bestow
Your needful counsel to our businesses,
Which craves the instant use.°
GLOUCESTER   I serve you, madam.
Your Graces are right welcome.   130

Flourish. Exeunt

❖

ACT 2
SCENE 2

Location: Before Gloucester's house

*Enter Kent [disguised as Caius]
and steward [Oswald], severally°*

OSWALD   Good dawning° to thee, friend. Art of this house?
KENT   Ay.
OSWALD   Where may we set our horses?
KENT   I'th' mire.
OSWALD   Prithee, if thou lov'st me,° tell me.   5
KENT   I love thee not.
OSWALD   Why then, I care not for thee.
KENT   If I had thee in Lipsbury pinfold,° I would make thee
care for° me.

---

121 **poise** weight   123 **differences** quarrels | **which** which letters   124 **from our home** while still at our palace in Cornwall   125 **attend dispatch** wait to be dispatched   129 **the instant use** immediate attention

0.1 *severally* at separate doors   1 **dawning** (it is not yet day)   5 **if thou lov'st me** if you bear good will toward me (but Kent deliberately takes the phrase in its literal, not courtly, sense)   8 **in Lipsbury pinfold** within the pinfold of the lips, between my teeth (a *pinfold* is a pound for stray animals)   9 **care for** be wary of (playing on *care not for*, "do not like," in line 7)

OSWALD Why dost thou use me thus? I know thee not. 10

KENT Fellow, I know thee.°

OSWALD What dost thou know me for?

KENT A knave, a rascal, an eater of broken meats;° a base, proud, shallow, beggarly, three-suited, hundred-pound, filthy worsted-stocking knave;° a lily-livered, action-taking, 15 whoreson, glass-gazing, superserviceable, finical rogue; one-trunk-inheriting slave;° one that wouldst be a bawd in way of good service,° and art nothing but the composition° of a knave, beggar, coward, pander, and the son and heir of a mongrel bitch; one whom I will beat into clamorous 20 whining if thou deny'st the least syllable of thy addition.°

OSWALD Why, what a monstrous fellow art thou thus to rail on one that is neither known of thee nor knows thee!

KENT What a brazen-faced varlet art thou to deny thou knowest me! Is it two days since I tripped up thy heels and 25 beat thee before the King? Draw, you rogue, for though it be night, yet the moon shines. I'll make a sop o'th' moonshine° of you, you whoreson, cullionly barbermonger.° Draw!

[*He brandishes his sword*]

OSWALD Away! I have nothing to do with thee.

KENT Draw, you rascal! You come with letters against the 30 King, and take Vanity the puppet's part° against the royalty of her father. Draw, you rogue, or I'll so carbonado° your shanks—draw, you rascal! Come your ways.°

OSWALD Help, ho! Murder! Help!

---

11 I know thee I know you for what you are (playing on *know thee not,* "am unacquainted with you," in line 10) **13 broken meats** scraps of food (such as were passed out to the most lowly) **14–15 three-suited . . . knave** a steward of a household, with an allowance of three suits a year and a comfortable income of one hundred pounds, dressed in dirty wool stockings appropriate to the servant class **15–17 a lily-livered . . . slave** a cowardly, litigious, insufferable, self-infatuated, officious, foppish rogue, whose personal property all fits into one trunk **17–18 bawd . . . service** pimp or pander as a way of providing whatever is wanted **18 composition** compound **21 thy addition** the titles I've given you **27 sop o'th' moonshine** something so perforated that it will soak up moonshine as a sop (floating piece of toast) soaks up liquor **28 cullionly barbermonger** base frequenter of barber shops, fop (*cullion* originally meant "testicle") **31 vanity . . . part** the part of Goneril (here personified as a character in a morality play) **32 carbonado** cut crosswise, like meat for broiling **33 come your ways** come on

KENT   Strike, you slave! Stand, rogue, stand, you neat° slave,   35
     strike!   [*He beats him*]
OSWALD   Help, ho! Murder! Murder!

> *Enter Bastard, [Edmund, with his rapier drawn],*
> *Cornwall, Regan, Gloucester, servants*

EDMUND   How now, what's the matter?° Part!
KENT   With you,° goodman boy,° an° you please! Come, I'll
     flesh° ye. Come on, young master.   40
GLOUCESTER   Weapons? Arms? What's the matter here?
CORNWALL   Keep peace, upon your lives! [*Kent and Oswald are
     parted*] He dies that strikes again. What is the matter?
REGAN   The messengers from our sister and the King.
CORNWALL   What's your difference?° Speak.   45
OSWALD   I am scarce in breath, my lord.
KENT   No marvel, you have so bestirred your valor. You cow-
     ardly rascal, nature disclaims in° thee. A tailor made thee.
CORNWALL   Thou art a strange fellow. A tailor make a man?
KENT   A tailor, sir. A stonecutter or a painter could not have   50
     made him so ill, though they had been but two years o'th'
     trade.
CORNWALL   Speak yet, how grew your quarrel?
OSWALD   This ancient ruffian, sir, whose life I have spared at
     suit of his gray beard—   55
KENT   Thou whoreson zed!° Thou unnecessary letter!—My
     lord, if you'll give me leave, I will tread this unbolted° villain
     into mortar and daub° the wall of a jakes° with him.—Spare
     my gray beard, you wagtail?°
CORNWALL   Peace, sirrah!   60
     You beastly knave, know you no reverence?
KENT
     Yes, sir, but anger hath a privilege.

---

35 **neat** (1) foppish (2) calflike (*neat* means "horned cattle")   38 **matter** trouble
(but Kent takes the meaning "cause for quarrel")   39 **with you** I'll fight with you;
my quarrel is with you | **goodman boy** (a contemptuous epithet, a title of mock
respect, addressed seemingly to Edmund) | **an** if   40 **flesh** initiate into combat
45 **difference** quarrel   48 **disclaims in** disowns   56 **zed** the letter z (regarded as
unnecessary and often not included in dictionaries of the time)   57 **unbolted** unsifted;
hence, coarse   58 **daub** plaster | **jakes** privy   59 **wagtail** bird wagging its tail
feathers in pert obsequiousness

CORNWALL   Why art thou angry?

KENT   That such a slave as this should wear a sword,
Who wears no honesty. Such smiling rogues as these,   65
Like rats, oft bite the holy cords° atwain
Which are too intrinse° t'unloose; smooth° every passion
That in the natures of their lords rebel,°
Bring oil to fire, snow to their colder moods,°
Renege, affirm,° and turn their halcyon beaks°   70
With every gale and vary° of their masters,
Knowing naught, like dogs, but following.°—
A plague upon your epileptic° visage!
Smile you° my speeches, as° I were a fool?
Goose, an I had you upon Sarum plain,   75
I'd drive ye cackling home to Camelot.°

CORNWALL   What, art thou mad, old fellow?

GLOUCESTER   How fell you out? Say that.

KENT   No contraries hold more antipathy
Than I and such a knave.   80

CORNWALL
Why dost thou call him knave? What is his fault?

KENT   His countenance likes° me not.

CORNWALL
No more, perchance, does mine, nor his, nor hers.

KENT   Sir, 'tis my occupation to be plain:
I have seen better faces in my time   85
Than stands on any shoulder that I see
Before me at this instant.

CORNWALL   This is some fellow
Who, having been praised for bluntness, doth affect°

---

66 **holy cords** sacred bonds of loyalty and order   67 **intrinse** intrinsicate, tightly knotted | **smooth** flatter, humor   68 **rebel** rebel against reason   69 **bring . . . moods** flatteringly fuel the flame of their masters' angry passions, while similarly exacerbating their downward mood swings   70 **renege, affirm** nay-say one moment (when their lords are in a denying mood) and serve as yes-men the next | **halcyon beaks** (the halcyon or kingfisher, if hung up, would supposedly turn its beak into the wind)   71 **gale and vary** shifting wind   72 **following** fawning and flattery   73 **epileptic** trembling and pale with fright and distorted with a grin   74 **smile you** do you smile at | **as** as if   75–76 **goose . . . Camelot** (the reference is obscure, but the general sense is that Kent, if given space and opportunity, would send Oswald packing like a cackling goose Camelot, the legendary seat of King Arthur and his Knights of the Round Table, was thought to have been in the general vicinity of Salisbury, Sarum, and Gloucester)   82 **likes** pleases   88 **affect** adopt the style of

A saucy roughness, and constrains the garb
Quite from his nature.° He cannot flatter, he;°   90
An honest mind and plain,° he must speak truth!
An they will take't, so; if not, he's plain.
These kind of knaves I know, which in this plainness
Harbor more craft and more corrupter ends
Than twenty silly-ducking observants   95
That stretch their duties nicely.°
KENT   Sir, in good faith,° in sincere verity,
Under th'allowance° of your great aspect,°
Whose influence,° like the wreath of radiant fire
On flickering Phoebus' front—°
CORNWALL   What mean'st by this?   100
KENT   To go out of my dialect, which you discommend so
   much. I know, sir, I am no flatterer. He that beguiled you in a
   plain accent was a plain knave, which for my part I will not
   be, though I should win your displeasure to entreat me to't.°
CORNWALL [*to Oswald*] What was th'offense you gave him?   105
OSWALD   I never gave him any.
   It pleased the King his master very late°
   To strike at me, upon his misconstruction;°
   When he, compact, and flattering his displeasure,°
   Tripped me behind; being down, insulted,° railed,   110

89–90 constrains . . . nature distorts plainness quite from its true purpose so that it
becomes instead a way of deceiving the listener   **90 he . . . he** he professes to be one
who abhors the use of flattering speech (said sardonically)   **91 an . . . plain** if people
will take his rudeness, fine; if not, his excuse is that he speaks plain truth
95–96 than . . . nicely than twenty foolishly bowing, obsequious courtiers who outdo
themselves in the punctilious performance of their courtly duties   **97 sir, in good faith**
(Kent assumes the wordy mannerisms of courtly flattery)   **98 th'allowance** the
approval | **aspect** (1) countenance (2) astrological position   **99 influence** astrological
power   **100 Phoebus' front** the sun's forehead   **102–04 he . . . to't** the man who used
plain speech to you craftily (see lines 93–96) and thereby taught you to suspect plain
speakers of being deceitful was in fact a plain rascal, which part I will not play, much
as it would please me to incur your displeasure if speaking thus would have that effect
(Kent would prefer to displease Cornwall, since Cornwall is pleased only by flatterers,
and Kent has assumed until now that plain speech was the best way to offend, but he
now argues mockingly that he can no longer speak plainly, since his honest utterance
would be interpreted as duplicity)   **107 late** recently   **108 upon his misconstruction**
as a result of the King's misunderstanding (me)   **109 when . . . displeasure** whereupon
Kent, in cahoots with the King and his party, and wishing to gratify the King's anger
at me   **110 being down, insulted** when I was down, he exulted over me

And put upon him° such a deal of man
That worthied him, got praises of the King
For him attempting who was self-subdued;°
And, in the fleshment of this dread exploit,°
Drew on me here again.

KENT   None of these rogues and cowards   115
But Ajax is their fool.°

CORNWALL   Fetch forth the stocks!
You stubborn, ancient knave, you reverend° braggart,
We'll teach you.

KENT   Sir, I am too old to learn.
Call not your stocks for me. I serve the King,
On whose employment I was sent to you.   120
You shall do small respect, show too bold malice
Against the grace° and person of my master,
Stocking his messenger.

CORNWALL   Fetch forth the stocks!
As I have life and honor, There shall he sit till noon.

REGAN   Till noon? Till night, my lord, and all night too.   125

KENT   Why, madam, if I were your father's dog
You should° not use me so.

REGAN   Sir, being° his knave, I will.

CORNWALL   This is a fellow of the selfsame color°
Our sister speaks of.—Come, bring away° the stocks!   130

Stocks brought out

GLOUCESTER   Let me beseech Your Grace not to do so.
His fault is much, and the good King his master
Will check° him for't. Your purposed low correction
Is such as basest and contemned'st° wretches
For pilferings and most common trespasses   135
Are punished with. The King must take it ill
That he, so slightly valued in his messenger,

---

111 and put upon him and acted with a bravado that earned him an accolade
113 for . . . self-subdued for assailing one (myself) who chose not to resist   **114 and
. . . exploit** and, in the excitement of his first success in this fearless deed (said
ironically)   **115–16 none . . . fool** you never find any rogues and cowards of this sort
who do not outdo the blustering Ajax in their boasting   **117 reverend** (because old)
122 grace sovereignty, royal grace   **127 should** would   **128 being** since you are
129 color complexion, character   **130 away** along   **133 check** rebuke, correct
134 contemned'st most despised

Should have him thus restrained.

CORNWALL   I'll answer° that.

REGAN   My sister may receive it much more worse
To have her gentleman abused, assaulted,   140
For following her affairs. Put in his legs.

                     [Kent is put in the stocks]

Come, my good lord, away.

           Exeunt [all but Gloucester and Kent]

GLOUCESTER

I am sorry for thee, friend. 'Tis the Duke's pleasure,
Whose disposition, all the world well knows,
Will not be rubbed° nor stopped. I'll entreat for thee.   145

KENT   Pray, do not, sir. I have watched° and traveled hard.
Some time I shall sleep out; the rest I'll whistle.
A good man's fortune may grow out at heels.°
Give you° good morrow!

GLOUCESTER

The Duke's to blame in this. 'Twill be ill taken.   *Exit* 150

KENT   Good King, that must approve° the common saw,°
Thou out of heaven's benediction com'st
To the warm sun! [*He takes out a letter*]
Approach, thou beacon to this under globe,°
That by thy comfortable° beams I may   155
Peruse this letter. Nothing almost sees miracles
But misery.° I know 'tis from Cordelia,
Who hath most fortunately been informed
Of my obscurèd° course, "and shall find time
From this enormous state, seeking to give   160
Losses their remedies."° All weary and o'erwatched,°

---

138 answer be answerable for   **145 rubbed** hindered, obstructed (a term from bowls)
146 watched gone sleepless   **148 a . . . heels** even good men suffer decline in fortune
at times (to be out at heels is literally to be threadbare, coming through one's stock-
ings)   **149 give you** God give you   **151 approve** prove true | **saw** proverb ("to run
out of God's blessing into the warm sun," meaning "to go from better to worse,"
from a state of bliss into the pitiless world; Kent sees Lear as heading for trouble)
154 beacon . . . globe the sun (daylight is coming soon)   **155 comfortable** comforting
156–57 nothing . . . misery scarcely anything can make one appreciate miracles like
being in a state of misery; to the miserable, any relief seems miraculous   **159 obscurèd**
disguised   **159–61 "and shall . . . remedies"** "and who, in the fullness of time, will
bring relief from the monstrous state of affairs under which we suffer, seeking to remedy what has been destroyed" (the passage may be corrupt; Kent may be reading from
his letter)   **161 o'erwatched** exhausted with staying awake

Take vantage,° heavy eyes, not to behold
This shameful lodging.°
Fortune, good night. Smile once more; turn thy wheel!°

                                                  [He sleeps]

❖

ACT 2
SCENE 3

Location: Scene continues. Kent is dozing in the stocks

                                                     Enter Edgar

EDGAR   I heard myself proclaimed,
  And by the happy° hollow of a tree
  Escaped the hunt. No port° is free, no place
  That° guard and most unusual vigilance
  Does not attend my taking.° Whiles I may scape   5
  I will preserve myself, and am bethought°
  To take the basest and most poorest shape
  That ever penury, in contempt of man,°
  Brought near to beast. My face I'll grime with filth,
  Blanket my loins, elf° all my hairs in knots,   10
  And with presented° nakedness outface
  The winds and persecutions of the sky.
  The country gives me proof° and precedent
  Of Bedlam° beggars who with roaring voices
  Strike° in their numbed and mortifièd° arms   15
  Pins, wooden pricks,° nails, sprigs of rosemary;
  And with this horrible object,° from low° farms,
  Poor pelting° villages, sheepcotes, and mills,
  Sometimes with lunatic bans,° sometimes with prayers,

---

162 vantage advantage (of sleep)   **163 lodging** the stocks   **164 wheel** (since Kent is at the bottom of Fortune's wheel, any turning should improve his situation)

2 happy luckily found   **3 port** (see 2.1.80 and note)   **4 that** in which   **5 attend my taking** lie in wait to capture me   **6 bethought** resolved   **8 in . . . man** in order to show how contemptible humankind is   **10 elf** tangle into elflocks   **11 presented** exposed to view, displayed   **13 proof** example   **14 Bedlam** (see the note to 1.2.124–25.)   **15 strike** stick | **mortifièd** deadened   **16 wooden pricks** skewers   **17 object** spectacle | **low** lowly   **18 pelting** paltry   **19 bans** curses

Enforce their charity.° Poor Turlygod! Poor Tom!°   20
That's something yet. Edgar I nothing am.°

Exit

❖

ACT 2
SCENE 4

Location: Scene continues before Gloucester's house.
Kent still dozing in the stocks

Enter Lear, Fool, and Gentleman

LEAR 'Tis strange that they° should so depart from home
And not send back my messenger.

GENTLEMAN   As I learned,
The night before there was no purpose in them
Of this remove.°

KENT   Hail to thee, noble master!

LEAR Ha?   5
Mak'st thou this shame thy pastime?

KENT   No, my lord.

FOOL Ha, ha, he wears cruel° garters. Horses are tied by the
heads, dogs and bears by th' neck, monkeys by th' loins, and
men by th' legs. When a man's overlusty at legs,° then he
wears wooden netherstocks.°   10

LEAR What's he that hath so much thy place mistook
To° set thee here?

KENT   It is both he and she:
Your son and daughter.

LEAR No.

KENT Yes.   15

LEAR No, I say.

---

20 enforce their charity manage to beg something | **poor . . . Tom** (Edgar practices
the begging role he is about to adopt; beggars were known as "poor Toms")
Turlygod (meaning unknown)   **21 that's . . . am** there's some kind of existence for
me as poor Tom; I am Edgar no longer

1 they Cornwall and Regan   **4 remove** change of residence   **7 cruel** (1) unkind
(2) crewel (compare the Quarto spelling, "crewell"), a thin yarn of which hose were
made   **9 overlusty at legs** given to running away, or overly active sexually
10 netherstocks stockings   **12 to** as to

KENT   I say yea.

LEAR   No, no, they would not.

KENT   Yes, they have.

LEAR   By Jupiter, I swear no.   20

KENT   By Juno, I swear ay.

LEAR   They durst not do't!
    They could not, would not do't. 'Tis worse than murder
    To do upon respect° such violent outrage.
    Resolve° me with all modest haste which way
    Thou mightst deserve, or they impose, this usage,   25
    Coming from us.

KENT   My lord, when at their home°
    I did commend° Your Highness' letters to them,
    Ere I was risen from the place that showed
    My duty kneeling,° came there a reeking° post,
    Stewed° in his haste, half breathless, panting forth   30
    From Goneril his mistress salutations;
    Delivered letters, spite of intermission,°
    Which presently° they read; on° whose contents
    They summoned up their meiny,° straight took horse,
    Commanded me to follow and attend   35
    The leisure of their answer, gave me cold looks;
    And meeting here the other messenger,
    Whose welcome, I perceived, had poisoned mine—
    Being the very fellow which of late
    Displayed so saucily° against Your Highness—   40
    Having more man than wit° about me, drew.
    He raised the house with loud and coward cries.
    Your son and daughter found this trespass worth
    The shame which here it suffers.

---

23 **upon respect** against my officers (who deserve respect)   24 **resolve** enlighten |
modest moderate   26 **their home** (Kent and Oswald went first to Cornwall's palace
after leaving Albany's palace)   27 **commend** deliver   28–29 **from . . . kneeling** from
the kneeling posture that showed my duty   29 **reeking** steaming (with heat of
travel)   30 **stewed** thoroughly heated, soaked   32 **spite of intermission** in disregard
of interrupting me, or, in spite of the interruptions caused by his being out of breath
33 **presently** instantly | **on** on the basis of   34 **meiny** retinue of servants, house-
hold   40 **displayed so saucily** behaved so insolently   41 **more man than wit** more
courage than good sense

FOOL   Winter's not gone yet if the wild geese fly that way.°   45
    Fathers that wear rags
      Do make their children blind,°
    But fathers that bear bags°
      Shall see their children kind.
    Fortune, that arrant whore,   50
    Ne'er turns the key° to th' poor.
But, for all this, thou shalt have as many dolors° for° thy
daughters as thou canst tell° in a year.

LEAR   Oh, how this mother swells up toward my heart!
Hysterica passio,° down, thou climbing sorrow!   55
Thy element's° below.—Where is this daughter?

KENT   With the Earl, sir, here within.

LEAR   Follow me not. Stay here.   *Exit*

GENTLEMAN
Made you no more offense but what you speak of?

KENT   None.   60
How chance° the King comes with so small a number?

FOOL   An° thou hadst been set i'th' stocks for that question,
thou'dst well deserved it.

KENT   Why, Fool?

FOOL   We'll set thee to school to an ant to teach thee there's no   65
laboring i'th' winter.° All that follow their noses are led by
their eyes but blind men, and there's not a nose among
twenty but can smell him that's stinking.° Let go thy hold
when a great wheel runs down a hill lest it break thy neck
with following; but the great one that goes upward, let him   70
draw thee after. When a wise man gives thee better counsel,
give me mine again. I would have none but knaves follow it,
since a fool gives it.

---

45 winter's . . . way the signs still point to continued and worsening fortune; the wild geese are still flying south   **47 blind** indifferent to their father's needs   **48 bags** of gold   **51 turns the key** opens the door   **52 dolors** griefs (with pun on "dollars," English word for an Austrian or Spanish coin) | **for** (1) on account of (2) in exchange for   **53 tell** (1) relate (2) count   **54, 55 mother,** *Hysterica passio* hysteria, giving the sensation of choking or suffocating   **56 element's** proper place is (hysteria, from the Greek *hystera*, womb, was thought to be produced by vapors ascending from the uterus or abdomen)   **61 chance** chances it   **62 an** if   **65–66 we'll . . . winter** Just as the ant knows not to labor in the winter, the wise man knows not to labor for one whose fortunes are fallen   **66–68 all . . . stinking** one who is out of favor can be easily detected (he smells of misfortune) and so is easily avoided by timeservers

That sir which serves and seeks for gain,
  And follows but for form,   75
Will pack° when it begins to rain
  And leave thee in the storm.
But I will tarry; the fool will stay,
  And let the wise man fly.
The knave turns fool that runs away;°   80
  The fool no knave, pardie.°

        Enter Lear and Gloucester

KENT   Where learned you this, Fool?

FOOL   Not i'th' stocks, fool.

LEAR   Deny to speak with me? They are sick? They are weary?
They have traveled all the night? Mere fetches,°   85
The images° of revolt and flying off.°
Fetch me a better answer.

GLOUCESTER   My dear lord,
You know the fiery quality of the Duke,
How unremovable and fixed he is
In his own course.   90

LEAR   Vengeance! Plague! Death! Confusion!°
Fiery? What quality? Why, Gloucester, Gloucester,
I'd speak with the Duke of Cornwall and his wife.

GLOUCESTER   Well, my good lord, I have informed them so.

LEAR   Informed them? Dost thou understand me, man?   95

GLOUCESTER   Ay, my good lord.

LEAR   The King would speak with Cornwall. The dear father
Would with his daughter speak, commands, tends° service.
Are they informed of this? My breath and blood!°
Fiery? The fiery Duke? Tell the hot Duke that—   100
No, but not yet. Maybe he is not well.
Infirmity doth still neglect all office
Whereto our health is bound;° we are not ourselves
When nature, being oppressed, commands the mind

---

76 pack be off   **80 the knave . . . away** deserting one's master is the greatest folly
81 pardie *par Dieu* (French), "by God"   **85 fetches** pretexts, dodges   **86 images**
signs | **flying off** desertion   **91 confusion!** destruction!   **98 tends** attends, waits
for   **99 my . . . blood!** by my very life (an oath)   **102–03 infirmity . . . bound** sickness always prompts us to neglect all duties which in good health we are bound to
perform

To suffer with the body. I'll forbear,   105
And am fallen out with my more headier will,
To take the indisposed and sickly fit
For the sound man.°   [*Looking at Kent*]
                        Death on my state!° Wherefore
Should he sit here? This act persuades me
That this remotion° of the Duke and her   110
Is practice° only. Give me my servant forth.°
Go tell the Duke and 's wife I'd speak with them,
Now, presently.° Bid them come forth and hear me,
Or at their chamber door I'll beat the drum
Till it cry sleep to death.°   115
GLOUCESTER   I would have all well betwixt you.   *Exit*
LEAR   Oh, me, my heart, my rising heart! But down!
FOOL   Cry to it, nuncle, as the cockney° did to the eels when
she put 'em i'th' paste° alive. She knapped° 'em o'th' cox-
combs° with a stick and cried, "Down, wantons,° down!" 120
'Twas her brother that, in pure kindness to his horse, but-
tered his hay.°

        Enter Cornwall, Regan, Gloucester, [and] servants

LEAR   Good morrow to you both.
CORNWALL   Hail to your Grace!
                        Kent here set at liberty
REGAN   I am glad to see your Highness.
LEAR   Regan, I think you are. I know what reason   125
I have to think so. If thou shouldst not be glad,

106–08 **and . . . man** and now disapprove of my more impetuous will in having
rashly supposed that those who are indisposed and sickly were in sound health
108 **death . . . state!** (a common oath, here ironically appropriate to a king whose
royal authority is dying)   110 **remotion** removal, inaccessibility   111 **practice**
deception | **forth** out of the stocks   113 **presently** at once   115 **cry sleep to death**
puts an end to sleep by the noise   118 **cockney** a Londoner, ignorant of ways of
cooking eels   119 **paste** pastry pie | **knapped** rapped   119–20 **coxcombs** heads
120 **wantons** playful creatures, sexy rogues (a term of affectionate abuse; the
cockney wife is trying to coax and wheedle the eels into laying down their lives for
the making of the pastry pie—a plea that is about as ineffectual as Lear's imploring
his rising heart to subside)   121–22 **'twas . . . hay** (another city ignorance; the act
is well intended, but horses do not like greasy hay; as with Lear, good intentions
are not enough; the *brother* is related to the cockney wife in that they are both
misguidedly tenderhearted)

I would divorce me from thy mother's tomb,
Sepulch'ring an adultress.° [*To Kent*] Oh, are you free?
Some other time for that.—Belovèd Regan,
Thy sister's naught.° Oh, Regan, she hath tied   130
Sharp-toothed unkindness, like a vulture, here.

                       [*He lays his hand on his heart*]

I can scarce speak to thee. Thou'lt not believe
With how depraved a quality°—Oh, Regan!
REGAN   I pray you, sir, take patience. I have hope
You less know how to value her desert   135
Than she to scant her duty.°
LEAR   Say?° How is that?
REGAN   I cannot think my sister in the least
Would fail her obligation. If, sir, perchance
She have restrained the riots of your followers,
'Tis on such ground and to such wholesome end   140
As clears her from all blame.
LEAR   My curses on her!
REGAN   Oh, sir, you are old;
Nature in you stands on the very verge
Of his confine.° You should be ruled and led
By some discretion that discerns your state°   145
Better than you yourself. Therefore, I pray you,
That to our sister you do make return.
Say you have wronged her.
LEAR   Ask her forgiveness?
Do you but mark how this becomes the house:°
[*Kneeling*] "Dear daughter, I confess that I am old;   150
Age is unnecessary. On my knees I beg
That you'll vouchsafe me raiment, bed, and food."
REGAN   Good sir, no more. These are unsightly tricks.
Return you to my sister.

127–28 I would . . . adultress I would cease to honor your dead mother's tomb, since it would surely contain the dead body of an adultress (only such a fantasy of illegitimacy could explain to Lear filial ingratitude of the monstrous sort that now confronts him) **130 naught** wicked **133 quality** disposition **134–36 I have . . . duty** I trust this is more a matter of your undervaluing her merit than of her falling slack in her duty to you **136 say?** come again? **143–44 nature . . . confine** your life has almost completed its allotted scope **145 by . . . state** by some discreet person who understands your situation and condition **149 becomes the house** suits domestic decorum and the royal family line (said with bitter irony)

LEAR [*rising*]   Never, Regan.
    She hath abated° me of half my train,   155
    Looked black upon me, struck me with her tongue
    Most serpentlike upon the very heart.
    All the stored vengeances of heaven fall
    On her ingrateful top!° Strike her young bones,
    You taking° airs, with lameness!
CORNWALL   Fie, sir, fie!   160
LEAR   You nimble lightnings, dart your blinding flames
    Into her scornful eyes! Infect her beauty,
    You fen-sucked° fogs drawn by the powerful sun
    To fall and blister!°
REGAN   O the blest gods! So will you wish on me   165
    When the rash mood is on.
LEAR   No, Regan, thou shalt never have my curse.
    Thy tender-hafted° nature shall not give
    Thee o'er to harshness. Her eyes are fierce, but thine
    Do comfort and not burn. 'Tis not in thee   170
    To grudge my pleasures, to cut off my train,
    To bandy° hasty words, to scant my sizes,°
    And, in conclusion, to oppose the bolt°
    Against my coming in. Thou better know'st
    The offices of nature, bond of childhood,°   175
    Effects° of courtesy, dues of gratitude.
    Thy half o'th' kingdom hast thou not forgot,
    Wherein I thee endowed.
REGAN   Good sir, to th' purpose.°
LEAR   Who put my man i'th' stocks?   *Tucket within*
CORNWALL   What trumpet's that?
REGAN   I know't—my sister's. This approves° her letter,   180
    That she would soon be here.

                          Enter steward [Oswald]

                          Is your lady come?

---

155 **abated** deprived   159 **ingrateful top** ungrateful head   160 **taking** infectious
163 **fen-sucked** (it was supposed that the sun sucked up poisons from fens or marshes)
164 **to fall and blister** to fall upon her and blister her beauty   168 **tender-hafted** gentle
(literally, set in a tender *haft*, handle or frame)   172 **bandy** volley, exchange | **scant
my sizes** diminish my allowances   173 **oppose the bolt** lock the door   175 **the offices
... childhood** the natural duties and filial obligations due to parents   176 **effects** outward manifestations   178 **to th' purpose** get to the point   180 **approves** confirms

LEAR   This is a slave, whose easy-borrowed° pride
   Dwells in the fickle grace° of her he follows.—
   Out, varlet,° from my sight!
CORNWALL   What means Your Grace?
LEAR   Who stocked my servant? Regan, I have good hope   185
   Thou didst not know on't.

                          Enter Goneril

              Who comes here? O heavens,
   If you do love old men, if your sweet sway
   Allow° obedience, if you yourselves are old,
   Make it your cause; send down, and take my part!
   [*To Goneril*] Art not ashamed to look upon this beard?°   190
                [*Goneril and Regan join hands*]
   Oh, Regan, will you take her by the hand?
GONERIL   Why not by th' hand, sir? How have I offended?
   All's not offense that indiscretion finds
   And dotage terms so.°
LEAR   O sides,° you are too tough!
   Will you yet hold?—How came my man i'th' stocks?   195
CORNWALL   I set him there, sir; but his own disorders
   Deserved much less advancement.°
LEAR   You? Did you?
REGAN   I pray you, father, being weak, seem so.°
   If till the expiration of your month
   You will return and sojourn with my sister,   200
   Dismissing half your train, come then to me.
   I am now from° home, and out of that provision
   Which shall be needful for your entertainment.°
LEAR   Return to her? And fifty men dismissed?
   No! Rather I abjure all roofs, and choose   205
   To wage° against the enmity o'th'air,

---

182 easy-borrowed easily put on   **183 grace** favor   **184 varlet** worthless fellow
188 allow approve, sanction   **190 beard** (a sign of age and presumed entitlement to
respect)   **193–94 all's . . . so** not everything that the poor judgment and dotage of
old age deem offensive is actually so   **194 sides** sides of the chest (stretched by the
swelling heart)   **197 much less advancement** far less honor, far worse treatment
198 seem so don't act as if you were strong   **202 from** away from   **203 entertainment** proper reception   **206 wage** wage war

To be a comrade with the wolf and owl—
Necessity's sharp pinch. Return with her?
Why, the hot-blooded° France, that dowerless took
Our youngest born—I could as well be brought   210
To knee° his throne and, squirelike, pension beg
To keep base life afoot. Return with her?
Persuade me rather to be slave and sumpter°
To this detested groom.   [*He points to Oswald*]

GONERIL   At your choice, sir.

LEAR   I prithee, daughter, do not make me mad.   215
I will not trouble thee, my child. Farewell.
We'll no more meet, no more see one another.
But yet thou art my flesh, my blood, my daughter—
Or rather a disease that's in my flesh,
Which I must needs call mine. Thou art a boil,   220
A plague-sore, or embossèd° carbuncle
In my corrupted blood. But I'll not chide thee;
Let shame come when it will, I do not call° it.
I do not bid the thunder-bearer° shoot,
Nor tell tales of thee to high-judging° Jove.   225
Mend when thou canst; be better at thy leisure.
I can be patient. I can stay with Regan,
I and my hundred knights.

REGAN   Not altogether so.
I looked not for° you yet, nor am provided   230
For your fit welcome. Give ear, sir, to my sister;
For those that mingle reason with your passion
Must be content to think you old,° and so—
But she knows what she does.

LEAR   Is this well spoken?

REGAN   I dare avouch° it, sir. What, fifty followers?   235
Is it not well? What should you need of more?
Yea, or so many, sith that° both charge° and danger

---

209 hot-blooded spirited, youthful; choleric   **211 knee** fall on my knees before
213 sumpter packhorse; hence, drudge   **221 embossèd** swollen, tumid   **223 call**
summon   **224 the thunder-bearer** Jove   **225 high-judging** judging from on high
230 looked not for did not expect   **232–33 for . . . old** for those who dispassionately
consider your intemperate outbursts must conclude that you are old   **235 avouch**
vouch for   **237 sith that** since | **charge** expense

Speak 'gainst so great a number? How in one house
Should many people under two commands
Hold amity? 'Tis hard, almost impossible.   240
GONERIL   Why might not you, my lord, receive attendance
From those that she calls servants, or from mine?
REGAN   Why not, my lord? If then they chanced to slack° ye,
We could control° them. If you will come to me—
For now I spy a danger—I entreat you   245
To bring but five-and-twenty. To no more
Will I give place or notice.°
LEAR   I gave you all—
REGAN   And in good time you gave it.
LEAR   Made you my guardians, my depositaries,°
But kept a reservation° to be followed   250
With such a number. What, must I come to you
With five-and-twenty? Regan, said you so?
REGAN   And speak't again, my lord. No more with me.
LEAR   Those wicked creatures yet do look well-favored°
When others are more wicked; not being the worst   255
Stands in some rank of praise.° [*To Goneril*] I'll go with thee.
Thy fifty yet doth double five-and-twenty,
And thou art twice her love.
GONERIL   Hear me, my lord:
What need you five-and-twenty, ten, or five,
To follow° in a house where twice so many   260
Have a command to tend you?
REGAN   What need one?
LEAR   Oh, reason not° the need! Our basest beggars
Are in the poorest thing superfluous.°
Allow not° nature more than nature needs,°
Man's life is cheap as beast's. Thou art a lady;   265

---

243 slack neglect   **244 control** correct   **247 place or notice** houseroom or recognition   **249 depositaries** trustees   **250 kept a reservation** reserved a right   **254 well-
favored** attractive, fair of feature   **256 stands . . . praise** achieves, by necessity,
some relative deserving of praise   **260 follow** be your attendants   **262 reason not**
do not dispassionately analyze   **262–63 our . . . superfluous** even our most destitute beggars have some wretched possessions beyond what they absolutely need
264 allow not if you do not allow | **needs** to survive

If only to go warm were gorgeous,
Why, nature needs not what thou gorgeous wear'st,
Which scarcely keeps thee warm.° But, for true need—
You heavens, give me that patience, patience I need!
You see me here, you gods, a poor old man,   270
As full of grief as age, wretched in both.
If it be you that stirs these daughters' hearts
Against their father, fool me not so much
To° bear it tamely; touch me with noble anger,
And let not women's weapons, water drops,   275
Stain my man's cheeks. No, you unnatural hags,
I will have such revenges on you both
That all the world shall—I will do such things—
What they are yet I know not, but they shall be
The terrors of the earth. You think I'll weep;   280
No, I'll not weep.   *Storm and tempest*
I have full cause of weeping; but this heart
Shall break into a hundred thousand flaws°
Or ere° I'll weep. Oh, Fool, I shall go mad!
                     Exeunt [Lear, Gloucester, Kent, Gentleman, and Fool]
CORNWALL   Let us withdraw. 'Twill be a storm.   285
REGAN   This house is little. The old man and 's people
Cannot be well bestowed.°
GONERIL   'Tis his own blame° hath° put himself from rest,°
And must needs taste° his folly.
REGAN   For his particular,° I'll receive him gladly,   290
But not one follower.
GONERIL   So am I purposed. Where is my lord of Gloucester?
CORNWALL   Followed the old man forth.

                                   Enter Gloucester

                              He is returned.

266–68 if . . . warm if fashions in clothes were determined only by the need for warmth, this natural standard wouldn't justify the rich robes you wear to be gorgeous—which don't serve well for warmth in any case   273–74 fool . . . to do not make me so foolish as to   283 flaws fragments   284 or ere before   287 bestowed lodged   288 blame fault | hath that he has, or, that has | from rest out of the house; also, lacking peace of mind   289 taste experience   290 for his particular as for him individually

GLOUCESTER   The King is in high rage.

CORNWALL   Whither is he going?

GLOUCESTER   He calls to horse, but will I know not whither.   295

CORNWALL   'Tis best to give him way. He leads himself.°

GONERIL [*to Gloucester*]
   My lord, entreat him by no means° to stay.

GLOUCESTER   Alack, the night comes on, and the bleak winds
   Do sorely ruffle.° For many miles about
   There's scarce a bush.

REGAN   Oh, sir, to willful men   300
   The injuries that they themselves procure
   Must be their schoolmasters. Shut up your doors.
   He is attended with a desperate train,
   And what they may incense him to, being apt
   To have his ear abused,° wisdom bids fear.   305

CORNWALL   Shut up your doors, my lord; 'tis a wild night.
   My Regan counsels well. Come out o'th' storm.

                                                    Exeunt

❧

ACT 3
SCENE 1

Location: An open place in Gloucestershire

Storm still. Enter Kent [disguised as
Caius] and a Gentleman, severally°

KENT   Who's there, besides foul weather?

GENTLEMAN   One minded like the weather, most unquietly.

KENT   I know you. Where's the King?

GENTLEMAN   Contending with the fretful elements;
   Bids the wind blow the earth into the sea   5
   Or swell the curlèd waters 'bove the main,°
   That things° might change or cease; tears his white hair,
   Which the impetuous blasts with eyeless rage

---

296 **give . . . himself** give him his own way; he is guided only by his own willfulness
297 **entreat . . . means** by no means entreat him   299 **ruffle** bluster   304-05 **being . . .**
abused (he) being inclined to hearken to wild counsel

0.2 *severally* at separate doors   6 **main** mainland   7 **things** all things

Catch in their fury and make nothing of;°
Strives in his little world of man° to outstorm   10
The to-and-fro-conflicting wind and rain.
This night, wherein the cub-drawn° bear would couch,°
The lion and the belly-pinchèd wolf
Keep their fur dry, unbonneted he runs
And bids what will take all.°

KENT   But who is with him?   15

GENTLEMAN   None but the Fool, who labors to outjest°
His heart-struck injuries.°

KENT   Sir, I do know you,
And dare upon the warrant of my note
Commend a dear thing to you.° There is division,
Although as yet the face of it is covered   20
With mutual cunning, twixt Albany and Cornwall;
Who have—as who have not, that their great stars
Throned and set high?°—servants, who seem no less,°
Which are to France the spies and speculations°
Intelligent of° our state. What hath been seen,   25
Either in snuffs and packings° of the dukes,
Or the hard rein which both of them hath borne
Against the old kind King,° or something deeper,
Whereof perchance these are but furnishings°—
But true it is, from France there comes a power°   30
Into this scattered° kingdom, who already,
Wise in° our negligence, have secret feet°
In some of our best ports and are at point°
To show their open banner. Now to you:
If on my credit° you dare build so far°   35

---

9 make nothing of blow about contemptuously   **10 little world of man** microcosm, which is an epitome of the macrocosm or universe   **12 cub-drawn** famished, with udders sucked dry (and hence ravenous) | **couch** lie close in its den   **15 bids . . . all** (a cry of desperate defiance; "take all" is the cry of a gambler in staking his last)   **16 outjest** exorcise or relieve by jesting   **17 heart-struck injuries** injuries that strike to the very heart   **18–19 and . . . to you** and dare, on the strength of what I know about you, entrust a precious undertaking to you   **22–23 as . . . high** as who does not, among those whom a mighty destiny has enthroned on high   **23 no less** no other than servants   **24 speculations** scouts, spies   **25 intelligent of** supplying intelligence pertinent to   **26 snuffs and packings** resentments and intrigues   **27–28 or . . . king** or the harsh reining in they both have inflicted on King Lear   **29 furnishings** outward shows   **30 power** army   **31 scattered** divided   **32 wise in** taking advantage of | **feet** footholds   **33 at point** ready   **35 credit** trustworthiness | **so far** so far as

To make your speed to Dover, you shall find
Some that will thank you, making just report°
Of how unnatural and bemadding sorrow
The King hath cause to plain.°
I am a gentleman of blood and breeding,° 40
And from some knowledge and assurance° offer
This office° to you.
GENTLEMAN   I will talk further with you.
KENT   No, do not.
For confirmation that I am much more
Than my outwall,° open this purse and take 45
What it contains.   [*He gives a purse and a ring*]
                      If you shall see Cordelia—
As fear not but° you shall—show her this ring,
And she will tell you who that fellow° is
That yet you do not know. Fie on this storm!
I will go seek the King. 50
GENTLEMAN   Give me your hand. Have you no more to say?
KENT   Few words, but, to effect,° more than all yet:
That when we have found the King—in which your pain
That way, I'll this°—he that first lights on him
Holla the other. 55
                              Exeunt [separately]

❖

ACT 3
SCENE 2

Location: An open place, as before

Storm still. Enter Lear and Fool

LEAR   Blow, winds, and crack your cheeks! Rage, blow!
You cataracts and hurricanoes,° spout
Till you have drenched° our steeples, drowned the cocks!°

---

37 **making just report** for making an accurate report   39 **plain** complain   40 **blood and breeding** good family and education   41 **assurance** confidence, certainty   42 **office** assignment   45 **outwall** exterior appearance   47 **fear not but** be assured that   48 **fellow** Kent   52 **to effect** in their consequences   53–54 **in which . . . this** in which task, you search in that direction while I go this way

2 **hurricanoes** waterspouts   3 **drenched** drowned | **cocks** weathercocks

You sulfurous and thought-executing fires,°
Vaunt-couriers° of oak-cleaving thunderbolts,   5
Singe my white head! And thou, all-shaking thunder,
Strike flat the thick rotundity o'th' world!
Crack nature's molds, all germens spill at once°
That makes ingrateful man!

FOOL   Oh, nuncle, court holy water° in a dry house is better   10
than this rainwater out o'door. Good nuncle, in, ask thy
daughters blessing.° Here's a night pities neither wise men
nor fools.

LEAR   Rumble thy bellyful! Spit, fire! Spout, rain!
Nor° rain, wind, thunder, fire are my daughters.   15
I tax° not you, you elements, with° unkindness;
I never gave you kingdom, called you children.
You owe me no subscription.° Then let fall
Your horrible pleasure. Here I stand your slave,
A poor, infirm, weak, and despised old man.   20
But yet I call you servile ministers,°
That will with two pernicious daughters join
Your high-engendered battles° 'gainst a head
So old and white as this. Oho! 'Tis foul.

FOOL

He that has a house to put 's head in has a good headpiece.°   25
      The codpiece that will house
         Before the head has any,
      The head and he shall louse;
         So beggars marry many.
      The man that makes his toe   30
         What he his heart should make

---

4 **thought-executing fires** lightning that acts with the quickness of thought
5 **vaunt-couriers** forerunners   8 **crack . . . at once** crack the molds in which nature
makes all life; destroy all seeds at once   10 **court holy water** flattery   11–12 **ask . . .
blessing** (for Lear to do so would be to acknowledge their authority)   15 **nor** nei-
ther   16 **tax** accuse | **with** of   18 **subscription** allegiance   21 **ministers** agents
23 **high-engendered battles** battalions engendered in the heavens   25 **headpiece**
(1) helmetlike covering for the head (2) head for common sense   26–33 **The codpiece
. . . wake** a man who houses his genitals in a sexual embrace before he has a roof over
his head can expect the lice-infested penury of a penniless marriage; and anyone who
unwisely places his affection on base things will be afflicted with sorrow and sleep-
lessness (the *codpiece* is a covering for the genitals worn by men with their close-fit-
ting hose; here representing the genitals themselves) the *corn* is a bunion on the toe

Shall of a corn cry woe,
        And turn his sleep to wake.°
For there was never yet fair woman but she made mouths in
    a glass.°   35
LEAR   No, I will be the pattern of all patience;
    I will say nothing.

Enter Kent, [disguised as Caius]

KENT   Who's there?
FOOL   Marry,° here's grace° and a codpiece;° that's a wise man
    and a fool.   40
KENT   Alas, sir, are you here? Things that love night
    Love not such nights as these. The wrathful skies
    Gallow the very wanderers of the dark°
    And make them keep° their caves. Since I was man,
    Such sheets of fire, such bursts of horrid thunder,   45
    Such groans of roaring wind and rain I never
    Remember to have heard. Man's nature cannot carry°
    Th'affliction° nor the fear.
LEAR   Let the great gods,
    That keep this dreadful pother° o'er our heads,
    Find out their enemies now. Tremble, thou wretch,   50
    That hast within thee undivulgèd crimes
    Unwhipped of justice! Hide thee, thou bloody hand,
    Thou perjured, and thou simular° of virtue
    That art incestuous! Caitiff,° to pieces shake,
    That under covert and convenient seeming°   55
    Has practiced on° man's life! Close pent-up guilts,
    Rive your concealing continents and cry
    These dreadful summoners grace!° I am a man

34–5 made . . . glass practiced making attractive faces in a mirror   39 marry (an oath, originally "by the Virgin Mary") | grace royal grace | codpiece (often prominent in the Fool's costume)   43 gallow . . . dark frighten the very wild beasts of the night   44 keep occupy, remain inside   47 carry endure   48 th'affliction the physical affliction   49 pother hubbub, turmoil   53 simular pretender   54 caitiff wretch   55 convenient seeming deception fitted to the purpose   56 practiced on plotted against   56–58 close . . . grace! you secret and buried consciousnesses of guilt, burst open the hiding places that conceal you, and pray for mercy! (*summoners* are the officers who cited offenders to appear before ecclesiastical courts)

More sinned against than sinning.

FOOL   Alack, bareheaded?
Gracious my lord, hard by here is a hovel;   60
Some friendship will it lend you 'gainst the tempest.
Repose you there while I to this hard house—
More harder than the stones whereof 'tis raised,
Which° even but now, demanding° after you,
Denied me to come in—return and force   65
Their scanted° courtesy.

LEAR   My wits begin to turn.
Come on, my boy. How dost, my boy? Art cold?
I am cold myself.—Where is this straw, my fellow?
The art of our necessities is strange,
And can make vile things precious. Come, your hovel.—   70
Poor fool and knave, I have one part in my heart
That's sorry yet for thee.

FOOL [*sings*]
          "He that has and a little tiny wit,
               With heigh-ho, the wind and the rain,
          Must make content with his fortunes fit,   75
               Though the rain it raineth every day."°

LEAR   True, boy.—Come, bring us to this hovel.

                                   Exit [*with Kent*]

FOOL   This is a brave night to cool a courtesan.° I'll speak a
prophecy ere I go:

          When priests are more in word than matter;°   80
          When brewers mar° their malt with water;
          When nobles are their tailors' tutors,°
          No heretics burned but wenches' suitors,°

---

64 **which** the occupants of which | **demanding** I inquiring   66 **scanted** stinted
73–76 **"he . . . day"** (derived from the popular song that Feste sings in *Twelfth Night*,
5.1.389 ff.)   78 **this . . . courtesan** this night is stormy enough to cool even the lust
of a courtesan (*brave* means "fine, excellent")   80 **when priests . . . matter** when
priests do not practice what they preach (this and the next three lines satirize the
present state of affairs)   81 **mar** adulterate   82 **are . . . tutors** can instruct their
own tailors about fashion   83 **no heretics . . . suitors** when the prevailing heresy is
lechery (a heresy, in other words, against love rather than against true religion),
punished by burning not at the stake but by means of venereal infection

Then shall the realm of Albion°
Come to great confusion.   85

When every case in law is right,°
No squire in debt, nor no poor knight;
When slanders do not live in tongues,°
Nor cutpurses come not to throngs;
When usurers tell° their gold i'th' field,°   90
And bawds and whores do churches build,
Then comes the time, who° lives to see't,
That going shall be used with feet.°

This prophecy Merlin° shall make, for I live before his time.

Exit

❖

ACT 3
SCENE 3

Location: Gloucester's house

Enter Gloucester and Edmund [with lights]

GLOUCESTER Alack, alack, Edmund, I like not this unnatural
dealing. When I desired their leave that I might pity° him,
they took from me the use of mine own house, charged me
on pain of perpetual displeasure neither to speak of him, entreat for him, or any way sustain him.   5
EDMUND Most savage and unnatural!

---

84 realm of Albion kingdom of England (the Fool is parodying a pseudo-Chaucer-
ian prophetic verse)   **86 right** just (this and the next five lines offer a utopian vision
of justice and charity that will never be realized in this corrupted world)   **88 when
slanders . . . tongues** when no tongues speak slanders   **90 tell** count | **i'th' field**
openly, without fear   **92 who** whoever   **93 that . . . feet** that walking will be done
on foot (a comical anticlimax: nothing will have been changed; don't expect these
utopian dreams to have materialized)   **94 Merlin** (a great wizard of the court of
King Arthur, who came after Lear; the fool's comical inversion ends his song on a
note of paradox and impossibility)

2 pity be merciful to, relieve

GLOUCESTER Go to;° say you nothing. There is division between the dukes, and a worse matter than that. I have received a letter this night; 'tis dangerous to be spoken; I have locked the letter in my closet.° These injuries the King 10
now bears will be revenged home;° there is part of a power° already footed.° We must incline to° the King. I will look° him and privily relieve him. Go you and maintain talk with the Duke, that my charity be not of° him perceived. If he ask for me, I am ill and gone to bed. If I die for't, as no 15
less is threatened me, the King my old master must be relieved. There is strange things toward,° Edmund. Pray you, be careful.   *Exit*

EDMUND This courtesy forbid thee° shall the Duke
Instantly know, and of that letter too.   20
This seems a fair deserving, and must draw me
That which my father loses—no less than all.°
The younger rises when the old doth fall.

                                                                                   Exit

                                    ❖

                               ACT 3
                              SCENE 4

          Location: An open place. Before a hovel

       Enter Lear, Kent [disguised as Caius], and Fool

KENT Here is the place, my lord. Good my lord, enter.
    The tyranny of the open night's too rough
    For nature° to endure.   *Storm still*
LEAR   Let me alone.
KENT Good my lord, enter here.
LEAR   Wilt break my heart?°

---

7 **go to** no more of that   10 **closet** private chamber   11 **home** thoroughly | **power** armed force   12 **footed** landed | **incline to** side with | **look** look for   14 **of** by   17 **toward** impending   19 **courtesy forbid thee** kindness (to Lear) which you were forbidden to show   21–22 **this . . . all** this betraying by me of my father is something he has brought on himself, and will surely confer upon me the earldom of Gloucester and all his wealth

3 **nature** human nature   4 **wilt . . . heart?** do you want to relieve my physical wants and thereby force me to remember my daughters' ingratitude?

KENT   I had rather break mine own. Good my lord, enter.   5
LEAR   Thou think'st 'tis much that this contentious storm
    Invades us to the skin. So 'tis to thee,
    But where the greater malady is fixed°
    The lesser is scarce felt. Thou'dst shun a bear,
    But if thy flight lay toward the roaring sea   10
    Thou'dst meet the bear i'th' mouth.° When the mind's free,°
    The body's delicate.° This tempest in my mind
    Doth from my senses take all feeling else
    Save what beats there. Filial ingratitude!
    Is it not as° this mouth should tear this hand   15
    For lifting food to't? But I will punish home.°
    No, I will weep no more. In such a night
    To shut me out? Pour on; I will endure.
    In such a night as this? Oh, Regan, Goneril,
    Your old kind father, whose frank° heart gave all—   20
    Oh, that way madness lies; let me shun that!
    No more of that.
KENT   Good my lord, enter here.
LEAR   Prithee, go in thyself; seek thine own ease.
    This tempest will not give me leave° to ponder
    On things would° hurt me more. But I'll go in.   25
    [*To the Fool*] In, boy; go first. You houseless poverty—
    Nay, get thee in. I'll pray, and then I'll sleep.
                      Exit [*Fool into the hovel*]
    Poor naked wretches, wheresoe'er you are,
    That bide° the pelting of this pitiless storm,
    How shall your houseless heads and unfed sides,°   30
    Your looped and windowed° raggedness, defend you
    From seasons such as these? Oh, I have ta'en
    Too little care of this! Take physic, pomp;°
    Expose thyself to feel what wretches feel,

---

8 fixed lodged, implanted   **11 i'th' mouth** head-on | **free** free of anxiety   **12 the
body's delicate** the body's importunate needs can assert themselves   **15 as** as if
16 home fully   **20 frank** liberal   **24 will . . . leave** keeps me too preoccupied
25 things would things (such as filial ingratitude) that would   **29 bide** endure
30 unfed sides lean ribs   **31 looped and windowed** full of openings like windows
and loopholes   **33 take physic, pomp** cure yourself, distempered great ones

That thou mayst shake the superflux° to them   35
And show the heavens more just.

EDGAR [*within*]   Fathom and half, fathom and half!° Poor Tom!

Enter Fool [from the hovel]

FOOL   Come not in here, nuncle; here's a spirit. Help me, help me!

KENT   Give me thy hand. Who's there?   40

FOOL   A spirit, a spirit! He says his name's poor Tom.

KENT   What art thou that dost grumble° there i'th' straw? Come forth.

Enter Edgar [disguised as a madman]

EDGAR   Away!° The foul fiend follows me! Through the sharp hawthorn blows the cold wind.° Hum! Go to thy bed and   45
warm thee.

LEAR   Didst thou give all to thy daughters? And art thou come to this?

EDGAR   Who gives anything to poor Tom? Whom the foul fiend hath led through fire and through flame, through ford   50
and whirlpool, o'er bog and quagmire; that hath laid knives under his pillow and halters in his pew, set ratsbane by his porridge,° made him proud of heart to ride on a bay trotting horse over four-inched bridges to course his own shadow for a traitor.° Bless thy five wits!° Tom's a-cold. Oh, do de, do de,   55
do de. Bless thee from whirlwinds, star-blasting,° and taking!° Do poor Tom some charity, whom the foul fiend vexes.

---

35 **superflux** superfluity (with suggestion of *flux,* "bodily discharge," introduced by *physic,* "purgative," in line 33)   37 **fathom and half** (a sailor's cry while taking soundings, hence appropriate to a deluge)   42 **grumble** mutter, mumble   44 **away!** keep away!   44–45 **through . . . wind** (possibly a line from a ballad)   51–53 **that hath . . . porridge** (the fiend has laid in poor Tom's way tempting means to despairing suicide, the most damnable of sins: knives under his pillow when he is asleep, nooses in his church pew when he should be at prayer, and rat poison set beside his soup when he should eat)   53–55 **made him . . . traitor** (the next temptation is a prideful act of great bravado that would be impossible without the devil's aid: riding a horse over bridges only four inches wide in pursuit of one's own shadow)   55 **five wits** (either the five physical senses—sight, hearing, etc.—or the five faculties of the mind: common wit, imagination, fantasy, estimation, and memory)   56 **star-blasting** being blighted by influence of the stars | **taking** infection, evil influence, enchantment

There° could I have him now—and   there—and there
again—and there.   *Storm still*

LEAR   Has his daughters brought him to this pass?°—   60
Couldst thou save nothing? Wouldst thou give 'em all?

FOOL   Nay, he reserved a blanket,° else we had been all shamed.

LEAR   Now, all the plagues that in the pendulous° air
Hang fated° o'er men's faults light on thy daughters!

KENT   He hath no daughters, sir.   65

LEAR   Death, traitor! Nothing could have subdued nature
To such a lowness but his unkind daughters.
Is it the fashion that discarded fathers
Should have thus little mercy on their flesh?°
Judicious° punishment! 'Twas this flesh begot   70
Those pelican° daughters.

EDGAR   Pillicock sat on Pillicock° Hill. Alow, alow, loo, loo!

FOOL   This cold night will turn us all to fools and mad-men.

EDGAR   Take heed o'th' foul fiend. Obey thy parents; keep thy
word's justice;° swear not; commit not° with man's sworn   75
spouse; set not thy sweet heart on proud array. Tom's a-cold.

LEAR   What hast thou been?

EDGAR   A servingman,° proud in heart and mind, that curled
my hair, wore gloves° in my cap, served the lust of my mistress' heart, and did the act of darkness with her; swore as   80
many oaths as I spake words, and broke them in the sweet
face of heaven. One that slept in the contriving of lust and
waked to do it. Wine loved I deeply, dice dearly, and in
woman out-paramoured the Turk.° False of heart, light of
ear,° bloody of hand; hog in sloth, fox in stealth, wolf in   85

---

58 **there** (perhaps he slaps at lice and other vermin as if they were devils)   60 **pass**
miserable plight   62 **reserved a blanket** kept a wrap (for his nakedness)   63 **pendulous**
suspended, overhanging   64 **fated** having the power of fate   69 **have . . . flesh** punish
themselves, as Edgar has done (probably with pins and thorns stuck in his flesh)
70 **judicious** appropriate to the crime   71 **pelican** greedy (young pelicans supposedly
smote their parents and fed on the blood of their mothers' breasts)   72 **Pillicock** (from
an old rhyme, suggested by the sound of *pelican*; *Pillicock* in nursery rhyme seems to
have been a euphemism for penis; *Pillicock Hill*, for the Mount of Venus)   75 **justice**
integrity | **commit not** do not commit adultery (Edgar's mad homily contains
fragments of the Ten Commandments)   78 **servingman** either a "servant" in the
language of courtly love or an ambitious servant in a household   79 **gloves** my
mistress's favors   84 **out-paramoured the Turk** outdid the Sultan in keeping mistresses
84–85 **light of ear** listening intently for information that can be used criminally

greediness, dog in madness, lion in prey.° Let not the creaking of shoes nor the rustling of silks° betray thy poor heart
to woman. Keep thy foot out of brothels, thy hand out of
plackets,° thy pen from lenders' books,° and defy the foul
fiend. Still through the hawthorn blows the cold wind; says   90
suum, mun, nonny.° Dolphin my boy,° boy, sessa!° Let him
trot by.   *Storm still*

LEAR   Thou wert better in a grave than to answer with thy un-
covered body this extremity of the skies. Is man no more
than this? Consider him well. Thou ow'st the worm no silk,   95
the beast no hide, the sheep no wool, the cat no perfume.°
Ha! Here's three on 's are sophisticated; thou art the thing itself.° Unaccommodated° man is no more but such a poor,
bare, forked animal as thou art. Off, off, you lendings!
Come, unbutton here.   [*Tearing off his clothes*]   100

FOOL   Prithee, nuncle, be contented; 'tis a naughty° night to
swim in. Now a little fire in a wild° field were like an old
lecher's heart—a small spark, all the rest on 's° body cold.

Enter Gloucester, with a torch

Look, here comes a walking fire.

EDGAR   This is the foul fiend Flibbertigibbet!° He begins at cur-   105
few and walks till the first cock;° he gives the web and the
pin,° squinnies° the eye and makes the harelip, mildews the
white° wheat, and hurts the poor creature of earth.

---

86 prey preying   **86–87 creaking . . . silks** (telltale noises of lovers in a secret
assignation)   **89 plackets** slits in skirts or petticoats | **thy pen . . . books** do not
sign a contract for a loan   **91 suum . . . nonny** (imitative of the wind?) | **dolphin
my boy** (a slang phrase or bit of song?) | **sessa** away, cease (?)   **95–96 thou . . .
perfume** stripped of your finery, you are not indebted to the silkworm for silk, cattle
for hide, the sheep for wool, or the civet cat for the perfume derived from its anal
pouch   **97–98 here . . . itself** the three of us here (Kent, the Fool, and Lear) are
decked out in the sophistication of supposedly civilized society; you (Edgar) are the
unadorned, natural essence, the natural man   **98 unaccommodated** unfurnished
with the trappings of civilization, such as clothing   **101 naughty** bad, nasty   **102 wild**
barren, uncultivated   **103 on 's** of his   **105 Flibbertigibbet** (a devil from Elizabethan
folklore whose name appears in Samuel Harsnett's *Declaration of Egregious Popish
Impostures*, 1603, and elsewhere)   **105–06 he . . . cock** he walks from nightfall till
dawn   **106–07 web and the pin** cataract of the eye   **107 squinnies** squints
108 white ripening, ready for harvest

Swithold° footed thrice the 'old;°
He met the nightmare and her ninefold;°   110
       Bid her alight,
       And her troth plight,
And aroint thee, witch, aroint thee!°

KENT   How fares Your Grace?

LEAR   What's he?   115

KENT   Who's there? What is't you seek?

GLOUCESTER   What are you there? Your names?

EDGAR   Poor Tom, that eats the swimming frog, the toad, the tadpole, the wall newt and the water;° that in the fury of his heart, when the foul fiend rages, eats cow dung for salads,   120 swallows the old rat and the ditch-dog,° drinks the green mantle° of the standing° pool; who is whipped from tithing to tithing° and stock-punished° and imprisoned; who hath had three suits° to his back, six shirts to his body,
       Horse to ride, and weapon to wear;   125
       But mice and rats and such small deer°
       Have been Tom's food for seven long year.
Beware my follower.° Peace, Smulkin!° Peace, thou fiend!

GLOUCESTER

What, hath your Grace no better company?

EDGAR   The Prince of Darkness° is a gentleman. Modo he's   130 called, and Mahu.

GLOUCESTER [to Lear]

Our flesh and blood, my lord, is grown so vile
That it doth hate what gets it.°

EDGAR   Poor Tom's a-cold.

---

109 Swithold Saint Withold, an Anglo-Saxon exorcist, who here provides defense against the *nightmare*, or demon thought to afflict sleepers, by commanding the nightmare to *alight*, stop riding over the sleeper, and *plight* her *troth*, vow true faith, promise to do no harm (or, an error for *Swithin*) | **footed . . . 'old** thrice traversed the wold (tract of hilly upland)   **110 ninefold** nine offspring (with possible pun on *fold, foal*)   **113 aroint thee** begone   **119 water** water newt   **121 ditch-dog** dead dog in a ditch   **122 mantle** scum | **standing** stagnant   **122–23 from . . . to tithing** from one ward or parish to another   **123 stock-punished** placed in the stocks   **124 three suits** (like the menial servant at 2.2.14.)   **126 deer** animals   **128 follower** familiar, attendant devil | **Smulkin** a devil's name (in Samuel Harsnet's *Declaration*, as are *Modo* and *Mahu* in lines 129–30)   **130 the Prince of Darkness** the devil   **132–33 our . . . gets it** (1) children have become so hardened in sin that they hate their parents (2) life is so intolerable that humans cry out at having been born

GLOUCESTER   Go in with me. My duty cannot suffer°   135
    T'obey in all° your daughters' hard commands.
    Though their injunction be to bar my doors
    And let this tyrannous night take hold upon you,
    Yet have I ventured to come seek you out
    And bring you where both fire and food is ready.   140
LEAR   First let me talk with this philosopher.
    [*To Edgar*] What is the cause of thunder?
KENT   Good my lord,
    Take his offer. Go into th' house.
LEAR   I'll talk a word with this same learnèd Theban.°
    [*To Edgar*] What is your study?°   145
EDGAR   How to prevent° the fiend, and to kill vermin.
LEAR   Let me ask you one word in private.
                          [*Lear and Edgar talk apart*]
KENT [*to Gloucester*]
    Importune him once more to go, my lord.
    His wits begin t'unsettle.
GLOUCESTER   Canst thou blame him?
                              Storm still
    His daughters seek his death. Ah, that good Kent!   150
    He said it would be thus, poor banished man.
    Thou sayest the King grows mad; I'll tell thee, friend,
    I am almost mad myself. I had a son,
    Now outlawed from my blood;° he sought my life
    But lately, very late. I loved him, friend,   155
    No father his son dearer. True to tell thee,
    The grief hath crazed my wits. What a night's this!—
    I do beseech your Grace—
LEAR   Oh, cry you mercy,° sir.
    [*To Edgar*] Noble philosopher, your company.   160
EDGAR   Tom's a-cold.
GLOUCESTER [*to Edgar*]
    In, fellow, there, in th' hovel. Keep thee warm.

---

135 suffer permit me   **136 in all** in all matters   **144 Theban** one deeply versed in
"philosophy" or natural science   **145 study** special competence   **146 prevent**
thwart   **154 outlawed . . . blood** disowned, disinherited, and legally outlawed
159 cry you mercy I beg your pardon

LEAR [*starting toward the hovel*]
　Come, let's in all.
KENT 　　　　　　　　　This way, my lord.
LEAR 　　　　　　　　　　　　　　With him!
　I will keep still with my philosopher.
KENT [*to Gloucester*]
　Good my lord, soothe° him. Let him take the fellow.　　165
GLOUCESTER [*to Kent*]　Take you him on.°
KENT [*to Edgar*]　Sirrah, come on. Go along with us.
LEAR 　Come, good Athenian.°
GLOUCESTER 　No words, no words! Hush.
EDGAR 　Child Rowland° to the dark tower came;　　　170
　His word° was still, "Fie, foh, and fum,
　I smell the blood of a British man."°

　　　　　　　　　　　　　　　　　Exeunt

❖

ACT 3
SCENE 5

Location: Gloucester's house

Enter Cornwall and Edmund [with a letter]

CORNWALL 　I will have my revenge ere I depart his house.
EDMUND 　How, my lord, I may be censured,° that nature° thus
　gives way to loyalty, something fears° me to think of.
CORNWALL 　I now perceive it was not altogether your brother's
　evil disposition made him seek his° death, but a provoking　　5
　merit set awork by a reprovable badness in himself.°
EDMUND 　How malicious is my fortune, that I must repent to
　be just!° This is the letter he spoke of, which approves him

---

165 **soothe** humor　166 **take . . . on** go on ahead with Edgar　168 **Athenian**
philosopher　170 **Child Rowland**, etc. (probably a fragment of a ballad about the
hero of the Charlemagne legends; a *child* is a candidate for knighthood)　171 **word**
watchword　171–72 **"fie . . . man"** (this is essentially what the Giant says in "Jack,
the Giant Killer")

2 **censured** judged | **nature** attachment to family　3 **something fears** somewhat
frightens　5 **his** his father's　5–6 **but . . . himself** but the promptings of self-worth
stimulated by the reprehensible badness of the Earl of Gloucester　7–8 **how . . .
just!** how cruel of fate to oblige me to be upright and loyal by betraying my own
father!

an intelligent party to the advantages of France.° Oh, heavens! That this treason were not, or not I the detector! 10

CORNWALL   Go with me to the Duchess.

EDMUND   If the matter of this paper be certain, you have
mighty business in hand.

CORNWALL   True or false, it hath made thee Earl of Gloucester.
Seek out where thy father is, that he may be ready for our 15
apprehension.°

EDMUND [*aside*]
If I find him comforting° the King, it will stuff his suspicion°
more fully.—I will persevere in my course of loyalty, though
the conflict be sore between that and my blood.°

CORNWALL   I will lay trust upon thee, and thou shalt find a 20
dearer father in my love.

                                        Exeunt

♣

ACT 3
SCENE 6

*Location: Within a building on Gloucester's estate,
near or adjoining his house, or part of the house itself.
See 3.4.133–41. Cushions are provided, and stools*

Enter Kent [disguised as Caius] and Gloucester

GLOUCESTER   Here is better than the open air; take it thankfully.
I will piece° out the comfort with what addition I can. I will
not be long from you.

KENT   All the power of his wits have given way to his
impatience.° The gods reward your kindness! 5

                               Exit [Gloucester]

Enter Lear, Edgar [as poor Tom], and Fool

8–9 which . . . France which proves him to be a spy on behalf of the French
15–16 for our apprehension for our arresting of him   **17 if . . . comforting** if I find
Gloucester giving aid and comfort to | **his suspicion** suspicion of him   **19 blood**
family loyalty, filial instincts

2 piece eke   **5 impatience** rage, inability to endure more

EDGAR Frateretto° calls me, and tells me Nero is an angler° in the lake of darkness. Pray, innocent,° and beware the foul fiend.

FOOL Prithee, nuncle, tell me whether a madman be a gentleman or a yeoman?° 10

LEAR A king, a king!

FOOL No, he's a yeoman that has a gentleman to his son; for he's a mad yeoman that sees his son a gentleman before him.

LEAR To have a thousand with red burning spits
Come hizzing° in upon 'em— 15

EDGAR The foul fiend bites° my back.

FOOL He's mad that trusts in the tameness of a wolf, a horse's health,° a boy's love, or a whore's oath.

LEAR It shall be done; I will arraign them° straight. [*To Edgar*]
Come, sit thou here, most learnèd justicer.° [*To the Fool*] 20
Thou, sapient° sir, sit here. Now, you she-foxes!

EDGAR Look where he° stands and glares! Want'st thou eyes at trial,° madam? *Sings*
    "Come o'er the burn, Bessy, to me—"°

FOOL [*sings*] Her boat hath a leak, 25
    And she must not speak
Why she dares not come over to thee.

EDGAR The foul fiend haunts poor Tom in the voice of a nightingale.° Hoppedance° cries in Tom's belly for two white° herring. Croak° not, black angel; I have no food for thee. 30

---

6 **Frateretto** (another of the fiends from Harsnett) | **Nero is an angler** (Chaucer's "Monk's Tale," lines 2474–5, tells how Nero fished in the Tiber with nets of gold thread; in Rabelais, 2.30, Nero is described as a hurdy-gurdy player and Trajan an angler for frogs in the underworld) 7 **innocent** simpleton, fool (the Fool) 10 **yeoman** property owner below the rank of gentleman (the Fool's bitter jest in lines 12–13 is that such a man might go mad to see his son advanced over him) 15 **hizzing** hissing (Lear imagines his wicked daughters suffering torments in hell or being attacked by enemies) 16 **bites** (in the shape of a louse) 17–18 **tameness ... health** (wolves are untamable, and horses are prone to disease) 19 **arraign them** (Lear now imagines the trial of his cruel daughters) 20 **justicer** judge, justice 21 **sapient** wise 22 **he** (probably one of Edgar's devils, or, Lear) 22–23 **want'st ... trial** do you lack spectators at your trial? or, can't you see who's looking at you? 24 **come ... me** (first line of a ballad by William Birche, 1558; a *burn* is a brook; the Fool makes a ribald reply, in which the *leaky boat* suggests the woman's easy virtue or perhaps her menstrual period) 29 **nightingale** (Edgar pretends to take the Fool's singing for that of a fiend disguised as a nightingale) | **Hoppedance** (Harsnett mentions "Hoberdidance") | **white** unsmoked (contrasted with *black angel*, a demon) 30 **croak** (refers to the rumbling in Edgar's stomach, denoting hunger)

KENT [*to Lear*]   How do you, sir? Stand you not so amazed.°
   Will you lie down and rest upon the cushions?
LEAR   I'll see their trial first. Bring in their evidence.°
   [*To Edgar*] Thou robèd man° of justice, take thy place;
   [*To the Fool*] And thou, his yokefellow of equity,°   35
   Bench° by his side. [*To Kent*] You are o'th' commission;°
   Sit you, too.   [*They sit*]
EDGAR   Let us deal justly.   [*He sings*]
      Sleepest or wakest thou, jolly shepherd?
         Thy sheep be in the corn;°   40
      And for one blast of thy minikin mouth,
         Thy sheep shall take no harm.°
   Purr the cat° is gray.
LEAR   Arraign her first; 'tis Goneril, I here take my oath before
   this honorable assembly, kicked° the poor King her father.   45
FOOL   Come hither, mistress. Is your name Goneril?
LEAR   She cannot deny it.
FOOL   Cry you mercy, I took you for a joint stool.°
LEAR   And here's another,° whose warped looks proclaim
   What store° her heart is made on.° Stop her there!   50
   Arms, arms, sword, fire! Corruption in the place!°
   False justicer, why hast thou let her scape?
EDGAR   Bless thy five wits!
KENT   Oh, pity! Sir, where is the patience now
   That you so oft have boasted to retain?   55
EDGAR [*aside*]   My tears begin to take his part so much
   They mar my counterfeiting.
LEAR   The little dogs and all,
   Tray, Blanch, and Sweetheart, see, they bark at me.
EDGAR   Tom will throw his head at° them.—Avaunt, you curs!   60

31 amazed bewildered   **33 their evidence** the witnesses against them   **34 robèd
man** Edgar, with his blanket   **35 yokefellow of equity** partner in the law   **36 bench**
take your place on the bench | **o'th' commission** one commissioned to be a justice
40 corn grainfield   **41–42 and . . . harm** one shout from your dainty (*minikin*) mouth
can recall the sheep from the grainfield and thus save them from dangerous over-
eating   **43 purr the cat** (a devil or familiar from Harsnett; see the note for 3.4.104.
purr may be the sound the familiar makes)   **45 kicked** who kicked   **48 joint stool**
low stool made by a joiner, or maker of furniture with joined parts (proverbially,
the phrase "I took . . . stool" meant "I beg your pardon for failing to notice you";
the reference is also presumably to a real stool onstage)   **49 another** Regan   **50 store**
abundance, material | **on** of   **51 corruption in the place!** there is iniquity or
bribery in this court!   **60 throw his head at** threaten

Be thy mouth or black° or white,
Tooth that poisons if it bite,
Mastiff, greyhound, mongrel grim,
Hound or spaniel, brach or lym,°
Bobtail tike or trundle-tail,°   65
Tom will make him weep and wail;
For, with throwing thus my head,
Dogs leap the hatch,° and all are fled.
Do de, de, de. Sessa!° Come, march to wakes° and fairs and
market towns. Poor Tom, thy horn° is dry.   70

LEAR   Then let them anatomize° Regan; see what breeds about
her heart. Is there any cause in nature that makes these hard
hearts? [*To Edgar*] You, sir, I entertain° for one of my hundred; only I do not like the fashion of your garments. You
will say they are Persian;° but let them be changed.   75

KENT   Now, good my lord, lie here and rest awhile.

LEAR [*lying on cushions*]   Make no noise, make no noise. Draw
the curtains.° So, so. We'll go to supper i'th' morning.

                                                            [*He sleeps*]

FOOL   And I'll go to bed at noon.

                                        Enter Gloucester

GLOUCESTER [*to Kent*]
Come hither, friend. Where is the King my master?   80

KENT   Here, sir, but trouble him not; his wits are gone.

GLOUCESTER
Good friend, I prithee, take him in thy arms.
I have o'erheard a plot of death upon° him.
There is a litter ready; lay him in't
And drive toward Dover, friend, where thou shalt meet   85
Both welcome and protection. Take up thy master.
If thou shouldst dally half an hour, his life,
With thine and all that offer to defend him,

---

61 or black either black   **64 brach or lym** bitch-hound or bloodhound   **65 bobtail**
. . . trundle-tail mongrel dog with a docked or bobbed tail, or one that is curly-tailed
68 hatch lower half of a divided door   **69 sessa** away, cease | **wakes** parish festi-
vals   **70 horn** horn-bottle, used by beggars to drink from and to beg for alms
71 anatomize dissect   **73 entertain** take into my service   **75 Persian** (Lear madly
asks if Edgar's wretched blanket is a rich Persian fabric)   **78 curtains** bedcurtains
(they presumably exist only in Lear's mad imagination)   **83 upon** against

Stand in assurèd loss.° Take up, take up,
And follow me, that will to some provision°   90
Give thee quick conduct.°
KENT   Oppressèd nature sleeps.
This rest might yet have balmed° thy broken sinews,°
Which, if convenience° will not allow,
Stand in hard cure.°   [*To the Fool*]
        Come, help to bear thy master.
Thou must not stay behind.   [*They pick up Lear*]
GLOUCESTER   Come, come, away!   95
                                Exeunt [*all but Edgar*]
EDGAR   When we our betters see bearing our woes,°
We scarcely think our miseries our foes.°
Who alone suffers suffers most i'th' mind,
Leaving free things and happy shows behind;
But then the mind much sufferance doth o'erskip   100
When grief hath mates, and bearing fellowship.°
How light and portable° my pain seems now,
When that which makes me bend makes the King bow—
He childed as I fathered.° Tom, away!
Mark the high noises, and thyself bewray   105
When false opinion, whose wrong thoughts defile thee,
In thy just proof repeals and reconciles thee.°
What will hap more tonight, safe scape the King!°
Lurk, lurk.°
                                            [*Exit*]

❧

89 **stand . . . loss** will assuredly be lost   90 **provision** supplies, or, means of provid-
ing for safety   91 **conduct** guidance   92 **balmed** soothed, healed | **sinews** nerves
93 **convenience** circumstances   94 **stand . . . cure** will be hard to cure   96 **our woes**
woes like ours   97 **we . . . foes** we almost forget our own miseries (since we see how
human suffering afflicts even the great)   98–101 **who . . . fellowship** anyone who has
no companionship in suffering undergoes the mental anguish of forgetting entirely
the carefree ways and happy scenes that were once enjoyed, whereas fellowship
in grief enables the mind to rise above such suffering (misery loves company)
102 **portable** bearable, endurable   104 **he . . . fathered** he suffering cruelty from his
children as I from my father   105–07 **mark . . . thee** observe what is being said
about those in high places or about great events, and reveal your identity only when
the general opinion that now slanders you, at length establishing your innocence, recalls you from banishment and restores you to favor   108 **what . . . King!** whatever
else happens tonight, may the King escape safely!   109 **lurk** keep out of sight

ACT 3
SCENE 7

Location: Gloucester's house

Enter Cornwall, Regan, Goneril,
Bastard [Edmund], and Servants

CORNWALL [*to Goneril*] Post speedily° to my lord your husband; show him this letter. [*He gives a letter*] The army of France is landed.—Seek out the traitor Gloucester.

[Exeunt some Servants]

REGAN Hang him instantly.

GONERIL Pluck out his eyes.   5

CORNWALL Leave him to my displeasure. Edmund, keep you our sister° company. The revenges we are bound° to take upon your traitorous father are not fit for your beholding. Advise the Duke,° where you are going, to a most festinate° preparation; we are bound° to the like. Our posts° shall be   10
swift and intelligent° betwixt us. Farewell, dear sister; farewell, my lord of Gloucester.°

Enter steward [Oswald]

How now? Where's the King?

OSWALD My lord of Gloucester hath conveyed him hence.
Some five- or six-and-thirty of his° knights,   15
Hot questrists after him,° met him at gate,
Who, with some other of the lord's° dependents,
Are gone with him toward Dover, where they boast
To have well-armèd friends.

CORNWALL Get horses for your mistress.   [*Exit Oswald*]   20

GONERIL Farewell, sweet lord, and sister.

CORNWALL Edmund, farewell.   *Exeunt [Goneril and Edmund]*
                    Go seek the traitor Gloucester.
Pinion him like a thief; bring him before us.

[Exeunt Servants]

---

1 **post speedily** hurry   7 **sister** sister-in-law, Goneril ǀ **bound** intending; obliged
9 **the Duke** Albany ǀ **festinate** hasty   10 **are bound** intend, are committed ǀ **posts**
messengers   11 **intelligent** serviceable in bearing information, knowledgeable
12 **my . . . Gloucester** Edmund, the recipient now of his father's forfeited estate and
title (two lines later, Oswald uses the same title to refer to Edmund's father)   15 **his**
Lear's   16 **questrists after him** searchers for Lear   17 **the lord's** Gloucester's

Though well we may not pass upon his life°
Without the form of justice, yet our power   25
Shall do a court'sy° to our wrath, which men
May blame but not control.

Enter Gloucester, and servants [leading him]

                    Who's there? The traitor?
REGAN   Ingrateful fox! 'Tis he.
CORNWALL   Bind fast his corky° arms.
GLOUCESTER
    What means Your Graces? Good my friends, consider   30
    You are my guests. Do me no foul play, friends.
CORNWALL   Bind him, I say.   *[Servants bind him]*
REGAN   Hard, hard. Oh, filthy traitor!
GLOUCESTER   Unmerciful lady as you are, I'm none.
CORNWALL   To this chair bind him.—Villain, thou shalt find—
                    [Regan plucks Gloucester's beard]
GLOUCESTER   By the kind gods, 'tis most ignobly done   35
    To pluck me by the beard.
REGAN   So white,° and such a traitor?
GLOUCESTER   Naughty° lady,
    These hairs which thou dost ravish from my chin
    Will quicken° and accuse thee. I am your host.
    With robbers' hands my hospitable favors   40
    You should not ruffle thus.° What will you do?
CORNWALL   Come, sir, what letters had you late° from France?
REGAN   Be simple-answered,° for we know the truth.
CORNWALL   And what confederacy have you with the traitors
    Late footed° in the kingdom?
REGAN   To whose hands   45
    You have sent the lunatic King. Speak.
GLOUCESTER   I have a letter guessingly set down,°
    Which came from one that's of a neutral heart,
    And not from one opposed.

---

24 **pass upon his life** pass the death sentence upon him   26 **do a court'sy** bow
before, yield precedence   29 **corky** withered with age   37 **white** white-haired,
venerable | **naughty** wicked   39 **quicken** come to life   40–41 **with . . . thus** you
should not roughly handle my welcoming face with your hands as though you were
robbers   42 **late** lately   43 **simple-answered** straightforward in your answers   45 **late
footed** recently landed   47 **guessingly set down** conjecturally written

CORNWALL Cunning.   50
REGAN And false.
CORNWALL Where hast thou sent the King?
GLOUCESTER To Dover.
REGAN Wherefore to Dover? Wast thou not charged at peril°—
CORNWALL Wherefore to Dover? Let him answer that.   55
GLOUCESTER I am tied to th' stake,° and I must stand the course.°
REGAN Wherefore to Dover?
GLOUCESTER Because I would not see thy cruel nails
  Pluck out his poor old eyes, nor thy fierce sister
  In his anointed° flesh rash° boarish fangs.   60
  The sea, with such a storm as his bare head
  In hell-black night endured, would have buoyed up
  And quenched the stellèd fires;°
  Yet, poor old heart, he holp° the heavens to rain.
  If wolves had at thy gate howled that dern° time,   65
  Thou shouldst have said, "Good porter, turn the key."°
  All cruels else subscribe.° But I shall see
  The wingèd Vengeance° overtake such children.
CORNWALL See't shalt thou never.—Fellows, hold the chair.
  Upon these eyes of thine I'll set my foot.   70
GLOUCESTER He that will think° to live till he be old,
  Give me some help!
        [*Servants hold the chair as Cornwall grinds
        out one of Gloucester's eyes with his boot*]
        Oh, cruel! O you gods!
REGAN One side will mock another. Th'other too.
CORNWALL [*to Gloucester*]
  If you see Vengeance—
FIRST SERVANT   Hold your hand, my lord!
  I have served you ever since I was a child;   75

---

54 charged at peril commanded on peril of your life   **56 tied to th' stake** like a bear
to be baited with dogs | **the course** the dogs' attack   **60 anointed** consecrated with
holy oil | **rash** slash, stick   **62–3 would . . . fires** would have swelled high enough,
like a wave-lifted buoy, to quench the stars (*stellèd* means "starry" or "fixed")
64 holp helped   **65 dern** dire, dread   **66 turn the key** let them in   **67 all . . .
subscribe** all other cruel creatures would show forgiveness except you; this cruelty is
unparalleled   **68 the wingèd Vengeance** the swift vengeance of the avenging angel
of divine wrath   **71 will think** hopes

But better service have I never done you
Than now to bid you hold.

REGAN   How now, you dog?

FIRST SERVANT [*to Regan*]

If you did wear a beard upon your chin,
I'd° shake it on this quarrel.—What do you mean?°

CORNWALL   My villain?° [*He draws his sword*]   80

FIRST SERVANT [*drawing*]

Nay, then, come on, and take the chance of anger.°
                              [*They fight. Cornwall is wounded*]

REGAN [*to another Servant*]

Give me thy sword. A peasant stand up thus?
                    [*She takes a sword and runs at him behind°*]

FIRST SERVANT   Oh, I am slain! My lord, you have one eye left
To see some mischief° on him. Oh! [*He dies*]

CORNWALL   Lest it see more, prevent it. Out, vile jelly!   85
                    [*He puts out Gloucester's other eye*]

Where is thy luster now?

GLOUCESTER

All dark and comfortless. Where's my son Edmund?
Edmund, enkindle all the sparks of nature°
To quit° this horrid act.

REGAN   Out,° treacherous villain!

Thou call'st on him that hates thee. It was he   90
That made the overture° of thy treasons to us,
Who is too good to pity thee.

GLOUCESTER   Oh, my follies! Then Edgar was abused.°
            Kind gods, forgive me that, and prosper him!

REGAN [*to a Servant*]

Go thrust him out at gates and let him smell   95
His way to Dover.   *Exit [a Servant] with Gloucester*
            How is't, my lord? How look you?°

---

79 **I'd . . . quarrel** I'd pull your beard in vehement defiance in this cause | **what do you mean?** what are you thinking of, what do you think you're doing? (said perhaps to Cornwall)   80 **villain** servant, bondman (Cornwall's question implies, "How dare you do such a thing?")   81 **the chance of anger** the risks of an angry encounter   82.1 **she . . . behind** (this stage direction appears in the Quarto)   84 **mischief** injury   88 **nature** filial love   89 **quit** requite | **out** (an exclamation of anger or impatience)   91 **overture** disclosure   93 **abused** wronged   96 **how look you?** how is it with you?

CORNWALL   I have received a hurt. Follow me, lady.—
Turn out that eyeless villain. Throw this slave
Upon the dunghill.—Regan, I bleed apace.
Untimely comes this hurt. Give me your arm.   100
                    Exeunt [Cornwall, supported by Regan]
SECOND SERVANT   I'll never care what wickedness I do,
If this man come to good.
THIRD SERVANT   If she live long,
And in the end meet the old° course of death,
Women will all turn monsters.
SECOND SERVANT   Let's follow the old Earl, and get the Bedlam°   105
To lead him where he would. His roguish madness
Allows itself to anything.°
THIRD SERVANT   Go thou. I'll fetch some flax and whites of eggs
To apply to his bleeding face. Now, heaven help him!
                            Exeunt° [with the body]

❖

ACT 4
SCENE 1

Location: An open place

Enter Edgar [as poor Tom]

EDGAR   Yet better thus, and known to be contemned,
Than still contemned and flattered.° To be worst,
The lowest and most dejected° thing of fortune,
Stands still in esperance, lives not in fear.°
The lamentable change is from the best;   5
The worst returns to laughter.° Welcome, then,

---

103 **old** customary, natural   105 **Bedlam** lunatic discharged from the insane asylum and licensed to beg   106–07 **his . . . anything** his being a madman and derelict allows him to do anything we ask   109.1 *exeunt* (at some point after lines 99–100, the body of the slain First Servant must be removed.)

1–2 **yet . . . flattered** it is better to be openly despised as a beggar than continually despised behind one's back and flattered to one's face   3 **dejected** cast down   4 **stands . . . fear** gives one some cause for hope, having nothing to fear (since everything is already lost)   5–6 **the lamentable . . . laughter** any change from the best is grievous, just as any change from the worst is bound to be for the better

Thou unsubstantial air that I embrace!
The wretch that thou hast blown unto the worst
Owes nothing° to thy blasts.

Enter Gloucester, and an Old Man [leading him]

                              But who comes here?
My father, poorly led? World, world, O world!   10
But that thy strange mutations make us hate thee,
Life would not yield to age.°

OLD MAN   Oh, my good lord, I have been your tenant
And your father's tenant these fourscore years.

GLOUCESTER   Away, get thee away! Good friend, begone.   15
Thy comforts can do me no good at all;
Thee they may hurt.

OLD MAN   You cannot see your way.

GLOUCESTER   I have no way and therefore want no eyes;
I stumbled when I saw. Full oft 'tis seen
Our means secure us, and our mere defects   20
Prove our commodities.° O dear son Edgar,
The food of thy abusèd father's wrath!°
Might I but live to see thee in my touch,
I'd say I had eyes again!

OLD MAN   How now? Who's there?

EDGAR [*aside*]
O gods! Who is't can say, "I am at the worst"?   25
I am worse than e'er I was.

OLD MAN   'Tis poor mad Tom.

EDGAR [*aside*]   And worse I may be yet. The worst is not
So long as we can say, "This is the worst."°

OLD MAN [*to Edgar*]   Fellow, where goest?

GLOUCESTER   Is it a beggar-man?

OLD MAN   Madman and beggar too.   30

---

9 owes nothing can pay no more, is free of obligation   **11–12 but . . . age** if it were not for your hateful inconstancy, we would never be reconciled to old age and death   **20–21 our . . . commodities** our prosperity makes us proudly overconfident, whereas the sheer afflictions we suffer prove beneficial (by teaching us humility)   **22 the . . . wrath** on whom thy deceived father's wrath fed, the object of his anger   **23 in** by means of   **27–28 The worst . . . worst** So long as we can speak and act and delude ourselves with false hopes, our fortunes can, in fact, grow worse

GLOUCESTER   He has some reason,° else he could not beg.
I'th' last night's storm I such a fellow saw,
Which made me think a man a worm. My son
Came then into my mind, and yet my mind
Was then scarce friends with him. I have heard more since.   35
As flies to wanton° boys are we to th' gods;
They kill us for their sport.

EDGAR [*aside*]   How should this be?°
Bad is the trade that must play fool to sorrow,
Ang'ring itself and others.°—Bless thee, master!

GLOUCESTER   Is that the naked fellow?

OLD MAN   Ay, my lord.   40

GLOUCESTER   Then, prithee, get thee gone. If for my sake
Thou wilt o'ertake us° hence a mile or twain
I'th' way toward Dover, do it for ancient love,°
And bring some covering for this naked soul,
Which I'll entreat to lead me.

OLD MAN   Alack, sir, he is mad.   45

GLOUCESTER
'Tis the time's plague,° when madmen lead the blind.
Do as I bid thee, or rather do thy pleasure;
Above the rest,° begone.

OLD MAN   I'll bring him the best 'parel that I have,
Come on't what will.°   *Exit*

GLOUCESTER   Sirrah, naked fellow—   50

EDGAR
Poor Tom's a-cold. [*Aside*] I cannot daub it further.°

GLOUCESTER   Come hither, fellow.

EDGAR [*aside*]
And yet I must.—Bless thy sweet eyes, they bleed.

GLOUCESTER   Know'st thou the way to Dover?

---

31 reason sanity   **36 wanton** childishly cruel   **37 how . . . be?** how can he have
suffered so much, changed so much?   **38–39 bad . . . others** it's a bad business
to have to play the fool to my sorrowing father, vexing myself and others (with
this delay in revealing my true identity)   **42 o'ertake us** catch up to us (after you
have found clothing for Tom o' Bedlam)   **43 ancient love** the mutually trusting
relationship of master and tenant that you and I have long enjoyed   **46 'tis the
time's plague** it well expresses the spreading sickness of our present state
48 the rest all   **50 come . . . will** whatever comes of this as regards myself   **51 I . . .
further** I cannot keep up this pretense any longer (literally, "I cannot plaster up
the wall")

EDGAR   Both stile and gate, horseway and footpath. Poor Tom   55
hath been scared out of his good wits. Bless thee, good man's
son, from the foul fiend! Five fiends have been in poor Tom
at once: of lust, as Obidicut; Hobbididance, prince of dumb-
ness; Mahu, of stealing; Modo, of murder; Flibbertigibbet,°
of mopping and mowing,° who since° possesses chamber-   60
maids and waiting women. So, bless thee, master!

GLOUCESTER [*giving a purse*]
Here, take this purse, thou whom the heavens' plagues
Have humbled to all strokes.° That I am wretched
Makes thee the happier. Heavens, deal so still!
Let the superfluous and lust-dieted° man,   65
That slaves your ordinance,° that will not see
Because he does not feel,° feel your pow'r quickly!
So distribution should undo excess
And each man have enough. Dost thou know Dover?

EDGAR   Ay, master.   70

GLOUCESTER   There is a cliff, whose high and bending° head
Looks fearfully in the confinèd deep.°
Bring me but to the very brim of it
And I'll repair the misery thou dost bear
With something rich about me.° From that place   75
I shall no leading need.

EDGAR   Give me thy arm.
Poor Tom shall lead thee.

                                                    Exeunt

❖

58–9 Obidicut . . . Flibbertigibbet (fiends borrowed, as before in 3.4.104 and
129–30, from Harsnett) **60–61 mopping and mowing** making grimaces and mouths
60 since ever since then **63 have . . . strokes** have brought so low as to bear every
blow of Fortune **65 superfluous and lust-dieted** immoderately gluttonous and lux-
uriously fed **66 that . . . ordinance** who enslaves your divine ordinances to his own
corrupt will **66–67 that . . . feel** who is resistant to spiritual insight because, not
having suffered himself, he lacks the sympathy of fellow feeling **71 bending** overhanging **72 in . . . deep** into the sea below, which is confined by its shores
75 about me on my person

ACT 4
SCENE 2

Location: Before the Duke of Albany's palace

Enter Goneril [and] Bastard [Edmund]

GONERIL Welcome,° my lord. I marvel our mild husband
Not met° us on the way.

[Enter] steward [Oswald]

                        Now, where's your master?
OSWALD Madam, within, but never man so changed.
  I told him of the army that was landed;
  He smiled at it. I told him you were coming;   5
  His answer was "The worse." Of Gloucester's treachery
  And of the loyal service of his son
  When I informed him, then he called me sot°
  And told me I had turned the wrong side out.
  What most he should dislike seems pleasant to him;   10
  What like, offensive.
GONERIL *[to Edmund]* Then shall you go no further.
  It is the cowish° terror of his spirit,
  That dares not undertake.° He'll not feel wrongs
  Which tie him to an answer.° Our wishes on the way
  May prove effects.° Back, Edmund, to my brother;°   15
  Hasten his musters° and conduct his powers.°
  I must change names° at home and give the distaff°
  Into my husband's hands. This trusty servant
  Shall pass between us. Ere long you are like° to hear,
  If you dare venture in your own behalf,   20

---

1 welcome (Goneril, who has just arrived home from Gloucestershire escorted by Edmund, bids him brief welcome before he must return) **2 not met** has not met **8 sot** fool **12 cowish** cowardly **13 undertake** venture **13–14 he'll . . . answer** he will ignore insults that, if he took notice, would oblige him to respond, to fight **14–15 our . . . effects** the hopes we discussed on our journey here (presumably concerning the supplanting of Albany by Edmund) may come to pass **15 brother** brother-in-law, Cornwall **16 musters** assembling of troops | **powers** armed forces **17 change names** exchange the roles of master and mistress of the household, and exchange the insignia of man and woman: the sword and the *distaff* | **distaff** spinning staff, symbolizing the wife's role **19 like** likely

A mistress's° command. Wear this; spare speech.
                              [*She gives him a favor*]
Decline your head. [*She kisses him*]
                              This kiss, if it durst speak,
Would stretch thy spirits up into the air.
Conceive,° and fare thee well.

EDMUND   Yours in the ranks of death.   *Exit*

GONERIL   My most dear Gloucester!   25
Oh, the difference of man and man!
To thee a woman's services are due;
My fool usurps my body.°

OSWALD   Madam, here comes my lord.   [*Exit°*]

                              Enter Albany

GONERIL   I have been worth the whistling.°

ALBANY   Oh, Goneril,   30
You are not worth the dust which the rude wind
Blows in your face. I fear your disposition;°
That nature which contemns° its origin
Cannot be bordered certain° in itself.
She that herself will sliver° and disbranch   35
From her material sap° perforce must wither
And come to deadly use.°

GONERIL   No more. The text° is foolish.

ALBANY   Wisdom and goodness to the vile seem vile;
Filths savor but themselves.° What have you done?   40
Tigers, not daughters, what have you performed?
A father, and a gracious agèd man,
Whose reverence even the head-lugged° bear would lick,

---

21 **mistress's** (with sexual double meaning)   24 **conceive** understand, take my meaning (with sexual double entendre, continuing from *stretch thy spirits* in the previous line and continued in *death*, line 25, and *a woman's services*, line 27)   28 **my fool . . . body** my husband claims possession of me but is unfitted to do so   29 s.d. **exit** (Oswald could exit later with Goneril, at line 88)   30 **worth the whistling** worth the attentions of men (alludes to the proverb, "it is a poor dog that is not worth the whistling")   32 **fear your disposition** mistrust your nature   33 **contemns** spurns   34 **bordered certain** safely restrained, kept within bounds   35 **sliver** tear off   36 **material sap** nourishing substance, the stock from which she grew   37 **to deadly use** to a bad end, to a destructive purpose   38 **the text** on which you have been preaching   40 **savor but themselves** hunger only for that which is filthy   43 **head-lugged** dragged by the head (or by the ring in its nose) and infuriated

Most barbarous, most degenerate, have you madded.°
Could my good brother° suffer you to do it?   45
A man, a prince, by him so benefited?
If that° the heavens do not their visible° spirits
Send quickly down to tame these vile offenses,
It will come,
Humanity must perforce prey on itself,   50
Like monsters of the deep.

GONERIL   Milk-livered° man,
That bear'st a cheek for blows, a head for wrongs,
Who hast not in thy brows an eye discerning
Thine honor from thy suffering,° that not know'st
Fools do those villains pity who are punished   55
Ere they have done their mischief.° Where's thy drum?°
France spreads his banners in our noiseless° land,
With plumèd helm thy state begins to threat,°
Whilst thou, a moral° fool, sits still and cries,
"Alack, why does he so?"°

ALBANY   See thyself, devil!   60
Proper deformity shows not in the fiend
So horrid as in woman.°

GONERIL   Oh, vain fool!

ALBANY   Thou changèd and self-covered thing, for shame,
Bemonster not thy feature.° Were't my fitness°
To let these hands obey my blood,°   65
They are apt° enough to dislocate and tear

---

44 madded driven mad   **45 brother** brother-in-law (Cornwall)   **47 if that** if |
visible manifested   **51 milk-livered** white-livered, cowardly   **53–54 discerning . . .
suffering** able to tell the difference between an insult to your honor and something
you should tolerate   **54–56 that not . . . mischief** you who fail to understand that
only fools like yourself are so tenderhearted as to pity villains (like Gloucester, Lear,
and Cordelia) who are apprehended and punished before they have committed a
crime   **56 where's thy drum?** where is your military preparedness?   **57 noiseless**
peaceful, unprepared for war   **58 thy state . . . threat** (France) begins to threaten
your kingdom   **59 moral** moralizing   **60 "alack . . . so?"** (an utterly ineffectual
response to invasion)   **61–62 proper . . . woman** the deformity that is appropriate
in a fiend's features is even uglier in a woman's (since it is so at variance with her
nominally feminine appearance)   **63–64 thou . . . feature** you creature whose
transformation into a fiend now overwhelms your womanliness, do not, however
evil you are, take on the outward form of a monster or fiend   **64 were't my fitness**
if it were suitable for me   **65 blood** passion   **66 apt** ready

Thy flesh and bones. Howe'er thou art a fiend,°
A woman's shape doth shield° thee.
GONERIL   Marry, your manhood! Mew!°

Enter a Messenger

ALBANY   What news?   70
MESSENGER   Oh, my good lord, the Duke of Cornwall's dead,
Slain by his servant, going to put out
The other eye of Gloucester.
ALBANY   Gloucester's eyes!
MESSENGER   A servant that he bred,° thrilled with remorse,°
Opposed° against the act, bending his sword   75
To° his great master, who, thereat enraged,
Flew on him and amongst them° felled him dead,
But not without that harmful stroke which since
Hath plucked him after.°
ALBANY   This shows you are above,
You justicers,° that these our nether° crimes   80
So speedily can venge! But, Oh, poor Gloucester!
Lost he his other eye?
MESSENGER   Both, both, my lord.—
This letter, madam, craves a speedy answer;
'Tis from your sister.   [*He gives her a letter*]
GONERIL [*aside*]   One way° I like this well;
But being widow, and my Gloucester with her,   85
May all the building in my fancy pluck
Upon my hateful life.° Another way
The news is not so tart.°—I'll read, and answer.   [*Exit*]

---

67 **howe'er . . . fiend** however much you may be a fiend in reality   68 **shield** (since
I, as a gentleman, cannot lay violent hands on a lady)   69 **mew** (an exclamation of
disgust, a derisive catcall: you speak of manhood in shielding me as a woman; some
manhood!)   74 **bred** kept in his household | **thrilled with remorse** deeply moved
with pity   75 **opposed** opposed himself   75–76 **bending . . . to** directing his sword
against   77 **amongst them** together with the others (?) in their midst (?) out of their
number (?)   79 **after** along (to death)   80 **justicers** (heavenly) judges   **nether** committed here below, on earth   84 **one way** (because Edmund is now Duke of
Gloucester, and Cornwall, a dangerous rival for the throne, is dead)   85–87 **but . . .
life** but she being now a widow, and Edmund in her company, may pull down my
imagined happiness (of having the entire kingdom with Edmund), leaving my hopes
in ruins   88 **tart** bitter, sour (see line 84 and note)

ALBANY   Where was his son° when they did take his° eyes?

MESSENGER   Come with my lady hither.

ALBANY   He is not here.   90

MESSENGER   No, my good lord. I met him back again.°

ALBANY   Knows he the wickedness?

MESSENGER   Ay, my good lord. 'Twas he informed against him,
   And quit the house on purpose that their punishment
   Might have the freer course.

ALBANY   Gloucester,° I live   95
   To thank thee for the love thou show'dst the King
   And to revenge thine eyes.—Come hither, friend.
   Tell me what more thou know'st.

                                                Exeunt

                                    ❧

                                ACT 4
                               SCENE 3

          Location: The French camp near Dover

            Enter Kent [disguised] and a Gentleman

KENT   Why the King of France is so suddenly gone back
   know you no reason?

GENTLEMAN   Something he left imperfect in the state,° which
   since his coming forth is thought of, which imports° to the
   kingdom so much fear and danger that his personal return   5
   was most required and necessary.

KENT   Who hath he left behind him general?

GENTLEMAN   The Marshal of France, Monsieur la Far.

KENT   Did your letters pierce the Queen to any demonstration
   of grief?   10

GENTLEMAN   Ay, sir. She took them, read them in my presence,
   And now and then an ample tear trilled° down
   Her delicate cheek. It seemed she was a queen

---

89 his son Edmund | his Gloucester's   91 back again on the way back (from
Albany's palace)   95 Gloucester the old Earl of Gloucester

3 imperfect in the state unsettled in state affairs   4 imports portends   12 trilled
trickled

Over her passion, who,° most rebel-like,
Sought to be king o'er her.

KENT   Oh, then it moved her?   15

GENTLEMAN   Not to a rage. Patience and sorrow strove
Who should express her goodliest.° You have seen
Sunshine and rain at once. Her smiles and tears
Were like a better way;° those happy smilets
That played on her ripe lip seemed not to know   20
What guests were in her eyes,° which parted thence
As pearls from diamonds dropped. In brief,
Sorrow would be a rarity° most beloved
If all could so become it.°

KENT   Made she no verbal° question?   25

GENTLEMAN

Faith, once or twice she heaved° the name of "father"
Pantingly forth, as if it pressed her heart;
Cried, "Sisters, sisters! Shame of ladies, sisters!
Kent! Father! Sisters! What, i'th' storm, i'th' night?
Let pity not be believed!"° There she shook   30
The holy water from her heavenly eyes,
And, clamor-moistened,° then away she started°
To deal with grief alone.

KENT   It is the stars,
The stars above us, govern our conditions,°
Else one self mate and make° could not beget   35
Such different issues.° You spoke not with her since?

GENTLEMAN   No.

KENT   Was this before the King returned?°

GENTLEMAN   No, since.

KENT   Well, sir, the poor distressèd Lear's i'th' town,
Who sometime in his better tune° remembers   40

---

14 who which   **17 who . . . goodliest** which of the two could portray her best
19 like a better way better than that, though similar   **20–21 seemed . . . eyes** seemed
oblivious of her tears   **23 a rarity** a precious thing, like a jewel   **24 if . . . it** if all
persons were as attractive in sorrow as she   **25 verbal** as distinguished from her
tears and looks   **26 heaved** breathed out with difficulty   **30 let . . . believed!** let no
show of pity be trusted (since they are proved to be so false)!   **32 clamor-moistened**
her outcry of grief assuaged by tears | **started** went   **34 conditions** characters
35 else . . . make otherwise, one couple (husband and wife)   **36 issues** offspring
38 before . . . returned before the King of France returned to his kingdom   **40 better tune** more composed state of mind

What we are come about, and by no means
Will yield° to see his daughter.

GENTLEMAN   Why, good sir?

KENT

A sovereign° shame so elbows him°—his own unkindness
That stripped her from his benediction, turned her°
To foreign casualties,° gave her dear rights   45
To his dog-hearted daughters—these things sting
His mind so venomously that burning shame
Detains him from° Cordelia.

GENTLEMAN   Alack, poor gentleman!

KENT

Of Albany's and Cornwall's powers° you heard not?   50

GENTLEMAN   'Tis so. They are afoot.°

KENT   Well, sir, I'll bring you to our master Lear
And leave you to attend him. Some dear cause°
Will in concealment wrap me up awhile.
When I am known aright, you shall not grieve   55
Lending me this acquaintance.° I pray you, go
Along with me.

                                            Exeunt

❖

ACT 4
SCENE 4

Location: The French camp

*Enter, with drum and colors,
Cordelia, Gentleman,° and soldiers*

CORDELIA   Alack, 'tis he! Why, he was met even now
As mad as the vexed sea, singing aloud,
Crowned with rank fumiter° and furrow weeds,°

---

42 **yield** consent   43 **sovereign** overruling | **elbows him** prods his memory, jostles
him, thrusts him back   44 **turned her** turned her out   45 **foreign casualties** chances of
fortune abroad   48 **detains him from** holds him back from seeing   50 **powers** troops,
armies   51 **afoot** on the march   53 **dear cause** important purpose   55–56 **grieve . . .
acquaintance** regret having made my acquaintance

0.2 *gentleman* (the Quarto specifies "Doctor" here and at line 11)   3 **fumiter** fumi-
tory, a weed or herb | **furrow weeds** weeds growing in plowed furrows

With hardocks,° hemlock, nettles, cuckooflowers,°
Darnel,° and all the idle° weeds that grow   5
In our sustaining corn.° A century° send forth!
Search every acre in the high-grown field
And bring him to our eye.   [*Exit a soldier or soldiers*]
                                   What can man's wisdom°
In the restoring his bereavèd sense,
He that helps him take all my outward° worth.   10
GENTLEMAN   There is means, madam.
    Our foster nurse of nature is repose,
    The which he lacks. That to provoke° in him
    Are many simples operative,° whose power
    Will close the eye of anguish.
CORDELIA   All blest secrets,   15
    All you unpublished virtues° of the earth,
    Spring° with my tears! Be aidant and remediate°
    In the good man's distress! Seek, seek for him,
    Lest his ungoverned rage° dissolve the life
    That wants the means to lead it.°

                                   Enter Messenger

MESSENGER   News, madam.   20
    The British powers° are marching hitherward.
CORDELIA   'Tis known before. Our preparation stands
    In expectation of them. O dear father,
    It is thy business that I go about;
    Therefore great France   25
    My mourning and importuned° tears hath pitied.
    No blown° ambition doth our arms incite,
    But love, dear love, and our aged father's right.
    Soon may I hear and see him!

                                   Exeunt

4 **hardocks** probably burdock, a coarse weedy plant | **cuckooflowers** flowers of
late spring, when the cuckoo is heard   5 **darnel** weed of the grass kind | **idle**
worthless   6 **sustaining corn** sustenance-giving grain | **a century** (literally, a troop
of one hundred men)   8 **what . . . wisdom** what medical knowledge can accomplish
10 **outward** material   13 **that to provoke** to induce that   14 **are . . . operative**
many herbal remedies are efficacious; or, there are many effective remedies (*simples*
are prepared from a single herb)   16 **unpublished virtues** little-known benign herbs
17 **spring** grow | **aidant and remediate** helpful and remedial   19 **rage** frenzy
20 **that . . . lead it** that lacks the means to live sanely   21 **powers** armies
26 **importuned** importunate   27 **blown** swollen

❖

ACT 4
SCENE 5

Location: Gloucester's house

Enter Regan and steward [Oswald]

REGAN But are my brother's powers° set forth?

OSWALD Ay, madam.

REGAN Himself in person there?

OSWALD Madam, with much ado.° Your sister is the better soldier.

REGAN
Lord Edmund spake not with your lord at home?   5

OSWALD No, madam.

REGAN
What might import° my sister's letters to him?

OSWALD I know not, lady.

REGAN Faith, he is posted° hence on serious matter.
It was great ignorance,° Gloucester's eyes being out,   10
To let him live. Where he arrives he moves
All hearts against us. Edmund, I think, is gone,
In pity of his° misery, to dispatch
His nighted° life; moreover to descry°
The strength o'th'enemy.   15

OSWALD I must needs after him, madam, with my letter.

REGAN Our troops set forth tomorrow. Stay with us;
The ways are dangerous.

OSWALD   I may not, madam.
My lady charged my duty° in this business.

REGAN Why should she write to Edmund? Might not you   20
Transport her purposes by word? Belike°
Something—I know not what. I'll love thee much;
Let me unseal the letter.

OSWALD   Madam, I had rather—

REGAN I know your lady does not love her husband,
I am sure of that; and at her late° being here   25

1 **my brother's powers** Albany's forces 4 **with much ado** after much fuss and
persuasion 7 **import** bear as their purport, express 9 **is posted** has hurried
10 **ignorance** error, folly 13 **his** Gloucester's 14 **nighted** benighted, blinded |
descry spy out 19 **charged my duty** laid great stress on my obedience 21 **belike** it
may be 25 **late** recently

She gave strange oeillades° and most speaking looks
To noble Edmund. I know you are of her bosom.°
OSWALD   I, madam?
REGAN   I speak in understanding; y'are,° I know't.
Therefore I do advise you, take this note:°   30
My lord is dead; Edmund and I have talked,°
And more convenient° is he for my hand
Than for your lady's. You may gather more.°
If you do find him, pray you, give him this;°
And when your mistress hears thus much° from you,   35
I pray, desire her call her wisdom to her.°
So, fare you well.
If you do chance to hear of that blind traitor,
Preferment° falls on him that cuts him off.
OSWALD   Would I could meet him, madam! I should show   40
What party I do follow.
REGAN   Fare thee well.

Exeunt [separately]

❖

ACT 4
SCENE 6

Location: Open place near Dover

*Enter Gloucester, and Edgar [in
peasant's clothes, leading his father]*

GLOUCESTER   When shall I come to th' top of that same hill?°
EDGAR   You do climb up it now. Look how we labor.
GLOUCESTER   Methinks the ground is even.
EDGAR   Horrible steep.
Hark, do you hear the sea?
GLOUCESTER   No, truly.

26 **oeillades** amorous glances   27 **of her bosom** in her confidence   29 **y'are** you are
30 **take this note** take note of this   31 **have talked** have come to an understanding
32 **convenient** fitting   33 **gather more** infer what I am trying to suggest   34 **this**
this information, or a love token, or possibly a letter (though only one letter,
Goneril's, is found on his dead body at 4.6.255)   35 **thus much** what I have told
you   36 **call . . . to her** recall herself to her senses   39 **preferment** advancement

1 **that same hill** the cliff we talked about (4.1.71–73)

EDGAR   Why, then, your other senses grow imperfect   5
   By your eyes' anguish.
GLOUCESTER   So may it be, indeed.
   Methinks thy voice is altered, and thou speak'st
   In better phrase and matter than thou didst.
EDGAR   You're much deceived. In nothing am I changed
   But in my garments.
GLOUCESTER   Methinks you're better spoken.   10
EDGAR
   Come on, sir, here's the place. Stand still. How fearful
   And dizzy 'tis to cast one's eyes so low!
   The crows and choughs° that wing the midway° air
   Show scarce so gross° as beetles. Halfway down
   Hangs one that gathers samphire°—dreadful trade!   15
   Methinks he seems no bigger than his head.
   The fishermen that walk upon the beach
   Appear like mice, and yond tall anchoring bark°
   Diminished to her cock;° her cock, a buoy
   Almost too small for sight. The murmuring surge,   20
   That on th'unnumbered idle pebble° chafes,
   Cannot be heard so high. I'll look no more,
   Lest my brain turn, and the deficient sight
   Topple down headlong.°
GLOUCESTER   Set me where you stand.
EDGAR   Give me your hand. You are now within a foot   25
   Of th'extreme verge. For all beneath the moon°
   Would I not leap upright.°
GLOUCESTER   Let go my hand.
   Here, friend, 's another purse; in it a jewel
   Well worth a poor man's taking.   [*He gives a purse*]
                         Fairies and gods
   Prosper it with thee!° Go thou further off.   30
   Bid me farewell, and let me hear thee going.

---

13 choughs jackdaws | **midway** halfway down   **14 gross** large   **15 samphire** (a
herb used in pickling)   **18 bark** small sailing vessel   **19 diminished . . . cock**
reduced to the size of her cockboat, small ship's boat   **21 th'unnumbered idle pebble**
innumerable, randomly shifting, pebbles   **23–24 lest . . . headlong** lest I become
dizzy, and my failing sight topple me headlong   **26 for . . . moon** for the whole
world   **27 upright** up and down, much less forward   **29–30 fairies . . . thee!** may
the fairies and gods cause this to multiply in your possession!

EDGAR [*moving away*]
  Now fare ye well, good sir.
GLOUCESTER   With all my heart.
EDGAR [*aside*]   Why I do trifle thus with his despair
  Is done to cure it.
GLOUCESTER [*kneeling*]   O you mighty gods!
  This world I do renounce, and in your sights   35
  Shake patiently my great affliction off.
  If I could bear it longer and not fall
  To quarrel with° your great opposeless° wills,
  My snuff° and loathèd part of nature° should
  Burn itself out. If Edgar live, oh, bless him!   40
  Now, fellow, fare thee well.   [*He falls forward*]
EDGAR   Gone, sir. Farewell.—
  And yet I know not how conceit° may rob
  The treasury of life, when life itself
  Yields° to the theft. Had he been where he thought,
  By this° had thought been past. Alive or dead?—   45
  Ho, you, sir! Friend! Hear you, sir! Speak!—
  Thus might he pass° indeed; yet he revives.—
  What° are you, sir?
GLOUCESTER   Away, and let me die.
EDGAR   Hadst thou been aught but gossamer, feathers, air,
  So many fathom down precipitating,   50
  Thou'dst shivered like an egg; but thou dost breathe,
  Hast heavy substance,° bleed'st not, speak'st, art sound.
  Ten masts at each° make not the altitude
  Which thou hast perpendicularly fell.
  Thy life's a miracle. Speak yet again.   55
GLOUCESTER   But have I fall'n or no?
EDGAR   From the dread summit of this chalky bourn.°
  Look up aheight;° the shrill-gorged° lark so far
  Cannot be seen or heard. Do but look up.

---

38 to quarrel with into rebellion against | **opposeless** irresistible **39 snuff** useless residue (literally, the smoking wick of a candle) | **of nature** of my life **42 conceit** imagination **44 yields** consents **45 by this** by this time **47 pass** die **48 what** who (Edgar now speaks in a new voice, differing from that of "poor Tom" and also from the "altered" voice he used at the start of this scene; see lines 7–10) **52 heavy substance** the substance of the flesh **53 at each** end to end **57 bourn** limit, boundary (the edge of the sea) **58 aheight** on high | **shrill-gorged** shrill-throated

GLOUCESTER Alack, I have no eyes. 60
  Is wretchedness deprived that benefit
  To end itself by death? 'Twas yet some comfort
  When misery could beguile° the tyrant's rage
  And frustrate his proud will.
EDGAR   Give me your arm.
                                   [*He lifts him up*]
  Up—so. How is't? Feel you your legs? You stand. 65
GLOUCESTER Too well, too well.
EDGAR   This is above all strangeness.
  Upon the crown o'th' cliff what thing was that
  Which parted from you?
GLOUCESTER   A poor unfortunate beggar.
EDGAR As I stood here below, methought his eyes
  Were two full moons; he had a thousand noses, 70
  Horns whelked° and waved like the enridgèd° sea.
  It was some fiend. Therefore, thou happy father,°
  Think that the clearest° gods, who make them honors
  Of men's impossibilities,° have preserved thee.
GLOUCESTER I do remember now. Henceforth I'll bear 75
  Affliction till it do cry out itself
  "Enough, enough," and die.° That thing you speak of,
  I took it for a man; often 'twould say
  "The fiend, the fiend." He led me to that place.
EDGAR Bear free° and patient thoughts.

  Enter Lear [mad, fantastically dressed with wild flowers]

                               But who comes here? 80
  The safer sense will ne'er accommodate
  His master thus.°

---

63 **beguile** outwit 71 **whelked** twisted, convoluted | **enridgèd** furrowed (by the wind) 72 **happy father** lucky old man 73 **clearest** purest, most righteous 73–74 **who . . . impossibilities** who win our awe and reverence by doing things impossible to men 76–77 **till . . . die** until affliction itself has had enough, or until I die 80 **free** free from despair 81–82 **the safer . . . thus** a person in his right senses would never dress himself in such a fashion (*his master* is the owner of the *safer sense* or sane mind; *his* means "its")

LEAR No, they cannot touch me for coining. I am the King himself.°

EDGAR Oh, thou side-piercing° sight! 85

LEAR Nature's above art in that respect.° There's your press money.° That fellow handles his bow like a crow-keeper.° Draw me a clothier's yard.° Look, look, a mouse! Peace, peace; this piece of toasted cheese will do't.° There's my gauntlet;° I'll prove it on° a giant. Bring up the brown bills.° 90 Oh, well flown, bird!° I'th' clout,° i'th' clout—hewgh!° Give the word.°

EDGAR Sweet marjoram.°

LEAR Pass.

GLOUCESTER I know that voice. 95

LEAR Ha! Goneril with a white beard? They flattered me like a dog° and told me I had white hairs in my beard ere the black ones were there.° To say ay and no to everything that I said ay and no to was no good divinity.° When the rain came to wet me once and the wind to make me chatter, when the 100 thunder would not peace at my bidding, there I found 'em, there I smelt 'em out.° Go to,° they are not men o' their words. They told me I was everything. 'Tis a lie. I am not ague-proof.°

83–84 they . . . himself they cannot prosecute me for minting coins; as king, I enjoy the exclusive royal prerogative for doing so (Lear goes on to discuss his need for money to pay his imaginary soldiers) **85 side-piercing** heartrending (with a suggestion of Christ's suffering on the cross) **86 nature's . . . respect** real life can offer more heart-piercing examples than art **86–87 press money** enlistment bonus **87 crowkeeper** laborer hired to scare away the crows **88 draw . . . yard** draw your bow to the full length of the arrow, a cloth-yard long **89 do't** capture the mouse, an imagined enemy **90 gauntlet** armored glove thrown down as a challenge | **prove it on** maintain it against | **brown bills** soldiers carrying pikes (painted brown), or the pikes themselves **91 well flown, bird** (Lear uses the language of hawking to describe the flight of an arrow) | **clout** target, bull's-eye | **hewgh** (the arrow's noise) **92 word** password **93 sweet marjoram** (a herb used to cure madness) **96–97 like a dog** as a dog fawns **97–98 told . . . there** told me I had the white-haired wisdom of old age before I had even attained the manliness of a beard **98–99 to say . . . divinity** to agree flatteringly with everything I said was not good theology, since the Bible teaches us to "let your yea be yea and your nay, nay" (James 5.12; see also Matthew 5.37 and 2 Cor. 1.18) **99–102 when . . . out** suffering wet, cold, and storm have taught me about the frailty of the human condition **102 go to** (an expression of impatience) **104 ague-proof** immune against illness (literally, fever)

GLOUCESTER   The trick° of that voice I do well remember.   105
  Is't not the King?
LEAR   Ay, every inch a king.
  When I do stare, see how the subject quakes.
  I pardon that man's life. What was thy cause?°
  Adultery?
  Thou shalt not die. Die for adultery? No.   110
  The wren goes to't, and the small gilded fly
  Does lecher in my sight.
  Let copulation thrive; for Gloucester's bastard son
  Was kinder to his father than my daughters
  Got 'tween the lawful sheets.   115
  To't, luxury,° pell-mell, for I lack soldiers.
  Behold yond simpering dame,
  Whose face between her forks presages snow,°
  That minces° virtue and does shake the head
  To hear of pleasure's name;°   120
  The fitchew nor the soilèd horse goes to't°
  With a more riotous appetite.
  Down from the waist they're centaurs,°
  Though women all above.
  But° to the girdle° do the gods inherit;°   125
  Beneath is all the fiends'.
  There's hell, there's darkness, there is the sulfurous pit,
  burning, scalding, stench, consumption. Fie, fie, fie! Pah,
  pah! Give me an ounce of civet,° good apothecary, sweeten
  my imagination. There's money for thee.   130
GLOUCESTER   Oh, let me kiss that hand!
LEAR   Let me wipe it first; it smells of mortality.
GLOUCESTER   Oh, ruined piece° of nature! This great world
  Shall so wear out to naught.° Dost thou know me?

---

105 **trick** peculiar characteristic 108 **cause** offense 116 **luxury** lechery
118 **whose . . . snow** whose frosty countenance seems to suggest frigidity between
her legs 119 **minces** affects, mimics 120 **of pleasure's name** the very name of
pleasure 121 **the fitchew . . . to't** neither the polecat nor the well-pastured horse
indulges in sexual pleasure 123 **centaurs** fabulous creatures with the head, trunk,
and arms of a man joined to the body and legs of a horse 125 **but** only | **girdle**
waist | **inherit** have possession 129 **civet** musk perfume 133 **piece** (1) fragment
(2) masterpiece 133–34 **this . . . naught** even so will the whole universe come to an
apocalyptic end

LEAR   I remember thine eyes well enough. Dost thou squinny° 135
at me? No, do thy worst, blind Cupid; I'll not love. Read
thou this challenge. Mark but the penning of it.

GLOUCESTER
Were all thy letters suns, I could not see.

EDGAR [*aside*]   I would not take° this from report. It is,°
And my heart breaks at it.   140

LEAR   Read.

GLOUCESTER   What, with the case° of eyes?

LEAR   Oho, are you there with me?° No eyes in your head, nor
no money in your purse? Your eyes are in a heavy case,°
your purse in a light, yet you see how this world goes.   145

GLOUCESTER   I see it feelingly.°

LEAR   What, art mad? A man may see how this world goes
with no eyes. Look with thine ears. See how yond justice
rails upon yond simple° thief. Hark in thine ear: change
places and, handy-dandy,° which is the justice, which is the 150
thief? Thou hast seen a farmer's dog bark at a beggar?

GLOUCESTER   Ay, sir.

LEAR   And the creature° run from the cur? There thou mightst
behold the great image of authority: a dog's obeyed in office.°
Thou rascal beadle,° hold thy bloody hand!   155
Why dost thou lash that whore? Strip thine own back;
Thou hotly lusts to use her in that kind°
For which thou whipp'st her. The usurer hangs the cozener.°
Through tattered clothes small vices do appear;
Robes and furred gowns hide all.° Plate° sin with gold,   160
And the strong lance of justice hurtless breaks;°
Arm it in rags, a pygmy's straw does pierce it.
None does offend, none, I say, none. I'll able° 'em.

---

135 **squinny** squint   139 **take** believe, credit | **it is** it is taking place, incredibly
enough   142 **case** mere sockets   143 **are . . . me?** is that your meaning, the point
you are making?   144 **heavy case** sad plight (with pun on *case* in line 142)
146 **feelingly** (1) by touch (2) keenly, painfully   149 **simple** of humble station
150 **handy-dandy** take your choice of hands (as in a well-known child's game)
153 **creature** poor fellow   154 **a dog's . . . office** even currish power commands sub-
mission   155 **beadle** parish officer, responsible for giving whippings   157 **kind** way
158 **the usurer . . . cozener** the moneylender (who can buy out justice) hangs the con
man   159–60 **through . . . all** beggars' small vices are apparent for all to see; rich
folk, in expensive clothes, succeed in hiding a great deal   160 **plate** arm in plate
armor   161 **hurtless breaks** splinters harmlessly   163 **able** empower, give warrant to

Take that of me,° my friend, who have the power
To seal th'accuser's lips. Get thee glass eyes,   165
And like a scurvy politician seem
To see the things thou dost not.° Now, now, now, now!
Pull off my boots. Harder, harder! So.

EDGAR *[aside]*   Oh, matter and impertinency° mixed,
Reason in madness!   170

LEAR   If thou wilt weep my fortunes, take my eyes.
I know thee well enough; thy name is Gloucester.
Thou must be patient. We came crying hither.
Thou know'st the first time that we smell the air
We wawl and cry. I will preach to thee. Mark.   175

GLOUCESTER   Alack, alack the day!

LEAR   When we are born, we cry that we are come
To this great stage of fools.—This'° a good block.°
It were a delicate° stratagem to shoe
A troop of horse with felt.° I'll put 't in proof,°   180
And when I have stol'n upon these son-in-laws,
Then, kill, kill, kill, kill, kill, kill!

Enter a Gentleman [with attendants]

GENTLEMAN   Oh, here he is. Lay hand upon him.—Sir,
Your most dear daughter—

LEAR   No rescue? What, a prisoner? I am even   185
The natural fool° of fortune. Use me well;
You shall have ransom. Let me have surgeons;
I am cut° to th' brains.

GENTLEMAN   You shall have anything.

LEAR   No seconds?° All myself?
Why, this would make a man a man of salt°   190
To use his eyes for garden waterpots,
Ay, and laying autumn's dust.

GENTLEMAN   Good sir.

---

164 take . . . me (1) learn that from me (2) take that protection from me   **165–67 get . . . dost not** if Gloucester were to fit himself out with spectacles (or perhaps with glass eyeballs, though they are not mentioned elsewhere until later in the seventeenth century), he would look wise like a hypocritical politician   **169 matter and impertinency** sense and nonsense   **178 this'** this is | **block** mold for a felt hat (Lear may refer to the weeds strewn in his hair, which he removes as though doffing a hat before preaching a sermon)   **179 delicate** subtle   **180 felt** padding to deaden the sound of the footfall | **in proof** to the test   **186 natural fool** born plaything   **188 cut** wounded   **189 seconds** supporters   **190 of salt** of salt tears

LEAR   I will die bravely,° like a smug° bridegroom. What?
I will be jovial.° Come, come, I am a king,
Masters,° know you that?   195

GENTLEMAN
You are a royal one, and we obey you.

LEAR   Then there's life° in't. Come, an° you get it, you shall get
it by running. Sa, sa, sa, sa.°

Exit [running, followed by attendants]

GENTLEMAN   A sight most pitiful in the meanest wretch,
Past speaking of in a king! Thou hast one daughter   200
Who redeems nature from the general curse°
Which twain° have brought her to.

EDGAR   Hail, gentle° sir.

GENTLEMAN   Sir, speed you.° What's your will?

EDGAR   Do you hear aught, sir, of a battle toward?°   205

GENTLEMAN   Most sure and vulgar.° Everyone hears that
Which° can distinguish sound.

EDGAR   But, by your favor,
How near's the other army?

GENTLEMAN   Near and on speedy foot. The main descry
Stands on the hourly thought.°   210

EDGAR   I thank you, sir; that's all.

GENTLEMAN   Though that° the Queen on special cause° is here,
Her army is moved on.

EDGAR   I thank you, sir.

Exit [Gentleman]

GLOUCESTER
You ever-gentle gods, take my breath from me;
Let not my worser spirit° tempt me again   215
To die before you please!

EDGAR   Well pray you, father.°

---

193 bravely (1) courageously (2) splendidly attired | **smug** trimly dressed (*bridegroom* continues the punning sexual suggestion of *die bravely*, "have sex successfully") **194 jovial** (1) jovelike, majestic (2) jolly **195 masters** good sirs **197 life** hope still | **an** if **198 sa . . . sa** (a hunting cry) **201 general curse** fallen condition of the human race **202 twain** (1) Goneril and Regan (2) Adam and Eve **203 gentle** noble **204 speed you** Godspeed, may God prosper you **205 toward** imminent **206 vulgar** in everyone's mouth, generally known **207 which** who **209–10 the main . . . thought** the full view of the main body is expected any hour now **212 though that** although | **on special cause** for a special reason, to minister to Lear **215 worser spirit** bad angel, or ill thoughts **217 father** (a term of respect to older men, as also in lines 72, 252, and 282, though with ironic double meaning throughout the scene)

GLOUCESTER Now, good sir, what° are you?

EDGAR A most poor man, made tame° to fortune's blows,
    Who, by the art of known and feeling° sorrows,   220
    Am pregnant° to good pity. Give me your hand.
    I'll lead you to some biding.°   *[He offers his arm]*

GLOUCESTER   Hearty thanks.
    The bounty and the benison of heaven
    To boot, and boot!°

Enter steward [Oswald]

OSWALD   A proclaimed prize!° Most happy!°
                         [He draws his sword]
    That eyeless head of thine was first framed flesh°   225
    To raise my fortunes. Thou old unhappy traitor,
    Briefly thyself remember.° The sword is out
    That must destroy thee.

GLOUCESTER   Now let thy friendly° hand
    Put strength enough to't.   *[Edgar intervenes]*

OSWALD   Wherefore, bold peasant,
    Durst thou support a published° traitor? Hence,   230
    Lest that° th'infection of his fortune take
    Like° hold on thee. Let go his arm.

EDGAR 'Chill° not let go, zir, without vurther 'cagion.°

OSWALD Let go, slave, or thou diest!

EDGAR Good gentleman, go your gait,° and let poor volk pass. 235
    An 'chud° ha' bin zwaggered° out of my life, 'twould not ha'
    bin zo long as 'tis by a vortnight.° Nay, come not near th' old
    man; keep out, 'che vor ye,° or Ise° try whether your costard°
    or my ballow° be the harder. 'Chill be plain with you.

---

218 what who (again, Edgar alters his voice to personate a new stranger assisting Gloucester; see line 48, earlier, and note) **219 tame** submissive **220 known and feeling** personally experienced and heartfelt **221 pregnant** prone **222 biding** abode **223–24 the bounty . . . and boot!** in addition to my thanks, I wish you the bounty and blessings of heaven **224 proclaimed prize** one with a price on his head | **happy** fortunate **225 framed flesh** born **227 thyself remember** say your prayers **228 friendly** welcome, since I desire death **230 published** proclaimed **231 lest that** lest **232 like** similar **233 'chill** I will (literally, a contraction of *Ich will*; Edgar adopts Somerset dialect, a stage convention regularly used for peasants) | **vurther 'cagion** further occasion **235 go your gait** go your own way **236 an 'chud** if I could | **zwaggered** swaggered, bullied **236–37 'twould . . . vortnight** it (my life) wouldn't have lasted a fortnight **238 'che vor ye** I warrant you | **Ise** I shall | **costard** head (literally, an apple) **239 ballow** cudgel

OSWALD   Out, dunghill!   240

EDGAR   'Chill pick your teeth, zir. Come, no matter vor your
    foins.°   [*They fight. Edgar fells him with his cudgel*]

OSWALD   Slave, thou hast slain me. Villain,° take my purse.
    If ever thou wilt thrive, bury my body
    And give the letters° which thou find'st about me°   245
    To Edmund, Earl of Gloucester. Seek him out
    Upon° the English party.° Oh, untimely death!
    Death!   [*He dies*]

EDGAR   I know thee well: a serviceable° villain,
    As duteous to the vices of thy mistress   250
    As badness would desire.

GLOUCESTER   What, is he dead?

EDGAR   Sit you down, father. Rest you.   [*Gloucester sits*]
    Let's see these pockets; the letters that he speaks of
    May be my friends. He's dead; I am only sorry
    He had no other deathsman.° Let us see.   255
           [*He finds a letter and opens it*]
    Leave,° gentle wax,° and, manners, blame us not.
    To know our enemies' minds we rip their hearts;
    Their papers is more lawful. [*Reads the letter.*]
        "Let our reciprocal vows be remembered. You have many
        opportunities to cut him° off; if your will want not,° time   260
        and place will be fruitfully° offered. There is nothing done°
        if he return the conqueror. Then am I the prisoner, and his
        bed my jail, from the loathed warmth whereof deliver me
        and supply° the place for your labor.°
           Your—wife, so I would say—affectionate servant,   265
          and for you her own for venture,° Goneril."
    Oh, indistinguished space of woman's will!°
    A plot upon her virtuous husband's life,
    And the exchange my brother! Here in the sands

---

242 **foins** thrusts   243 **villain** serf   245 **letters** letter (see 4.5.35 and note) |
about me upon my person   247 **upon** on | **party** side   249 **serviceable** officious
255 **deathsman** executioner   256 **leave** by your leave | **wax** wax seal on the letter
260 **him** Albany | **want not** is not lacking   261 **fruitfully** plentifully and with
results | **there is nothing done** we will have accomplished nothing   264 **supply**
fill | **for your labor** (1) as recompense for your efforts (2) as a place for your
amorous labors   266 **and for . . . venture** and one ready to venture her own fortunes for your sake   267 **indistinguished . . . will** limitless and incalculable expanse
of woman's appetite

Thee I'll rake up,° the post unsanctified°   270
Of murderous lechers; and in the mature time°
With this ungracious° paper strike° the sight
Of the death-practiced Duke. For him 'tis well°
That of thy death and business I can tell.

                                               [Exit with the body]

GLOUCESTER   The King is mad. How stiff is my vile sense,°   275
That I stand up and have ingenious° feeling
Of my huge sorrows! Better I were distract;°
So should my thoughts be severed from my griefs,
And woes by wrong imaginations° lose
The knowledge of themselves.   *Drum afar off*

                                            [Enter Edgar]

EDGAR   Give me your hand.   280
Far off, methinks, I hear the beaten drum.
Come, father, I'll bestow° you with a friend.

                 Exeunt, [Edgar leading his father]

❖

ACT 4
SCENE 7

Location: The French camp

Enter Cordelia, Kent [dressed still in
his disguise costume], and Gentleman°

CORDELIA   O thou good Kent, how shall I live and work
To match thy goodness? My life will be too short,
And every measure fail me.°

270 **rake up** cover up | **post unsanctified** unholy messenger   271 **in . . . time** when
the time is ripe   272 **ungracious** wicked | **strike** blast   273 **of . . . well** of Albany,
whose death is plotted; it's a good thing for him   275 **how . . . sense** how obstinate is
my deplorable sanity and power of sensation   276 **ingenious** conscious (Gloucester
laments that he remains sane and hence fully conscious of his troubles, unlike Lear)
277 **distract** distracted, crazy   279 **wrong imaginations** delusions   282 **bestow**
lodge (at the scene's end, Edgar leads off Gloucester; presumably, at line 282 or
else here, he must also dispose of Oswald's body in the trapdoor or by lugging it
offstage)

0.2 **Gentleman** ("*Doctor*" in Q)   3 **every . . . me** every attempt (to match your
goodness) will fall short

KENT   To be acknowledged, madam, is o'erpaid.
    All my reports go° with the modest truth,   5
    Nor more nor clipped,° but so.
CORDELIA   Be better suited.°
    These weeds° are memories° of those worser hours;
    I prithee, put them off.
KENT   Pardon, dear madam;
    Yet to be known shortens my made intent.°
    My boon I make it° that you know° me not   10
    Till time and I think meet.°
CORDELIA
    Then be't so, my good lord.   [*To the Gentleman*]
               How does the King?
GENTLEMAN   Madam, sleeps still.
CORDELIA   O you kind gods,
    Cure this great breach in his abusèd nature!   15
    Th'untuned and jarring senses, oh, wind up°
    Of this child-changèd° father!
GENTLEMAN   So please your Majesty
    That we may wake the King? He hath slept long.
CORDELIA   Be governed by your knowledge, and proceed
    I'th' sway° of your own will.—Is he arrayed?   20

        Enter Lear in a chair carried by servants

GENTLEMAN   Ay, madam. In the heaviness of sleep
    We put fresh garments on him.
    Be by, good madam, when we do awake him.
    I doubt not of his temperance.°
CORDELIA   Very well.   [*Music*]
GENTLEMAN   Please you, draw near.—Louder the music there!   25
CORDELIA [*kissing him*]
    O my dear father! Restoration hang
    Thy medicine on my lips, and let this kiss

---

5 **all my reports go** all my reports (of my service as Caius to Lear) conform 6 **nor . . . clipped** neither more nor less | **suited** dressed 7 **weeds** garments | **memories** remembrances 9 **yet . . . intent** to reveal my true identity now would alter my carefully made plan 10 **my . . . it** the favor I seek is | **know** acknowledge 11 **meet** appropriate 16 **wind up** tune (as by tightening the slackened string of an instrument) 17 **child-changèd** changed by children's cruelty 20 **I'th' sway** under the direction 24 **temperance** self-control, calm behavior

Repair those violent harms that my two sisters
Have in thy reverence° made!

KENT   Kind and dear princess!

CORDELIA   Had you° not been their father, these white flakes°   30
Did challenge° pity of them. Was this a face
To be opposed against the warring winds?
To stand against the deep° dread-bolted° thunder
In the most terrible and nimble stroke
Of quick cross° lightning? To watch°—poor perdu!°—   35
With this thin helm?° Mine enemy's dog,
Though he had bit me, should have stood that night
Against° my fire; and wast thou fain,° poor father,
To hovel thee with swine and rogues forlorn°
In short° and musty straw? Alack, alack!   40
'Tis wonder that thy life and wits at once
Had not concluded all.°—He wakes! Speak to him.

GENTLEMAN   Madam, do you; 'tis fittest.

CORDELIA
How does my royal lord? How fares your Majesty?

LEAR   You do me wrong to take me out o'th' grave.   45
Thou art a soul in bliss; but I am bound
Upon a wheel of fire,° that° mine own tears
Do scald like molten lead.

CORDELIA   Sir, do you know me?

LEAR   You are a spirit, I know. Where did you die?

CORDELIA   Still, still, far wide!°   50

GENTLEMAN
He's scarce awake. Let him alone awhile.

LEAR   Where have I been? Where am I? Fair daylight?
I am mightily abused.° I should ev'n die with pity
To see another thus.° I know not what to say.
I will not swear these are my hands. Let's see;   55

29 **reverence** venerable condition   30 **had you** even if you had | **flakes** locks of hair   31 **did challenge** would have demanded   33 **deep** bass-voiced | **dread-bolted** furnished with the dreadful thunderbolt   35 **cross** zigzag | **watch** stay awake (like a sentry on duty) | **perdu** lost one; a sentinel placed in a position of peculiar danger   36 **helm** helmet, scanty hair   38 **against** before, in front of | **fain** constrained   39 **rogues forlorn** abandoned vagabonds   40 **short** broken up and hence uncomfortable   42 **concluded all** come to an end altogether   47 **wheel of fire** (a hellish torment for the eternally damned) | **that** so that   50 **wide** wide of the mark, wandering   53 **abused** confused, deluded   54 **thus** thus confused, bewildered

I feel this pinprick. Would I were assured
Of my condition!

CORDELIA [*kneeling*] Oh, look upon me, sir,
And hold your hands in benediction o'er me.

[*He attempts to kneel*]

No, sir, you must not kneel.

LEAR   Pray, do not mock me.
I am a very foolish fond° old man,   60
Fourscore and upward, not an hour more nor less;
And, to deal plainly,
I fear I am not in my perfect mind.
Methinks I should know you, and know this man,
Yet I am doubtful; for I am mainly° ignorant   65
What place this is, and all the skill I have
Remembers not these garments, nor I know not
Where I did lodge last night. Do not laugh at me,
For, as I am a man, I think this lady
To be my child Cordelia.   70

CORDELIA [*weeping*] And so I am, I am.

LEAR Be your tears wet? Yes, faith. I pray, weep not.
If you have poison for me I will drink it.
I know you do not love me, for your sisters
Have, as I do remember, done me wrong.   75
You have some cause, they have not.

CORDELIA No cause, no cause.

LEAR Am I in France?

KENT In your own kingdom, sir.

LEAR Do not abuse° me.   80

GENTLEMAN Be comforted, good madam. The great rage,°
You see, is killed in him, and yet it is danger
To make him even o'er° the time he has lost.
Desire him to go in. Trouble him no more
Till further settling.°   85

CORDELIA Will't please Your Highness walk?°

LEAR You must bear with me.

---

60 fond in my dotàge **65 mainly** entirely **80 abuse** deceive (or perhaps Lear
feels hurt by the reminder of his having divided the kingdom) **81 rage** frenzy
83 even o'er fill in, go over in his mind **85 settling** composing of his mind
86 walk withdraw

Pray you now, forget and forgive.
I am old and foolish.

Exeunt [all but Kent and Gentleman]

GENTLEMAN

Holds it true,° sir, that the Duke of Cornwall was so slain?   90

KENT   Most certain, sir.

GENTLEMAN   Who is conductor° of his people?

KENT   As 'tis said, the bastard son of Gloucester.

GENTLEMAN   They say Edgar, his banished son, is with the Earl
of Kent in Germany.   95

KENT   Report is changeable. 'Tis time to look about;° the
powers of the kingdom° approach apace.

GENTLEMAN   The arbitrament° is like to be bloody. Fare you
well, sir.   [*Exit*]

KENT   My point and period will be throughly wrought,°   100
Or° well or ill, as° this day's battle's fought.

Exit

❖

ACT 5
SCENE 1

Location: The British camp near Dover

*Enter, with drum and colors, Edmund,
Regan, Gentlemen, and soldiers*

EDMUND   [*to a Gentleman*]

Know° of the Duke if his last purpose hold,°
Or whether since° he is advised by aught°
To change the course. He's full of alteration°
And self-reproving. Bring his constant pleasure.°

[*Exit Gentleman*]

90 holds it true is it still held to be true   **92 conductor** leader, general   **96 look about** be wary, take stock of the situation   **97 powers of the kingdom** British armies (marching against the French invaders)   **98 arbitrament** decision by arms, decisive encounter   **100 my . . . wrought** the conclusion of my destiny (literally, the full stop at the end of my life's sentence) will be thoroughly shaped   **101 or** either |
as according as

1 know inquire | **last purpose hold** most recent intention (to fight) remains firm
2 since since then | **advised by aught** persuaded by any consideration   **3 alteration**
vacillation   **4 constant pleasure** settled decision

REGAN   Our sister's man° is certainly miscarried.°   5

EDMUND   'Tis to be doubted,° madam.

REGAN   Now, sweet lord,
You know the goodness I intend° upon you.
Tell me, but truly—but then speak the truth—
Do you not love my sister?

EDMUND   In honored° love.

REGAN   But have you never found my brother's way   10
To the forfended° place?

EDMUND   That thought abuses° you.

REGAN   I am doubtful that you have been conjunct
And bosomed with her, as far as we call hers.°

EDMUND   No, by mine honor, madam.

REGAN   I never shall endure her. Dear my lord,   15
Be not familiar° with her.

EDMUND   Fear me not.°—She and the Duke her husband!

                  Enter, with drum and colors,
                  Albany, Goneril, [and] soldiers

GONERIL *[aside]*   I had rather lose the battle than that sister
Should loosen him and me.

ALBANY *[to Regan]*   Our very loving sister, well bemet.°   20
[to Edmund]
Sir, this I heard: the King is come to his daughter,
With others whom the rigor of our state°
Forced to cry out.° Where° I could not be honest,°
I never yet was valiant. For° this business,
It touches us as° France invades our land,   25
Not bolds the King, with others whom, I fear,
Most just and heavy causes make oppose.°

EDMUND   Sir, you speak nobly.

---

5 **man** Oswald | **miscarried** lost, perished 6 **doubted** feared 7 **intend** intend to confer 9 **honored** honorable 11 **forfended** forbidden (by the commandment against adultery) | **abuses** degrades, wrongs 12–13 **I . . . hers** I fear that you have been sexually intimate with her to the fullest extent possible 16 **familiar** intimate 17 **fear me not** don't worry about me on that score 20 **bemet** met 22 **rigor of our state** harshness of our rule 23 **cry out** rebel | **where** in a case where | **honest** honorable 24 **for** as for 25 **touches us as** concerns us insofar as 26–27 **not . . . oppose** not because the matter emboldens the King and others who, I fear, are driven into opposition by just and weighty grievances

REGAN   Why is this reasoned?°

GONERIL   Combine together 'gainst the enemy;

For these domestic and particular broils°   30

Are not the question here.

ALBANY   Let's then determine

With th'ancient of war° on our proceeding.

EDMUND

I shall attend you presently at your tent.

REGAN   Sister, you'll go with us?

GONERIL   No.   35

REGAN

'Tis most convenient.° Pray, go with us.

GONERIL [aside]   Oho, I know the riddle.°—I will go.

[As they are going out,] enter Edgar [disguised]

EDGAR [to Albany]

If e'er Your Grace had speech with man so poor,

Hear me one word.

ALBANY [to the others]   I'll overtake you.

                              Exeunt both the armies

                              Speak.

EDGAR [giving a letter]

Before you fight the battle, ope this letter.°   40

If you have victory, let the trumpet sound°

For him that brought it. Wretched though I seem,

I can produce a champion that will prove°

What is avouchèd° there. If you miscarry,°

Your business of the world hath so an end,   45

And machination° ceases. Fortune love you!

ALBANY   Stay till I have read the letter.

EDGAR   I was forbid it.

When time shall serve, let but the herald cry

And I'll appear again.   Exit [Edgar]   50

---

28 **why . . . reasoned?** why are we arguing about reasons for fighting, instead of fighting?   30 **particular broils** private quarrels   32 **th'ancient of war** the veteran officers   36 **convenient** proper, fitting   37 **I know the riddle** I understand the reason for Regan's enigmatic demand that I accompany her, which is that she wants to keep me away from Edmund   40 **this letter** Goneril's letter to Edmund found on Oswald's body   41 **sound** sound a summons   43 **prove** in trial by combat   44 **avouchèd** affirmed | **miscarry** lose the battle and die   46 **machination** plotting (against your life)

ALBANY   Why, fare thee well. I will o'erlook° thy paper.

Enter Edmund

EDMUND   The enemy's in view. Draw up your powers.
                              [*He offers Albany a paper*]
    Here is the guess° of their true strength and forces
    By diligent discovery;° but your haste
    Is now urged on you.

ALBANY   We will greet the time.°   *Exit*   55

EDMUND   To both these sisters have I sworn my love,
    Each jealous° of the other as the stung
    Are of the adder. Which of them shall I take?
    Both? One? Or neither? Neither can be enjoyed
    If both remain alive. To take the widow   60
    Exasperates, makes mad her sister Goneril,
    And hardly shall I carry out my side,°
    Her husband being alive. Now then, we'll use
    His countenance° for the battle, which being done,
    Let her who would be rid of him devise   65
    His speedy taking off.° As for the mercy
    Which he intends to Lear and to Cordelia,
    The battle done and they within our power,
    Shall° never see his pardon, for my state
    Stands on me to defend, not to debate.°   70

Exit

❖

ACT 5
SCENE 2

Location: The battlefield

Alarum° within. Enter, with drum and colors, Lear,
Cordelia, and soldiers, over the stage; and exeunt

Enter Edgar and Gloucester

---

51 o'erlook peruse   **53 guess** estimate   **54 discovery** reconnoitering   **55 we . . . time**
we will be ready for whatever happens   **57 jealous** suspicious   **62 carry . . . side**
carry out my end of the bargain in our *reciprocal vows* (4.6.259)   **64 countenance**
backing, authority of his name   **66 taking off** killing   **69 shall** they shall   **69–70 my**
state . . . debate my position depends upon maintenance by forceful action, not by talk

0.1 *alarum* trumpet call to arms

EDGAR   Here, father,° take the shadow of this tree
For your good host.° Pray that the right may thrive.
If ever I return to you again,
I'll bring you comfort.
GLOUCESTER   Grace go with you, sir!

Exit [Edgar]

Alarum and retreat° within. Enter Edgar

EDGAR   Away, old man! Give me thy hand. Away!   5
King Lear hath lost, he and his daughter ta'en.
Give me thy hand. Come on.
GLOUCESTER   No further, sir. A man may rot even here.
EDGAR   What, in ill thoughts again? Men must endure
Their going hence, even as their coming hither;   10
Ripeness° is all. Come on.
GLOUCESTER   And that's true too.

Exeunt

❖

ACT 5
SCENE 3

Location: The British camp

Enter, in conquest, with drum and colors, Edmund;
Lear and Cordelia, as prisoners; soldiers, Captain

EDMUND   Some officers take them away. Good guard°
Until their greater pleasures° first be known
That are to censure° them.
CORDELIA [*to Lear*]   We are not the first
Who with best meaning° have incurred the worst.
For thee, oppressèd King, I am cast down;   5
Myself could else outfrown false Fortune's frown.
Shall we not see these daughters and these sisters?°

---

1 **father** reverend old man   2 **host** shelterer   4.2 *retreat* trumpet signal for withdrawal   11 **ripeness** (humans shouldn't die before their time, just as fruit doesn't fall until it's ripe)

1 **good guard** guard them well   2 **their greater pleasures** the wishes of those in command   3 **censure** judge   4 **meaning** intentions   7 **shall . . . sisters?** aren't we even allowed to speak to Goneril and Regan before they order to prison their own father and sister?

LEAR   No, no, no, no! Come, let's away to prison.
We two alone will sing like birds i'th' cage.
When thou dost ask me blessing, I'll kneel down   10
And ask of thee forgiveness. So we'll live,
And pray, and sing, and tell old tales, and laugh
At gilded butterflies,° and hear poor rogues
Talk of court news; and we'll talk with them too—
Who loses and who wins; who's in, who's out—   15
And take upon 's° the mystery of things,
As if we were God's spies;° and we'll wear out,°
In a walled prison, packs and sects of great ones,
That ebb and flow by th' moon.°
EDMUND   Take them away.
LEAR   Upon such sacrifices, my Cordelia,   20
The gods themselves throw incense.° Have I caught thee?
He that parts us shall bring a brand from heaven
And fire us hence like foxes.° Wipe thine eyes;
The good years shall devour them, flesh and fell,
Ere they shall make us weep.° We'll see 'em starved first.   25
Come.   *Exit [with Cordelia, guarded]*
EDMUND   Come hither, Captain. Hark.
Take thou this note.   *[He gives a paper]*
                   Go follow them to prison.
One step I have advanced thee; if thou dost
As this instructs thee, thou dost make thy way   30
To noble fortunes. Know thou this: that men
Are as the time is.° To be tender-minded
Does not become a sword.° Thy great employment

---

13 **gilded butterflies** gaily dressed courtiers and other ephemeral types, or perhaps actual butterflies   16 **take upon 's** assume the burden of, or profess to understand 17 **God's spies** detached observers surveying the deeds of humanity from an eternal vantage point | **wear out** outlast   18–19 **packs . . . moon** followers and cliques attached to persons of high station, whose fortunes change erratically and constantly 21 **the gods . . . incense** (the gods make offerings to Cordelia instead of receiving them)   22–23 **he . . . foxes** nothing short of a firebrand from heaven will ever part us again (firebrands were used to smoke foxes from their lairs; compare also Samson's use of firebrands tied to the tails of foxes in order to punish the Philistines for denying him his wife, in Judges 15.4–5)   24–25 **the good . . . weep** the years will be good to us and will utterly foil our enemies' attempts to make us sorrowful as long as we are together (?)   32 **are . . . is** must adapt themselves to stern exigencies 33 **become a sword** suit a warrior

Will not bear question;° either say thou'lt do't
Or thrive by other means.
CAPTAIN   I'll do't, my lord.   35
EDMUND   About it, and write "happy"° when th'° hast done.
   Mark, I say, instantly, and carry it° so
   As I have set it down.
CAPTAIN   I cannot draw a cart, nor eat dried oats;
   If it be man's work, I'll do't.   *Exit Captain*   40

                    Flourish. Enter Albany, Goneril,
                    Regan, [another Captain, and] soldiers

ALBANY   Sir, you have showed today your valiant strain,
   And fortune led you well. You have the captives
   Who were the opposites° of this day's strife;
   I do require them of you, so to use them
   As we shall find their merits and our safety   45
   May equally determine.
EDMUND   Sir, I thought it fit
   To send the old and miserable King
   To some retention° and appointed guard,
   Whose age had charms in it, whose title more,
   To pluck the common bosom on his side   50
   And turn our impressed lances in our eyes
   Which do command them.° With him I sent the Queen,
   My reason all the same; and they are ready
   Tomorrow, or at further space,° t'appear
   Where you shall hold your session. At this time   55
   We sweat and bleed; the friend hath lost his friend,
   And the best quarrels in the heat are cursed
   By those that feel their sharpness.°

---

34 bear question admit of discussion   **36 write "happy"** call yourself fortunate |
th' thou   **37 carry it** carry it out   **43 opposites** enemies   **48 retention** confinement
49–52 whose . . . them whose advanced age had magic in it, and whose title as king
had even more, to win the sympathy of the commoners and turn against us the
weapons of those very troops whom we impressed into service (*in our eyes* may suggest
retaliation for the blinding of Gloucester)   **54 space** interval of time   **57–58 and . . .
sharpness** and even the best of causes, at this moment when the passions of battle
have not cooled, are viewed with hatred by those who have suffered the painful
consequences (Edmund pretends to worry that Lear and Cordelia would not receive
a fair trial)

The question of Cordelia and her father
Requires a fitter place.

ALBANY   Sir, by your patience,°   60
I hold you but a subject of° this war,
Not as a brother.

REGAN   That's as we list° to grace him.
Methinks our pleasure° might have been demanded°
Ere you had spoke so far. He led our powers,
Bore the commission of my place and person,   65
The which immediacy° may well stand up
And call itself your brother.

GONERIL   Not so hot!
In his own grace he doth exalt himself
More than in your addition.°

REGAN   In my rights,
By me invested, he compeers° the best.   70

GONERIL   That were the most° if he should husband you.

REGAN   Jesters do oft prove° prophets.

GONERIL   Holla, holla!
That eye that told you so looked but asquint.°

REGAN   Lady, I am not well, else I should answer
From a full-flowing stomach.° [*To Edmund*] General,   75
Take thou my soldiers, prisoners, patrimony;°
Dispose of them, of me; the walls is thine.°
Witness the world that I create thee here
My lord and master.

GONERIL   Mean you to enjoy him?

ALBANY   The let-alone° lies not in your good will.   80

EDMUND   Nor in thine, lord.

ALBANY   Half-blooded° fellow, yes.

REGAN [*to Edmund*]
Let the drum strike and prove my title thine.

---

60 **by your patience** if you please   61 **subject of** subordinate in   62 **list** please
63 **pleasure** wish | **demanded** asked about   66 **immediacy** nearness of connection
69 **your addition** the titles you confer   70 **compeers** is equal with   71 **that . . . most**
that investiture would be most complete   72 **prove** turn out to be   73 **asquint** (jealousy proverbially makes the eye look *asquint*, "furtively, suspiciously")   75 **full-
flowing stomach** full tide of angry rejoinder   76 **patrimony** inheritance   77 **the
walls is thine** the citadel of my heart and body surrenders completely to you   80 **let-
alone** preventing, denying   81 **half-blooded** only partly of noble blood, bastard

ALBANY   Stay yet; hear reason. Edmund, I arrest thee
  On capital treason; and, in thy attaint°
  This gilded serpent.   [*Pointing to Goneril*]
                        For your claim, fair sister,   85
  I bar it in the interest of my wife;
  'Tis she is subcontracted to this lord,
  And I, her husband, contradict your banns.°
  If you will marry, make your loves to me;°
  My lady is bespoke.
GONERIL   An interlude!°   90
ALBANY   Thou art armed, Gloucester. Let the trumpet sound.
  If none appear to prove upon thy person
  Thy heinous, manifest, and many treasons,
  There is my pledge.   [*He throws down a glove*]
                        I'll make° it on thy heart,
  Ere I taste bread, thou art in nothing less°   95
  Than I have here proclaimed thee.
REGAN   Sick, oh, sick!
GONERIL [*aside*]   If not, I'll ne'er trust medicine.°
EDMUND [*throwing down a glove*]
  There's my exchange. What° in the world he is
  That names me traitor, villain-like he lies.
  Call by the trumpet. He that dares approach,   100
  On him, on you—who not?—I will maintain
  My truth and honor firmly.
ALBANY   A herald, ho!
EDMUND   A herald, ho, a herald!

                        Enter a Herald

ALBANY [*to Edmund*]
  Trust to thy single virtue;° for thy soldiers,
  All levied in my name, have in my name   105
  Took their discharge.
REGAN   My sickness grows upon me.

---

84 in thy attaint as partner in your corruption and as one who has (unwittingly) provided the *attaint* or impeachment against you   **88 banns** public announcement of a proposed marriage   **89 make ... me** sue to me for permission   **90 an interlude!** a play; you are being melodramatic, or, what a farce this is!   **94 make** prove   **95 in nothing less** in no respect less guilty   **97 medicine** poison   **98 what** whoever   **104 single virtue** unaided prowess

ALBANY [*to Soldiers*]
　She is not well. Convey her to my tent.
　　　　　　　　　　　　　　　[*Exit Regan, supported*]
　Come hither, herald. Let the trumpet sound,
　And read out this. [*He gives a paper*]
CAPTAIN　Sound, trumpet!　　　　　　*A trumpet sounds*　110
HERALD [*reads*]　"If any man of quality or degree° within the
　lists° of the army will maintain upon Edmund, supposed Earl
　of Gloucester, that he is a manifold traitor, let him appear by
　the third sound of the trumpet. He is bold in his defense."
EDMUND　Sound!　　　　　　　　　　*First trumpet*　115
HERALD　Again!　　　　　　　　　　*Second trumpet*
HERALD　Again!　　　　　　　　　　*Third trumpet*
　　　　　　　　　　　　　　Trumpet answers within

　　　Enter Edgar, armed, [*with a trumpeter before him*]

ALBANY　Ask him his purposes, why he appears
　Upon this call o'th' trumpet.
HERALD　　　　　　　　　　What° are you?
　Your name, your quality, and why you answer　　　　120
　This present summons?
EDGAR　　　　　　　　　Know my name is lost,
　By treason's tooth bare-gnawn and canker-bit.°
　Yet am I noble as the adversary
　I come to cope.°
ALBANY　　　　　　　Which is that adversary?
EDGAR
　What's he that speaks for Edmund, Earl of Gloucester?　125
EDMUND　Himself. What say'st thou to him?
EDGAR　　　　　　　　　　　　Draw thy sword,
　That, if my speech offend a noble heart,
　Thy arm may do thee justice. Here is mine.
　　　　　　　　　　　　　　[*He draws his sword*]
　Behold, it is the privilege of mine honors,°
　My oath, and my profession.° I protest,　　　　　130

---

111 quality or degree noble birth or rank (also in line 120)　**112 lists** roster
119 what who　**122 canker-bit** eaten as by the caterpillar　**124 cope** encounter
129 of mine honors of my knighthood　**130 profession** knighthood

Maugre° thy strength, place, youth, and eminence,
Despite thy victor° sword and fire-new° fortune,
Thy valor, and thy heart,° thou art a traitor—
False to thy gods, thy brother, and thy father,
Conspirant 'gainst this high-illustrious prince,   135
And from th'extremest upward° of thy head
To the descent° and dust below thy foot
A most toad-spotted° traitor. Say thou° no,
This sword, this arm, and my best spirits are bent°
To prove upon thy heart, whereto I speak,   140
Thou liest.
EDMUND   In wisdom° I should ask thy name.
But since thy outside looks so fair and warlike,
And that thy tongue some say° of breeding breathes,
What safe and nicely° I might well delay
By rule of knighthood, I disdain and spurn.°   145
Back do I toss those treasons to thy head,°
With the hell-hated° lie o'erwhelm thy heart,
Which—for they yet glance by and scarcely bruise°—
This sword of mine shall give them instant way,°
Where they shall rest forever.°—Trumpets, speak!   150
                    [*He draws.*] *Alarums. Fight.* [*Edmund falls*]
ALBANY [*to Edgar*]
Save° him, save him!
GONERIL   This is practice,° Gloucester.
By th' law of arms thou wast not bound to answer
An unknown opposite. Thou art not vanquished,
But cozened° and beguiled.
ALBANY   Shut your mouth, dame,

---

131 maugre in spite of   **132 victor** victorious | **fire-new** newly minted   **133 heart**
courage   **136 upward** top   **137 descent** lowest extreme   **138 toad-spotted**
venomous, or having spots of infamy | **say thou** If you say   **139 bent** prepared
141 wisdom prudence   **143 say** smack, taste, indication   **144 safe and nicely**
prudently and punctiliously   **145 I . . . spurn** I disdain to insist on my right to refuse
combat with one of lower rank   **146 treasons . . . head** accusations of treason in
your teeth   **147 hell-hated** hated as hell is hated   **148 which . . . bruise** which
charges of treason—since as yet they merely glance off my armor and do no harm
149 give . . . way provide them an immediate pathway (to your heart)   **150 where . . .**
forever my victory in trial by combat will prove forever that the charges of treason
apply to you   **151 save** spare (Albany wishes to spare Edmund's life so that he may
confess and be found guilty) | **practice** trickery, or (said sardonically) astute
management   **154 cozened** tricked

Or with this paper shall I stopple° it.—Hold, sir.°   155
Thou worse than any name, read thine own evil.
                                        [*He shows the letter*]
[*To Goneril*] No tearing, lady; I perceive you know it.
GONERIL   Say if I do, the laws are mine, not thine.
Who can arraign me for't?
ALBANY   Most monstrous! Oh!
Know'st thou this paper?
GONERIL   Ask me not what I know.   160
                                                    Exit
ALBANY   Go after her. She's desperate; govern° her.
                                        [*Exit a soldier*]
EDMUND   What you have charged me with, that have I done,
And more, much more. The time will bring it out.
'Tis past, and so am I. But what art thou
That hast this fortune on° me? If thou'rt noble,   165
I do forgive thee.
EDGAR   Let's exchange charity.°
I am no less in blood than thou art, Edmund;
If more, the more th' hast° wronged me.
My name is Edgar, and thy father's son.
The gods are just, and of our pleasant° vices   170
Make instruments to plague us.
The dark and vicious place where thee he got°
Cost him his eyes.
EDMUND   Th' hast spoken right. 'Tis true.
The wheel is come full circle; I am here.°
ALBANY [*to Edgar*]   Methought thy very gait did prophesy   175
A royal nobleness. I must embrace thee.
                                        [*They embrace*]
Let sorrow split my heart if ever I
Did hate thee or thy father!
EDGAR   Worthy prince, I know't.

---

155 **stopple** stop up | **hold, sir** (addressed to Edgar or, more probably, Edmund)
161 **govern** restrain   165 **fortune on** victory over   166 **charity** forgiveness (for
Edmund's wickedness toward Edgar and Edgar's having slain Edmund)   168 **th'**
hast thou hast   170 **pleasant** pleasurable   172 **got** begot   174 **the wheel . . . here**
(alludes both to the wheel of fortune and to the idea of a completed circle whereby
crime meets its appropriate punishment; Edmund sees that everything has at last
come around to where it began)

ALBANY   Where have you hid yourself?
How have you known the miseries of your father?   180
EDGAR   By nursing them, my lord. List° a brief tale,
And when 'tis told, oh, that my heart would burst!
The bloody proclamation to escape°
That followed me so near—oh, our lives' sweetness,
That we the pain of death would hourly die   185
Rather than die at once!°—taught me to shift
Into a madman's rags, t'assume a semblance
That very dogs disdained; and in this habit°
Met I my father with his bleeding rings,°
Their precious stones° new lost; became his guide,   190
Led him, begged for him, saved him from despair;
Never—oh, fault!—revealed myself unto him
Until some half hour past, when I was armed.
Not sure, though hoping, of this good success,°
I asked his blessing, and from first to last   195
Told him our pilgrimage. But his flawed° heart—
Alack, too weak the conflict to support—
Twixt two extremes of passion, joy and grief,
Burst smilingly.
EDMUND   This speech of yours hath moved me,
And shall perchance do good. But speak you on;   200
You look as you had something more to say.
ALBANY   If there be more, more woeful, hold it in,
For I am almost ready to dissolve,°
Hearing of this.
EDGAR   This would have seemed a period°
To such as love not sorrow; but another,   205
To amplify too much, would make much more
And top extremity.° Whilst I
Was big in clamor,° came there in a man

---

181 list listen to   **183 the . . . escape** in order to escape the death-threatening
proclamation   **184–86 oh . . . at once!** oh, the perversity of our attachment to our
lives' sweetness, that we prefer to suffer continually the fear of death rather than die
at once and be done with it!   **188 habit** garb   **189 rings** sockets   **190 stones** eyeballs
194 success outcome   **196 flawed** cracked   **203 dissolve** in tears   **204 a period** the
limit   **205–07 but . . . extremity** but another sorrowful circumstance, adding to
what is already too much, would increase it and exceed the limit   **208 big in clamor**
loud in my lamenting

Who, having seen me in my worst estate,
Shunned my abhorred society; but then, finding   210
Who 'twas that so endured, with his strong arms
He fastened on my neck and bellowed out
As° he'd burst heaven, threw him on my father,°
Told the most piteous tale of Lear and him
That ever ear received, which in recounting   215
His° grief grew puissant,° and the strings of life°
Began to crack. Twice then the trumpets sounded,
And there I left him tranced.°

ALBANY   But who was this?

EDGAR   Kent, sir, the banished Kent, who in disguise
Followed his enemy king° and did him service   220
Improper for a slave.

Enter a Gentleman [with a bloody knife]

GENTLEMAN
Help, help, oh, help!

EDGAR   What kind of help?

ALBANY   Speak, man.

EDGAR   What means this bloody knife?

GENTLEMAN   'Tis hot, it smokes.°
It came even from the heart of—Oh, she's dead!

ALBANY   Who dead? Speak, man.   225

GENTLEMAN   Your lady, sir, your lady! And her sister
By her is poisoned; she confesses it.

EDMUND   I was contracted to them both. All three
Now marry in an instant.

EDGAR   Here comes Kent.

Enter Kent

ALBANY   Produce the bodies, be they alive or dead.   230
                              [Exit Gentleman]
This judgment of the heavens, that makes us tremble,
Touches us not with pity.—Oh, is this he?

---

213 as as if   **threw . . . father** threw himself on my father's body   **216 his** Kent's |
puissant powerful | **strings of life** heartstrings   **218 tranced** entranced, senseless
220 his enemy king the king who had rejected and banished him   **223 smokes**
steams

[*To Kent*] The time will not allow the compliment°
Which very manners urges.°
KENT   I am come
To bid my king and master aye good night.°   235
Is he not here?
ALBANY   Great thing of us forgot!
Speak, Edmund, where's the King? And where's Cordelia?
          Goneril and Regan's bodies [*are*] *brought out*
See'st thou this object,° Kent?
KENT   Alack, why thus?
EDMUND   Yet Edmund was beloved.
The one the other poisoned for my sake   240
And after slew herself.
ALBANY   Even so. Cover their faces.
EDMUND   I pant for life. Some good I mean to do,
Despite of mine own nature. Quickly send—
Be brief in it—to th' castle, for my writ
Is on the life of Lear and on Cordelia.   245
Nay, send in time.
ALBANY   Run, run, oh, run!
EDGAR   To who, my lord? Who has the office?° [*To Edmund*] Send
Thy token of reprieve.
EDMUND   Well thought on. Take my sword. The captain!
Give it the Captain.
EDGAR   Haste thee, for thy life.   250
                [*Exit one with Edmund's sword*]
EDMUND   He hath commission from thy wife and me
To hang Cordelia in the prison and
To lay the blame upon her own despair,
That she fordid° herself.
ALBANY
The gods defend her! Bear him hence awhile.   255
                [*Edmund is borne off*]

   Enter Lear, with Cordelia in his arms; [*Captain*]

---

233 **compliment** ceremony   234 **which . . . urges** which common courtesy requires
235 **aye good night** farewell forever (Kent believes he himself is near death, his
heartstrings having begun to crack) 238 **object** sight 247 **office** commission
254 **fordid** destroyed

LEAR   Howl, howl, howl! Oh, you are men of stones!
  Had I your tongues and eyes, I'd use them so
  That heaven's vault should crack. She's gone forever.
  I know when one is dead and when one lives;
  She's dead as earth. Lend me a looking glass;   260
  If that her breath will mist or stain the stone,°
  Why, then she lives.

KENT   Is this the promised end?°

EDGAR   Or image° of that horror?

ALBANY   Fall and cease!°

LEAR   This feather stirs; she lives! If it be so,
  It is a chance which does redeem all sorrows   265
  That ever I have felt.

KENT [*kneeling*]   O my good master!

LEAR   Prithee, away.

EDGAR   'Tis noble Kent, your friend.

LEAR   A plague upon you, murderers, traitors all!
  I might have saved her; now she's gone forever!
  Cordelia, Cordelia! Stay a little. Ha?   270
  What is't thou say'st? Her voice was ever soft,
  Gentle, and low, an excellent thing in woman.
  I killed the slave that was a-hanging thee.

CAPTAIN   'Tis true, my lords, he did.

LEAR   Did I not, fellow?
  I have seen the day, with my good biting falchion°   275
  I would have made them skip. I am old now,
  And these same crosses spoil me.°—Who are you?
  Mine eyes are not o'th' best; I'll tell you straight.°

KENT   If Fortune brag of two she loved and hated,
  One of them we behold.°   280

LEAR   This is a dull sight.° Are you not Kent?

KENT   The same,
  Your servant Kent. Where is your servant Caius?°

---

261 **stone** crystal or polished stone of which the mirror is made   262 **is . . . end?** (Kent may mean "Is this what all our hopes have come to?" Edgar replies by invoking the Last Judgment)   263 **image** representation | **fall and cease!** let all things cease to be!   275 **falchion** light sword   277 **crosses spoil me** adversities take away my strength   278 **I'll . . . straight** I'll recognize you in a moment   279–80 **if . . . behold** if Fortune were to brag of two persons whom she has subjected to the greatest fall from her favor into her hatred, Lear would have to be one of them   281 **this . . . sight** my vision is clouding, or, this is a dismal spectacle   282 **Caius** (Kent's disguise name)

LEAR   He's a good fellow, I can tell you that;
   He'll strike, and quickly too. He's dead and rotten.
KENT   No, my good lord, I am the very man—   285
LEAR   I'll see that straight.°
KENT   That from your first of difference and decay°
   Have followed your sad steps—
LEAR   You are welcome hither.
KENT   Nor no man else.° All's cheerless, dark, and deadly.
   Your eldest daughters have fordone° themselves,   290
   And desperately° are dead.
LEAR   Ay, so I think.
ALBANY   He knows not what he says, and vain is it
   That we present us to him.
EDGAR   Very bootless.°

                          Enter a Messenger

MESSENGER   Edmund is dead, my lord.
ALBANY   That's but a trifle here.   295
   You lords and noble friends, know our intent:
   What comfort to this great decay may come°
   Shall be applied. For° us, we will resign,
   During the life of this old majesty,
   To him our absolute power;   [*to Edgar and Kent*]
                          you, to your rights,   300
   With boot and such addition as your honors°
   Have more than merited. All friends shall taste
   The wages of their virtue, and all foes
   The cup of their deservings.—Oh, see, see!
LEAR   And my poor fool° is hanged! No, no, no life?   305
   Why should a dog, a horse, a rat have life,
   And thou no breath at all? Thou'lt come no more,
   Never, never, never, never, never!
   Pray you, undo this button. Thank you, sir.

286 **see that straight** attend to that in a moment   287 **from . . . decay** from the beginning of your quarrel (with Cordelia) to your decline of fortune   289 **nor . . . else** no, not I nor anyone else, or, I am the *very man* (line 286), him and no one else   290 **fordone** destroyed   291 **desperately** in despair   293 **bootless** in vain   297 **what . . . come** whatever means of comforting this ruined king and state of affairs may present themselves   298 **for** as for   301 **with . . . honors** with advantage and such further distinctions or titles as your honorable conduct in this war   305 **poor fool** Cordelia (*Fool* is here a term of endearment)

Do you see this? Look on her, look, her lips,   310
Look there, look there!   *He dies*
EDGAR   He faints.—My lord, my lord!
KENT   Break, heart, I prithee, break!
EDGAR   Look up, my lord.
KENT   Vex not his ghost.° Oh, let him pass! He hates him
That would upon the rack° of this tough world
Stretch him out longer.
EDGAR   He is gone indeed.   315
KENT   The wonder is he hath endured so long.
He but usurped his life.
ALBANY   Bear them from hence. Our present business
Is general woe.   [*To Kent and Edgar*]
Friends of my soul, you twain
Rule in this realm, and the gored state sustain.   320
KENT   I have a journey,° sir, shortly to go.
My master calls me; I must not say no.
EDGAR   The weight of this sad time we must obey;
Speak what we feel, not what we ought to say.
The oldest hath borne most; we that are young   325
Shall never see so much nor live so long.
Exeunt,° with a dead march

Notes

Copy text: the First Folio, except for those 300 or so lines found
only in the First Quarto of 1608 [Q1]. Unless otherwise indicated,
adopted readings are from the corrected state of Q1. A few readings are supplied from the Second Quarto of 1619 [Q2]. All readings subsequent to 1619 are marked as supplied by "eds." Act and
scene divisions are as marked in F, except that F does not mark 2.3
and 2.4, and omits 4.3 entirely, so that 4.4 is marked "*Scena Tertia*" and similarly with 4.5 and 4.6 (though 4.7 is marked "*Scena
Septima*"). The line numbers follow those in this edition. Other ab-

---

313 **ghost** departing spirit   314 **rack** torture rack (with suggestion, in the Folio and
Quarto spelling, "wracke," of shipwreck, disaster)   321 **journey** to another world,
to death   326.1 *exeunt* (presumably the dead bodies are borne out in procession)

breviations: s.d. stands for stage direction; stage directions not present in the original texts are marked in this text by brackets.

1.1. 5 equalities qualities **18–20 account . . . yet** [eds.] account, though . . .
for: yet **32 liege** Lord **55 words** word **66 issue** issues **65 Speak**
[Q1; not in F] **71 possesses** professes **87 interested** [eds.] interest
101 [Q1; not in F] **107 mysteries** [eds.] miseries [F] mistresse [Q1]
132 turns turne **153 as a** as **154 nor** nere **158** LEAR *Kear*
161 KENT *Lent* **163** CORNWALL [eds.] *Cor.* **164 the** thy **170 sentence**
sentences **188** GLOUCESTER *Cor.* **214 best object** obiect **226 well**
will **249 respects of fortune** respect and Fortunes **269 Ye** [eds.] The
282 shame them with shame **283.1** *Exeunt* [eds.] *Exit* **289 hath**
not hath **301 hit** sit
1.2. 1 [and elsewhere] EDMUND *Bast.* **21 top** [eds.] to' **51 waked** wake
89–91 EDMUND **Nor . . . earth** [Q1; not in F] **121 Fut, I I** **123 Edgar**
[Q1; not in F] **123 and pat** [eds.] Pat [F] and out [Q1] **133–39 as . . .**
come, [Q1; not in F] **163 s.d.** [at line 162 in F]
1.3. 3 [and elsewhere] OSWALD [eds.] *Ste.* **17–21** [Q1; not in F]
26–7 I would . . . speak [Q1; not in F] **28 very** [Q1; not in F]
1.4. 1 well will **28 canst** canst thou **41.1** *Enter steward* [eds.; after line
42 in F] **46 daughter** Daughters **69.1** *Enter steward* [eds.; after line
70 in F] **87** KENT *Lear* **Fool** my Boy **122 Dost** Do'st thou
125–40 That . . . snatching [Q1; not in F] **145 crown** Crownes
161 fools Foole **180 nor crumb** not crum **199 it had** it's had
214–17 [Q1; not in F] **240 Oh . . . come** [Q1; not in F] **288 Yea . . .**
this [Q1; not in F] **327 You're** Your are **attasked** at task
1.5. 0.1 *Kent Kent, Gentleman* **46 s.d.** *Exit Exeunt*
2.1. 2 you your **19.1** [after line 18 in F] **39 stand 's** stand **69 I should**
should I **70 ay, though** though **78 I never got him** [Q1; not in F]
78 s.d. [at line 76 in F, after "seeke it"] **79 why** wher **87 strange**
news strangenesse **100 spoil** wast **121 poise** prize **124 least**
thought best though **130** *Flourish. Exeunt* [eds.] *Exeunt. Flourish*
2.2. 20 clamorous clamours **39 an** if **45 What's** What is **57 you'll**
you will **69 Bring . . . their** Being . . . the **70 Renege** Reuenge
71 gale gall **74 Smile** Smoile **75 an** if **92 take't** take it **100 flick-**
ering flicking **114 dread** dead **117 their** there **122 respect** respects
132.1 [at line 140 in F] **134–8 His . . . with** [Q1; not in F] **136 con-**
temned'st [eds.] temnest [Q1] **138 King** King his Master, needs
143 [Q1; not in F] **144 Come . . . away** [assigned in F to Cornwall]
good [Q1; not in F] **144.1** *Exeunt* [eds.] *Exit* **145 Duke's** Duke
2.3. 18 sheepcotes Sheeps-Coates
2.4. 2 messenger Messengers **9 man's** man **18–19** [Q1; not in F]
30 panting painting **33 whose** those **55** *Hysterica* [eds.] *Historica*
61 the the the **75 have** hause **125 you** your **127 mother's** Mother

179 s.d. [after line 178 in F]   181.1 [at line 180 in F, after "Stockes"]
183 **fickle** fickly   185 s.d. [after line 183 in F]   209 **hot-blooded** hot-
bloodied   281 s.d. [after "weeping" in line 282 in F]   293 s.d. [after
line 292 in F]   294 **Whither** Whether [also in line 295]   298 **bleak** high

3.1. 7–15 **tears . . . all** [Q1; not in F]   10 **outstorm** [eds.] outscorne [Q1]
30–42 [Q1; not in F]

3.2. 3 **drowned** drown   37.1 [after line 35 in F]   49 **pother** pudder
84–5 [these lines follow line 91 in F]

3.3. 15 **for 't** for it

3.4. 7 **skin. So 'tis** skinso: 'tis   10 **thy** they   12 **This** the   27 s.d. [at line
26 in F]   31 **looped** lop'd   38.1 *Enter Fool* [F, after line 36: "*Enter
Edgar, and Foole*"]   44.1 [after line 36 in F]   45 **blows the cold wind**
blow the windes   50 **through fire** though Fire   50 **ford** Sword   55,
56 **Bless** Blisse   83 **deeply** deerely   91 **sessa** [eds.] *Sesey*   103.1 [after
line 99 in F]   105 **fiend** [Q1; not in F]   106 **till the** at   107 **squinnies**
[eds.] squints [F] squemes [Q1]   123 **stock-punished** stockt, punish'd
hath had hath   162 **in th'** into th'

3.5. 8 **he** which hee   21 **dearer** deere

3.6. 5.1 *Exit* [at line 3 in F]   16–52 [Q1; not in F]   21 **justicer** [eds.] Ius-
tice [Q1]   21 **Now** [Q2] no [Q1]   22–23 **eyes at trial, madam?** eyes,
at tral madam   24 **burn** [eds.] broome [Q1]   32 **cushions** [eds.] cush-
ings [Q1]   34 **robèd** robbed   48 **joint** [eds.] ioyne [Q1]   50 **on** [eds.]
an [Q1]   63 **mongrel grim** Mongrill, Grim   64 **lym** [eds.] Hym
65 **Bobtail tike or trundle-tail** Or Bobtaile tight, or Troudle taile
69 **Sessa** sese   72 **makes** make   79.1 [after line 75 in F]   91–94 KENT
Oppressèd . . . behind [Q1; not in F]   95 GLOUCESTER [not in F]
96–109 [Q1; not in F]

3.7. 10 **festinate** [eds.] festiuate   17 **lord's dependents** Lords, dependents
22 s.d. *Exeunt* [eds.] *Exit* [at line 21 in F]   60 **rash** sticke   65 **dern**
sterne   74 FIRST SERVANT *Seru.* [also *Seru.* or *Ser.* at lines 78, 81, 83]
82 [F provides a stage direction: "*Killes him*"]   101–09 [Q1; not in F]
101 SECOND SERVANT *Seruant* [and called "1 *Ser*" at line 105 in Q1]
102 THIRD SERVANT 2 *Seruant* [Q1]   106 **Roguish** [Qa; not in Qb]
108 THIRD SERVANT 2 *Ser.*   109.1 *Exeunt* Exit

4.1. 2 **flattered. To be worst** flattered to be worst,   41 **Then . . . gone** Get
thee away   57–61 **Five . . . master** [Q1; not in F]   59 **Flibbertigibbet**
[eds.] *Stiberdigebit* [Q1]   60 **mopping and mowing** [eds.] Mobing, &
Mohing [Q1]

4.2. 0.1 *Bastard Bastard, and Steward*   2 s.d. *steward* [Q1; placed at
scene beginning in F]   30 **whistling** whistle   32–51 **I fear . . . deep**
[Q1; not in F]   33 **its** [eds.] ith [Q1]   48 **these** [eds.] this [Q1]
54–60 **that . . . so** [Q1; not in F]   58 **to threat** thereat [Q1 corrected]
61 **shows** seemes   63–9, 70 [Q1; not in F]   76 **threat enraged** threat-
enrag'd   80 **justicers** [Q1 corrected] Iustices

4.3. 1–57 [scene omitted in F] **11 sir** [eds.] say [Q1] **16 strove** [eds.]
streme [Q1] **20 seemed** [eds.] seeme [Q1] **22 dropped. In** dropt in
32 then her, then **44 benediction, turned her** benediction turnd her,
57 s.d. *Exeunt* [eds.] *Exit* [Q1]
4.4 [F reads *"Scena Tertia"*] **3 fumiter** [eds.] femiter [Q1] Fenitar [F]
6 century Centery **18 distress** desires **28 right** Rite
4.5 [F reads *"Scena Quarta"*] **7 letters** Letter **22 Something** Some
things **26 oeillades** [eds.] Eliads **40 meet him** meet
4.6 [F reads *"Scena Quinta"*] **17 walk** walk'd **57 summit** Somnet
66–7 strangeness. / Upon . . . cliff what [eds.] strangenesse, / Vpon . . .
Cliffe. What **71 enridgèd** enraged **83 coining** crying **97 white** the
white **123 they're** they are **156 thine** thy **159 Through** Thorough
small great **160 Plate sin** [eds.] Place sinnes **192 Ay . . . dust** [Q1;
not in F] **200 one** a **213.1** *Exit* [after "moved on" in line 213 in F]
230 Durst Dar'st **233 'cagion** 'casion **258–9 not. / To** not / To
261–2 done if . . . conqueror. Then [eds.] *done. If . . . Conqueror then*
276 and . . . venture [Q1; not in F] **267 indistinguished** indinguish'd
280 s.d. *Drum afar off* [after line 278 in F]
4.7. 24 doubt not doubt **24–5** CORDELIA Very . . . there [Q1; not in F]
32 warring iarring **33–6 To stand . . . helm** [Q1; not in F] **58 hands**
hand **59 No, sir** [Q1; not in F] **82–3 and . . . lost** [Q1; not in F]
90–101 [Q1; not in F]
5.1. 11–13 [Q1; not in F] **17 me not** not **18–19** [Q1; not in F]
23–8 Where . . . nobly [Q1; not in F] **34** [Q1; not in F]
39 s.d. *Exeunt . . . armies* [after line 39 in F] **47 love** loues
5.3. 13 and hear poor rogues and heare (poore Rogues) **39–40** [Q1; not
in F] **48 and appointed guard** [Q1 corrected; not in F] **45–60 At . . .**
place [Q1; not in F] **56 We** [Q1 corrected] mee [Q1 uncorrected]
58 sharpness [Q1 corrected] sharpes [Q1 uncorrected] **71** GONERIL
Alb. **84 attaint** arrest **85 sister** Sisters **86 bar** [eds.] bare **98 he is**
hes **103** EDMUND A herald, ho, a herald [Q1; not in F] **103.1** *Enter
a Herald* [after line 102 in F] **104** ALBANY [not in F] **100** CAPTAIN
Sound, trumpet [Q1; not in F] **115** EDMUND Sound [Q1; not in F]
121–2 lost, / By . . . canker-bit. lost / By Treasons tooth: bare-gnawne,
and Canker-bit, **129 the** my priuiledge, The **132 Despite** Despise
143 tongue some say of tongue (some say) of **146 those** these
148 scarcely scarely **150.1** *Fight* [eds.] *Fights.* [*"Alarums. Fights"* is
opposite "Saue him, saue him," in line 151 in F.] **152 arms** Warre
158 stopple stop **160** GONERIL *Bast.* **160 16 s.d.** *Exit* [at line 159
after "for 't" in F] **204–21 This . . . slave** [Q1; not in F] **213 him**
[eds.] me [Q1] **237.1** [after line 230 in F] **251 The captain** [Q1; not
in F] **258 you** your **275** CAPTAIN *Gent.* **277 them** him **289 You
are** [eds.] Your are [F] You'r [Q1] **294.1** [after "to him" in line
294 in F] **315 rack** wracke

The above textual notes list all instances in which material not in F is included from Q1. To enable the reader to compare further the F and Q1 texts, a list is provided here of material not in Q1 that is to be found in F. There are some 100 lines in all.

1.1. 37–42 while . . . now   46–7 Since . . . state   61–2 and . . . rivers   80–2 to whose . . . interested   85–6 LEAR Nothing? CORDELIA Nothing   162 ALBANY, CORNWALL Dear sir, forbear.

1.2. 101–6 This . . . graves   152–7 I pray . . . brother

1.4. 245 ALBANY Pray . . . patient   258 Of . . . you   305–17 This . . . unfitness

2.4. 6 KENT No, my lord   21 KENT By Juno . . . ay   45–54 FOOL Winter's . . . year   94–5 GLOUCESTER Well . . . man   99–100 Are they . . . Fiery? The   136–41 LEAR Say . . . blame   294–5 CORNWALL Whither . . . horse

3.1. 22–9 Who . . . furnishings

3.2. 78–94 FOOL This . . . time. *Exit*

3.4. 17–18 In . . . endure   26–7 In . . . sleep   37–8 Fathom . . . Tom

3.6. 12–13 FOOL No . . . him   79 FOOL And . . . noon

4.1. 6–9 Welcome . . . blasts

4.2. 26 Oh, the . . . man

4.6. 160–75 Plate . . . lips

5.2. 11 GLOUCESTER And . . . too

5.3. 77Dispose . . . thine   90 GONERIL An interlude   144 What . . . delay   225 ALBANY Speak, man   311–12 Do you . . . look there

Lear and Cordelia in Prison. Watercolor by William Blake. The Tate Gallery, London. This scene is unrepresented in the play, although anticipated by Lear's speech "Come, let's away to prison; / We too alone will sing like birds i'th' cage" (5.3.8–9). Blake depicts a type of reverse pieta, in that the child shelters the parent.

The Texts of
King Lear

Like many of Shakespeare's plays, *King Lear* exists in multiple early versions. To understand how scholars refer to these versions, it helps to first know two terms. A *quarto* is a book formed from a sheet of paper folded twice so that each side of the sheet forms four (hence "quarto") pages of text; when cut this way, one sheet of paper provides a total of eight pages for printing. A quarto was a comparatively inexpensive and small book, unlike a *folio*, which is a large volume formed from a sheet folded once, so that a total of four pages are provided from one sheet of paper.

A quarto version of *King Lear* (Q1) appeared in the Stationer's Register (an index of licensed books) in November 1607: *Mr. William Shakespeare His True chronicle Historie of the Life and death of King Lear and his three Daughters, With the unfortunate life of Edgar, son, and heir to the Earle of Gloucester, and his sullen and assumed humor of Tom of Bedlam. . . .* A second quarto, based on Q1, appeared in 1619. The other principal text of *King Lear* appears in the folio version published in 1623 (F), an expensively produced and handsome volume that gathered all of Shakespeare's plays. There, the play is titled not as a chronicle history but as *The Tragedy of King Lear.*

Q1 and F differ in ways large and small. Q1, typically, has no act or scene divisions (a feature that arrived only with the attempt of the folio version's publishers to attribute a classical format to the plays). F lacks nearly 300 lines that appear in Q1 and has 100 lines that don't. It is thus sometimes conjectured that each was based on different copies or that together they represent "a degraded state of a lost complete original that contained all the mutually exclusive material," "or, that each represents in some form a stage in the development or existence of the play" (Michael Warren, "Shakespearean Tragedy Printed and Performed," 2003, p. 78). Other possible explanations propose printing house errors, cuts for performance, the vagaries of memorial reconstruction by actors, and even authorial revision.

In 1723 Alexander Pope began the editorial tradition of conflating Q1 and F into one text "in an effort to provide readers with all of what Shakespeare wrote" (R. A. Foakes, ed., *King Lear*, 1997, p. 116). (See the "Further Reading" section at the end of this Longman Cultural Edition for an annotated list of different presentations of the text.) David Bevington's edition of *King Lear*, presented in our volume, is a similar conflation. Some scholars have argued that Q1 and F should be treated as distinct, separate versions of the play (Michael Warren and Gary Taylor, eds., *The Division of the Kingdoms*, 1983).

Although the differences between these versions do not affect the plot or general structure, they do shape certain scenes in important ways. For instance, the last nine lines of *King Lear* 3.7 in Q1, where the servants comment on Cornwall and Regan's villainy and propose to comfort Gloucester, provide quite a different closure to the horror that has followed than do Cornwall's unmitigated comments in the folio version ("Throw this slave / Upon the dunghill.—Regan, I bleed apace. / Untimely comes this hurt. Give me your arm." (3.7.98–100)). Other significant differences can be found by comparing Bevington's textual notes for 3.6.16–52, 91–109 (only Q has both the mock trial and Edgar's soliloquy); for 4.2.32–51, 63–70 (F lacks Albany's extended censure of Goneril); and for 4.2.54–60 (F lacks Goneril's reminder of Albany's political duty to defend the realm). Only F contains the fool's prophecy at 3.2.78–94. Only Q has the conversation between Kent and a gentleman in 4.3, in which we receive an account of Cordelia's compassion for her father and his own reluctance to meet her. (This contradicts 4.6, in which Lear does not know that Cordelia is no longer in France.)

A final set of striking alternatives occurs in the different endings of Q1 and F, represented in the original versions, below. Note that F provides the stage direction for Lear's death "(*He dis*)"(5.2.312), and Kent speaks, "Break heart, I prythee break" whereas Q gives this injunction to Lear. As Michael Warren observes,

> As in F, Edgar comments on the movements of Lear's fainting, but in Q Lear speaks again, uttering words that are ascribed in F to Kent. . . . In this version Lear expresses his personal desire for his release and dies a willed death, not, as F may be interpreted as indicating, in some condition of happy illusion. These sequences present different scenarios for stage action; they permit different modes of interpretation of the different emotional and intellectual responses to Lear's death. ("Shakespearean Tragedy Printed and Performed," p. 79)

Another difference is that Edgar speaks the closing lines in F, but Albany does in Q. Each text, comments Warren,

> presents a different interpretive opportunity. . . . In F Edgar's response to Albany's invitation to rule is oblique but presumably positive. In Q[1], however, he is apparently unresponsive, and in the context of Albany's final speech his silence suggests that he is not accepting the throne. . . . [T]he two endings are irreconcilable; . . . Each is justifiable theatrically and intellectually. (pp. 79–80)

The facsimiles of Q1 and F presented here also allow us to see the editorial changes in spelling, punctuation, and lineation that go into producing a modernized text. Readers interested in more detailed discussions of these matters should consult the "Further Reading" section later in this edition.

The Historie of King Lear.

Kent. That from your life of difference and decay,
Haue followed your sad steps.　　*Lear.* You'r welcome hither.

Kent. Nor no man else, als chearles, darke and deadly,
Your eldest daughters haue foredoome themselues,
And desperatly are dead.　　*Lear.* So thinke I to.

Duke. He knowes not what he sees, and vaine it is,
That we present vs to him,　　*Edg.* Very bootlesse.　　*Enter*

Capt. Edmund is dead my Lord.　　　　　　　*Captaine.*

Duke. Thats but a trifle heere, you Lords and noble friends,
Know our intent, what comfort to this decay may come, shall be
applied : for vs we wil resigne during the life of this old maiesty,
to him our absolute power, you to your rights with boote, and
such addition as your honor haue more then merited, all friends
shall tast the wages of their vertue, and al foes the cup of their de-
seruings, O see, see.

Lear. And my poore foole is hangd, no, no life, why should a
dog, a horse, a rat of life and thou no breath at all, O thou wilt
come no more, neuer, neuer, neuer, pray you vndo this button,
thanke you sir, O, o, o, o.　　*Edg.* He faints my Lord, my Lord.

Lear. Breake hart, I prethe breake.　*Edgar.* Look vp my Lord.

Kent. Vex not his ghost, O let him passe,
He hates him that would vpon the wracke,
Of this tough world stretch him out longer.

Edg. O he is gone indeed.

Kent. The wonder is, he hath endured so long,
He but vsurpt his life.

Duke. Beare them from hence, our present busines
Is to generall woe, friends of my soule, you twaine
Rule in this kingdome, and the goard state sustaine.

Kent. I haue a iourney sir, shortly to go,
My maister cals, and I must not say no.

Duke. The waight of this sad time we must obey,
Speake what we feele, not what we ought to say,
The oldest haue borne most, we that are yong,
Shall neuer see so much, nor liue so long.

FINIS.

The final scene, first Quarto.

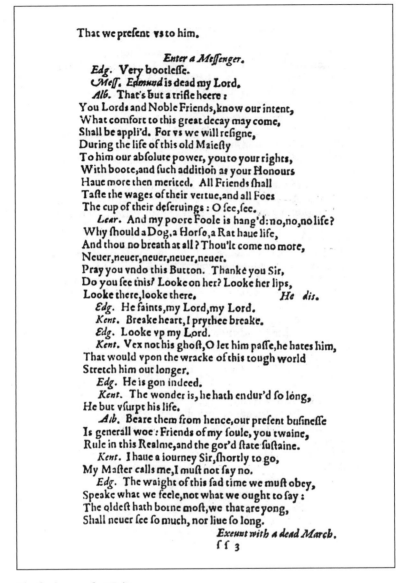

That we prefent vs to him.

Enter a Meſſenger.
Edg. Very bootleſſe.
Meſſ. *Edmund* is dead my Lord.
Alb. That's but a trifle heere :
You Lords and Noble Friends, know our intent,
What comfort to this great decay may come,
Shall be appli'd. For vs we will reſigne,
During the life of this old Maieſty
To him our abſolute power, you to your rights,
With boote, and ſuch addition as your Honours
Haue more then merited. All Friends ſhall
Taſte the wages of their vertue, and all Foes
The cup of their deſeruings : O ſee, ſee.
    Lear. And my poore Foole is hang'd : no, no, no life ?
Why ſhould a Dog, a Horſo, a Rat haue life,
And thou no breath at all ? Thou'lt come no more,
Neuer, neuer, neuer, neuer, neuer.
Pray you vndo this Button. Thanke you Sir,
Do you ſee this ? Looke on her ? Looke her lips,
Looke there, looke there.   *He dis.*
    Edg. He faints, my Lord, my Lord.
    Kent. Breake heart, I prythee breake.
    Edg. Looke vp my Lord.
    Kent. Vex not his ghoſt, O let him paſſe, he hates him,
That would vpon the wracke of this tough world
Stretch him out longer.
    Edg. He is gon indeed.
    Kent. The wonder is, he hath endur'd ſo long,
He but vſurpt his life.
    Alb. Beare them from hence, our preſent buſineſſe
Is generall woe : Friends of my ſoule, you twaine,
Rule in this Realme, and the gor'd ſtate ſuſtaine.
    Kent. I haue a iourney Sir, ſhortly to go,
My Maſter calls me, I muſt not ſay no.
    Edg. The waight of this ſad time we muſt obey,
Speake what we feele, not what we ought to ſay :
The oldeſt hath borne moſt, we that are yong,
Shall neuer ſee ſo much, nor liue ſo long.
                    Exeunt with a dead March.
                    ſ ſ 3

The final scene, first Folio.

CONTEXTS

Shakespeare's Narrative and Dramatic Sources

The tale of an ancient British king named Lear who divided his kingdom to disastrous effect was a familiar one in a Tudor-Stuart literary culture, avid for national history and the examples it offered (whether those examples be to emulate or eschew). The earliest account is that of Geoffrey of Monmouth (c. 1135), but a variety of contemporary texts were available to Shakespeare: prose chronicles, a play, and verse accounts.[1] In general, these other versions share several features that Shakespeare altered. Offered in this section are excerpts from Raphael Holinshed's *Chronicles* (1587) and the anonymous play *King Leir* (1605); also included is the source for the Gloucester plot, Sir Philip Sidney's *The Countess of Pembrokes Arcadia* (1590).

Shakespeare's most important alteration is to the king's dowry test in Act 1. In the Holinshed and *King Leir* sources all three daughters are unmarried, and the father's request for their testaments of love is designed to choose the daughter who will succeed him. The king's plan thus seems a good tactic for ensuring the political

---

[1] Geoffrey of Monmouth, *Historia Regium Britanniae* (translated by Aaron Thompson, London 1718); Raphael Holinshed, *The Historie of England in the First and Second Volumes of Chronicles* (London, 1587); John Higgins, *Mirror for Magistrates* (London, 1574); Edmund Spenser, *The Faerie Queene* (London, 1596); and *The True Chronicle Historie of King Leir . . . lately acted* (London, 1605). All are available in Geoffrey Bullough's *Narrative and Dramatic Sources of Shakespeare*, vol. 7 (1973).

integrity of his kingdom in the absence of a male heir. Cordelia's reticence is usually explained as originating in a desire to point out her sisters' hypocrisy.

Shakespeare's play has Goneril and Regan already married to the two lords whose names, Albany and Cornwall, indicate their sovereignty over opposite ends of the kingdom. (These husbands are Lear's choices in the sources, but they arrive only after Cordelia is disinherited.) Hence it is the rich middle compass of Britain, "a third more opulent" (1.1.84), that is officially unbequeathed, reserved for a daughter whose husband is yet to be determined (Lear means to "set [his] rest / On her kind nursery" (1.1.120–121). Shakespeare includes two rival suitors—Burgundy (ruler of a province of France) and the King of France—who are in the British court at the time of the distribution of lands. In all the sources, there is only one suitor, the King of France (or "Aganippus"), who arrives well after the fact of the dowry division, drawn (in one text) by rumors of the three "British nymphs" and oblivious to the catastrophe that precedes him. Shakespeare isolates the question of Cordelia's marriage, and her refusal to flatter her father is more enigmatic.

This concentration of effects is also evident in Shakespeare's compression of the time scheme, which gives a sense of inexorability to the chain of events. In the sources, Lear continues to reign for some years until (variously) either his sons-in-law or their wives become impatient and rebel, allowing the king some retinue. Only then, after being badly treated in the matter of his followers, does the king flee for France, to Cordelia and her husband. Aganippus raises an army, and all return to rout Cornwall and Albany. Lear rules some further years until he dies peacefully, succeeded by Cordelia, who reigns until supplanted by her nephews. She commits suicide in prison, while her sisters (presumably) die natural deaths (the tale is told from her point of view in Higgins's account). Shakespeare's Lear can barely face the thought of Cordelia or of his treatment of her, let alone the woman herself, which is one reason the recourse to France never arises. The sources, in other words, present this tale as an incidence of trouble in high places, but not necessarily trouble without remedy or containment. Tragedy, such as it is, accrues to the figure of Cordelia alone.

The extant stories of Lear lack the Gloucester subplot, which Shakespeare modeled after an incident in Sir Philip Sidney's *Countesse of Pembrokes Arcadia*. Its focus is also a father who fails to recognize the true worth of his respective children, a theme of folkloric currency. Shakespeare's incorporation of this other strand creates an epidemic sense of the tension between generations, and he seeds in the figure of the ungrateful child the animus of tragic destruction.

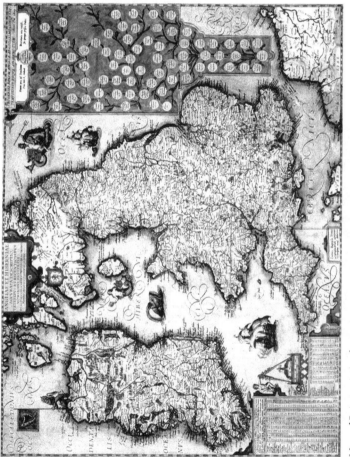

Map of Britain, 1606, by Jan Baptist Vrients. Albany is the northernmost portion (akin to modern Scotland); Cornwall is in the lower southwest. The map also shows, in the lower right-hand corner, the northwestern coast of France.

Raphael Holinshed (d. 1580?)

Shakespeare consulted Raphael Holinshed's Chronicles *(1577; later revised) for his history plays. Holinshed places Leir at about 800 BCE and describes him as a prince of "right noble demeanor." He seeks in the love test to "understand the affections of his daughters towards him, and preferre hir whome he best loved, to the succession over the kingdome." Some years later the dukes (his sons-in-law) rebel, "thinking it long yer the government of the land did come to their hands." As in Monmouth's* History, *Lear seeks the help of Aganippus and returns to rout "Henninus the duke of Cornewall" and "Maglanus the duke of Albania."*

from "The Second Booke of the Historie of England" in *The First and Second Volumes of Chronicles* (London, 1587); vol. 1, book 2, pp. 12–13, sig. B1r.

[Xll. 2. 59] LEIR the sonne of Baldud was admitted ruler over the Britaines, in the yeare of the world 3105, at what time Joas reigned in Juda. This Leir was a prince of right noble demeanor, governing his land and subjects in great wealth. He made the towne of Caerleir now called Leicester, which standeth upon the river of Sore. It is written that he had by his wife three daughters without other issue, whose names were Gonorilla, Regan, and Cordeilla, which daughters he greatly loved, but specially Cordeilla the yoongest farre above the two elder. When this Leir therefore was come to great yeres, & began to waxe unweldie through age, he thought to understand the affections of his daughters towards him, and preferre hir whome he best loved, to the succession over the kingdome. Wherupon he first asked Gonorilla the eldest, how well she loved him: who calling hir gods to record, protested that she 'loved him more than hir owne life, which by right and reason should be most deere unto hir'. With which answer the father being well pleased, turned to the second, and demanded of hir how well she loved him: who answered (confirming hir saiengs with great othes) that she loved him 'more than toong could expresse, and farre above all other creatures of the world.'

Then called he his yoongest daughter Cordeilla before him, and asked of hir what account she made of him, unto whome she made this answer as followeth: 'Knowing the great love and fatherlie zeale that you have alwaies borne towards me (for the which I maie not answere you otherwise than I thinke and as my conscience leadeth me) I protest unto you, that I have loved you ever, and will continuallie (while I live) love you as my naturall father. And if you would more understand of the love that I beare you, assertaine your selfe, that so much as you have, so much you are woorth, and so much I love you, and no more.'[1] The father being nothing content with this answer, married his two eldest daughters, the one unto Henninus the duke of Cornewall, and the other unto Maglanus the duke of Albania, betwixt whome he willed and ordeined that his land should be divided after his death, and the one halfe thereof immediatlie should be assigned to them in hand: but for the third daughter Cordeilla he reserved nothing.'[2]

Nevertheles it fortuned that one of the princes of Gallia (which now is called France) whose name was Aganippus, hearing of the beautie, womanhood, and good conditions of the said Cordeilla, desired to have hir in mariage, and sent over to hir father, requiring that he might have hir to wife: to whome answer was made, that he might have his daughter, but as for anie dower he could have none, for all was promised and assured to hir other sisters alreadie. Aganippus notwithstanding this answer of deniall to receive anie thing by way of dower with Cordeilla, tooke hir to wife, onlie moved thereto (I saie) for respect of hir person and amiable vertues. This Aganippus was one of the twelve kings that ruled Gallia in those daies, as in the British historie it is recorded. But to proceed.

After that Leir was fallen into age, the two dukes that had married his two eldest daughters, thinking it long yer the government of the land did come to their hands, arose against him in armour, and reft from him the governance of the land, upon conditions to be continued for terme of life: by the which he was put to his portion, that is, to live after a rate assigned to him for the maintenance of his estate, which in processe of time was diminished as well by Maglanus as by Henninus.[3] But the greatest griefe that Leir tooke, was to see the unkindnesse of his daughters, which seemed to thinke that all was too much which their father had, the same being never so little: in so much that going from the one to the other, he was brought to that miserie, that scarslie they would allow him one servant to wait upon him.

---

[1]Compare with the staggered brevity of Cordelia's reply in Shakespeare's *King Lear* at 1.1.76–107.

[2]Compare with Lear's far less prudent dispossession plan at 1.1.128–139.

[3]In some sources, Goneril and Regan are the instigating villains; here the sons-in-law also devise the plan for Lear's retirement.

In the end, such was the unkindnesse, or (as I maie saie) the unnaturalnesse which he found in his two daughters, notwithstanding their faire and pleasant words uttered in time past, that being constreined of necessitie, he fled the land, & sailed into Gallia, there to seeke some comfort of his yongest daughter Cordeilla, whom before time he hated. The ladie Cordeilla hearing that he was arrived in poore estate, she first sent to him privilie a certeine summe of monie to apparell himselfe withall, and to reteine a certeine number of servants that might attend upon him in honorable wise, as apperteined to the estate which he had borne: and then so accompanied, she appointed him to come to the court, which he did, and was so joifullie, honorablie, and lovinglie received, both by his sonne in law Aganippus, and also by his daughter Cordeilla, that his hart was greatlie comforted: for he was no lesse honored, than if he had beene king of the whole countrie himselfe.

Now when he had informed his sonne in law and his daughter in what sort he had been used by his other daughters, Aganippus caused a mightie armie to be put in a readinesse, and likewise a great navie of ships to be rigged, to passe over into Britaine with Leir his father in law, to see him againe restored to his kingdome. It was accorded, that Cordeilla should also go with him to take possession of the land, the which he promised to leave unto hir, as the rightful inheritour after his decesse, notwithstanding any former grant made to hir sisters or to their husbands in anie maner of wise.

Hereupon, when this armie and navie of ships were readie, Leir and his daughter Cordeilla with hir husband tooke the sea, and arriving in Britaine, fought with their enimies, and discomfited them in battell, in the which Maglanus and Henninus were slaine: and then was Leir restored to his kingdome, which he ruled after this by the space of two yeeres, and then died, fortie yeeres after he first began to reigne. His bodie was buried at Leicester in a vaut under the chanell of the river of Sore beneath the towne.

[. . .] Cordeilla after hir fathers deceasse ruled the land of Britaine right worthilie during the space of five yeeres, in which meane time hir husband died, and then about the end of those five yeeres, hir two nephewes Margan and Cunedag, sonnes to hir aforesaid sisters, disdaining to be under the government of a woman, levied warre against hir, and destroied a great part of the land, and finallie tooke hir prisoner, and laid hir fast in ward, wherewith she tooke such griefe, being a woman of a manlie courage, and despairing to recover libertie, there she slue hirselfe, when she had reigned (as before is mentioned) the tearme of five yeeres.

King Leir (1605)

This play was published anonymously, probably prior to Shakespeare's version; it is likely the same "King Leare" performed in 1594 by the Queen's and Sussex's Men acting companies. King Leir seeks in the love test to outmaneuver his youngest daughter who has vowed to marry only for love; he wants, instead, to "match her to some King within this Ile / And so establish such a perfit peace" (1.1.64–65). The king of France comes to Britain in the disguise of a pilgrim and falls in love with the dispossessed Cordella after overhearing her pledge herself to chastity and God's will rather than accept her father's command of a loveless marriage. (The play is set securely in Christian times.) Gonorill and Ragan plot to murder their father (their husbands are quite blameless), although Leir convinces the messenger sent to kill him not to follow through with those orders. The play includes a good counselor (Perillus) analogous to Kent, who accompanies Leir to France. The play ends with the king triumphant but also contrite, realizing the true nature of Cordella's love for him.

The play opens with Leir stating his concerns for his kingdom and receiving advice from various counselors, not only Perillus but also Skalliger, who is secretly acting on behalf of Gonorill and Ragan.

from *The True Chronicle History of King Leir and his three daughters, Gonorill, Ragan and Cordella. As it hath beene divers and sundry times lately acted* (London 1605)

ACTUS I

[Sc. l] *Enter King Leir and Nobles.*
[Leir] Thus to our griefe the obsequies performed
Of our (too late) deceast and dearest Queen,[1]
Whose soule I hope, possest of heavenly joyes,

---

[1]This mother is mentioned in *King Lear* only at 2.4.127–128.

Doth ride in triumph 'mongst the Cherubins,
Let us request your grave advice, my Lords,   5
For the disposing of our princely daughters,
For whom our care is specially imployd,
As nature bindeth to advaunce their states,
In royall marriage with some princely mates:
For wanting now their mothers good advice,   10
Under whose government they have receyved
A perfit patterne of a vertuous life:
Lest as it were a ship without a sterne,
Or silly sheepe without a Pastors care;
Although our selves doe dearely tender them,   15
Yet are we ignorant of their affayres:
For fathers best do know to governe sonnes;
But daughters steps the mothers counsell turnes.
A sonne we want for to succeed our Crowne,
And course of time hath cancelled the date   20
Of further issue from our withered loynes:
One foote already hangeth in the grave,
And age hath made deepe furrowes in my face:
The world of me, I of the world am weary,
And I would fayne resigne these earthly cares:[2]   25
And thinke upon the welfare of my soule
Which by no better meanes may be effected,
Then by resigning up the Crowne from me,
In equall dowry to my daughters three.
SKALLIGER.[3] A worthy care, my Leige, which well declares,   30
     The zeale you bare unto our *quondam*[4] Queene:
     And since your Grace hath licens'd me to speake,
     I censure thus; Your Majesty knowing well,
     What severall Suters your princely daughters have,
     To make them eche a Joynter[5] more or lesse,   35
     As is their worth, to them that love professe.

---

[2]Compare with *King Lear* 1.1.35.

[3]The untrustworthy councilor, in league with the two elder sisters.

[4]"Former."

[5]The property settled on a woman at the time of her marriage, to be owned by her even in the event of her husband's death.

LEIR. No more, nor lesse, but even all alike,
    My zeale is fixt, all fashioned in one mould:
    Wherefore unpartiall shall my censure be,
    Both old and young shall have alike for me.   40
NOBLE. My gracious Lord, I hartily do wish,
    That God had lent you an heyre indubitate,
    Which might have set upon your royall throne,
    When fates should loose the prison of your life,
    By whose succession all this doubt might cease;   45
    And as by you, by him we might have peace.
    But after-wishes ever come too late,
    And nothing can revoke the course of fate:
    Wherefore, my Liege, my censure deemes it best,
    To match them with some of your neighbour Kings,   50
    Bordring within the bounds of Albion,[6]
    By whose united friendship, this our state
    May be protected 'gainst all forrayne hate.
LEIR. Herein, my Lords, your wishes sort with mine,
    And mine (I hope) do sort with heavenly powers: 55
    For at this instant two neere neyghbouring Kings
    Of Cornwall and of Cambria,[7] motion love
    To my two daughters, *Gonorill* and *Ragan.*
    My youngest daughter, fayre *Cordella*, vowes
    No liking to a Monarch, unlesse love allowes.   60
    She is solicited by divers Peeres;[8]
    But none of them her partiall fancy heares.
    Yet, if my policy may her beguyle,
    Ile match her to some King within this Ile,[9]
    And so establish such a perfit peace,   65
    As fortunes force shall ne're prevayle to cease.
PERILLUS.[10] Of us & ours, your gracious care, my Lord,
    Deserves an everlasting memory,

---

[6]An ancient literary term for Great Britain.

[7]Modern-day Cumbria, a county in Northwest England.

[8]Various "noblemen."

[9]No such native son appears in Shakespeare's play; Leir means the "Irish king," line 190 (omitted from this excerpt).

[10]The king's loyal councilor, Kent's counterpart.

To be inrol'd in Chronicles of fame,
By never-dying perpetuity: 70
Yet to become so provident a Prince,
Lose not the title of a loving father:
Do not force love, where fancy cannot dwell,
Lest streames being stopt, above the banks do swell.
LEIR. I am resolv'd, and even now my mind   75
Doth meditate a sudden stratagem,[11]
To try which of my daughters loves me best:
Which till I know, I cannot be in rest.
This graunted, when they joyntly shall contend,
Eche to exceed the other in their love: 80
Then at the vantage will I take *Cordella*,
Even as she doth protest she loves me best,
Ile say, Then, daughter, graunt me one request,
To shew thou lovest me as thy sisters doe,
Accept a husband, whom my selfe will woo.   85
This sayd, she cannot well deny my sute,
Although (poore soule) her sences will be mute:
Then will I tryumph in my policy,
And match her with a King of Brittany.
SKALLIGER. Ile to them before, and bewray your secrecy.   90
PERILLUS. Thus fathers think their children to beguile,
And oftentimes themselves do first repent,
When heavenly powers do frustrate their intent.

> [*Exeunt.*]

　　　[Sc.3]
[. . .]　[*Skalliger tips off Gonorill and Ragan, who resent Cordella*]
LEIR. Deare *Gonorill*, kind *Ragan*, sweet *Cordella*,
Ye florishing branches of a Kingly stocke,
Sprung from a tree that once did flourish greene,
Whose blossomes now are nipt with Winters frost,
And pale grym death doth wayt upon my steps,   5
And summons me unto his next Assizes.[12]
Therefore, deare daughters, as ye tender the safety
Of him that was the cause of your first being,

---

[11]The dowry contest here arises from a relatively spontaneous decision.
[12]A court session.

Resolve a doubt which much molests my mind,
Which of you three to me would prove most kind;   10
Which loves me most, and which at my request
Will soonest yeeld unto their fathers hest.
[. . .]   [*Gonorill replies exorbitantly . . .*]
LEIR. O, how thy words revive my dying soule!
CORDELLA. O, how I doe abhorre this flattery!
[. . .]   [*Ragan pledges to subdue her will to her father's*]
LEIR. Did never *Philomel*[13] sing so sweet a note.   15
CORDELLA. Did never flatterer tell so false a tale.
LEIR. Speak now, *Cordella*, make my joyes at full,
   And drop downe Nectar from thy hony lips.
CORDELLA. I cannot paynt my duty forth in words,
   I hope my deeds shall make report for me: 20
   But looke what love the child doth owe the father,
   The same to you I beare, my gracious Lord.
GONORILL. Here is an answere answerlesse indeed:
   Were you my daughter, I should scarcely brooke it.
RAGAN. Dost thou not blush, proud Peacock as thou art,   25
   To make our father such a slight reply?
LEIR. Why how now, Minion, are you growne so proud?
   Doth our deare love make you thus peremptory?
   What, is your love become so small to us,
   As that you scorne to tell us what it is?   30
   Do you love us, as every child doth love
   Their father? True indeed, as some
   Who by disobedience short their fathers dayes,
   And so would you; some are so father-sick,
   That they make meanes to rid them from the world;   35
   And so would you: some are indifferent,
   Whether their aged parents live or dye;
   And so are you. But, didst thou know, proud gyrle,
   What care I had to foster thee to this,
   Ah, then thou wouldst say as thy sisters do: 40
   Our life is lesse, then love we owe to you.

---

[13]A name for the nightingale (due to her origin, according to Ovid's *Metamorphoses*, as a woman named Philomel who was turned into the bird after her brother-in-law raped her and cut out her tongue).

CORDELLA. Deare father, do not so mistake my words,
    Nor my playne meaning be misconstrued;
    My toung was never usde to flattery.
GONORILL. You were not best say I flatter: if you do,   45
    My deeds shall shew, I flatter not with you.
    I love my father better then thou canst.
CORDELLA. The prayse were great, spoke from anothers mouth:
    But it should seeme your neighbours dwell far off.
RAGAN. Nay, here is one, that will confirme as much   50
    As she hath sayd, both for my selfe and her.
    I say, thou dost not wish my fathers good.
CORDELLA. Deare father—
LEIR. Peace, bastard Impe, no issue of King *Leir*,
    I will not heare thee speake one little more.   55
    Call not me father, if thou love thy life,
    Nor these thy sisters once presume to name:
    Looke for no helpe henceforth from me nor mine;
    Shift as thou wilt, and trust unto thy selfe:
    My Kingdome will I equally devide   60
    'Twixt thy two sisters to their royall dowre,
    And will bestow them worthy their deserts:
    This done, because thou shalt not have the hope,
    To have a childs part in the time to come,
    I presently will dispossesse my selfe,   65
    And set up these upon my princely throne.
GONORILL. I ever thought that pride would have a fall.
RAGAN. Plaine dealing, sister: your beauty is so sheene,
    You need no dowry, to make you be a Queene.
                             [*Exeunt Leir, Gonorill, Ragan.*]
CORDELLA. Now whither, poore forsaken, shall I goe,   70
    When mine own sisters tryumph in my woe?
    But unto him which doth protect the just,
    In him will poore *Cordella* put her trust.
    These hands shall labour, for to get my spending:
    And so ile live untill my dayes have ending.   75
PERILLUS. Oh, how I grieve, to see my Lord thus fond,
    To dote so much upon vayne flattering words.
    Ah, if he but with good advice had weyghed,
    The hidden tenure of her humble speech,

Reason to rage should not have given place, 80
Nor poore *Cordella* suffer such disgrace.

[*Exit.*]

[Sc. 4] *Enter the Gallian King*[14] *with Mumford,*
and three Nobles more.

KING. Disswade me not, my Lords, I am resolv'd,
This next fayre wynd to sayle for Brittany,
In some disguise, to see if flying fame
Be not too prodigall in the wonderous prayse
Of these three Nymphes, the daughters of King *Leir*. 5
If present view do answere absent prayse,
And eyes allow of what our eares have heard,
And *Venus* stand auspicious to my vowes,
And Fortune favour what I take in hand;
I will returne seyz'd of as rich a prize 10
As *Jason*, when he wanne the golden fleece.

MUMFORD. Heavens graunt you may; the match were ful of honor,
And well beseeming the young Gallian King.
I would your Grace would favour me so much,
As make me partner of your Pilgrimage, 15
I long to see the gallant British Dames,
And feed mine eyes upon their rare perfections:
For till I know the contrary, Ile say,
Our Dames in Fraunce are more fayre then they.

[. . .]   [*The play's final scene*]

[Sc. 32] *Alarums and excursions, then sound victory.*
Enter Leir, Perillus, King, Cordella, and Mumford.

KING. Thanks be to God, your foes are overcome.
And you againe possessed of your right.

LEIR. First to the heavens, next, thanks to you, my sonne,
By whose good meanes I repossesse the same:
Which if it please you to accept your selfe, 5
With all my heart I will resigne to you:
For it is yours by right, and none of mine.
First, have you raisd, at your owne charge, a power
Of valiant Souldiers; (this comes all from you)

---

[14]The King of Gaul, the Roman name for France; Mumford is his companion.

Next have you ventured your owne persons scathe.   10
And lastly, (worthy *Gallia* never staynd)
My kingly title I by thee have gaynd.
KING. Thank heavens, not me, my zeale to you is such,
  Commaund my utmost, I will never grutch.
CORDELLA. He that with all kind love intreats his Queene,   15
  Will not be to her father unkind seene.
LEIR. Ah, my *Cordella*, now I call to mind,
  The modest answere, which I tooke unkind:
  But now I see, I am no whit beguild,
  Thou lovedst me dearely, and as ought a child.   20
  And thou (*Perillus*) partner once in woe,
  Thee to requite, the best I can, Ile doe:
  Yet all I can, I, were it ne're so much,
  Were not sufficient, thy true love is such.
  Thanks (worthy, *Mumford*) to thee last of all,   25
  Not greeted last, 'cause thy desert was small;
  No, thou hast Lion-like layd on to day,
  Chasing the Cornwall King and Cambria;
  Who with my daughters, daughters did I say?
  To save their lives, the fugitives did play.   30
  Come, sonne and daughter, who did me advaunce,
  Repose with me awhile, and then for Fraunce.
                    Sound Drummes and Trumpets.

Sir Philip Sidney (1554–1586)

*Sir Philip Sidney's prose romance presents the source for the Gloucester
plot as an incident in the travels of his heroes Pyrocles and Musidorus.
This pair, after hearing the tale of the wandering blind Paphlagonian
king and his good son Leonatus, come to their aid and vanquish the
bastard son. Unlike Gloucester in Shakespeare's play, the father here is
fully aware that he is succored by his good son, whom he had previously sought to kill on the advice of his bastard. He has been blinded by
this bastard, who has seized control of the kingdom. The king dies of
grief and relief only after the good son has been returned to the throne.
The bastard son appears only in the reports of his father and brother.*

from *The Countesse of Pembrokes Arcadia*
(London, 1590), Book 2, Chapter 10, pp. 143–147

There they perceaved an aged man, and a young, scarcely come to the age of a man, both poorly arayed, extreamely weather-beaten, the olde man blinde, the young man leading him: and yet through all those miseries, in both these seemed to appeare a kind of noblenesse, not sutable to that affliction. But the first words they heard, were these of the old man. Well *Leonatus* (said he) since I cannot perswade thee to lead me to that which should end my griefe, & thy trouble, let me now entreat thee to leave me: feare not, my miserie cannot be greater then it is, & nothing doth become me but miserie; feare not the danger of my blind steps, I cannot fall worse then I am. And doo not I pray thee, doo not obstinately continue to infect thee with my wretchednesse. But flie, flie from this region, onely worthy of me. Deare fataher (answered he) doo not take away from me the onely remnant of my happinesse: while I have power to doo your service, I am not wholly miserable. Ah my sonne (said he, and with that he groned, as if sorrow strave to breake his harte,) how evill fits it me to have such a sonne, and how much doth thy kindnessse upbraide my wickednesse? These dolefull speeches, and some others to like purpose (well shewing they had not bene borne to the fortune they were in,) moved the Princes to goe out unto them, and aske the younger what they were? Sirs, answered he, [. . .]

"This old man (whom I leade) was lately rightfull Prince of this countrie of *Paphlagonia*, by the hard-harted ungratefulnes of a sonne of his, deprived, not onely of his kingdome (whereof of forraine forces were ever able to spoyle him) but of his sight, the riches which Nature graunts to the poorest creatures. Whereby, and by other his unnatural dealings, he hath bin driven to such griefe, as even now he would have had me to have led him to the toppe of this rocke, thence to cast himselfe headlong to death: and so would have made me (who received my life of him) to be the worker of his destruction. But noble Gentlemen (said he) if either of you have a father, and feele what duetifull affection is engraffed in a sonnes hart, let me intreate you to convey this afflicted Prince to some place of rest and securitie. Amongst your worthie actes it shall be none of the least, that a King, of such might and fame, and so unjustly oppressed, is in any sort by you relieved.

But before they could make him answere, his father began to speake, Ah my sonne (said he) how evill an Historian are you, that leave out the chiefe knotte of all the discourse! my wickednes, my wickednes. And if thou doest it to spare my eares, (the onely sense nowe left me proper for knowledge) assure thy selfe thou dost mistake me. And I take witnesse of that Sunne which you see (with that he cast up his blinde eyes, as if he would hunt for light,) and wish my selfe in worse case then I do wish my selfe, which is as evill as may be, if I speake untruely; that nothing is so welcome to my thoughts, as the publishing of my shame. Therefore know you Gentlemen (to whom from my harte I wish that it may not prove ominous foretoken of misfortune to have mette with such a miser as I am) that whatsoever my sonne (O God, that trueth binds me to reproch him with the name of my sonne) hath said, is true. But besides those truthes, this also is true, that having had in lawful mariage, of a mother fitte to beare royall children, this sonne (such one as partly you see, and better shall knowe by my shorte declaration) and so enjoyed the expectations in the world of him, till he was growen to justifie their expectations (so as I needed envie no father for the chiefe comfort of mortalitie, to leave an other ones-selfe after me) I was caried by a bastarde sonne of mine (if at least I be bounde to beleeve the words of that base woman my concubine, his mother) first to mislike, then to hate, lastly to destroy, to doo my best to destroy, this sonne (I thinke you thinke) undeserving destruction. What waies he used to bring me to it, if I should tell you, I should tediously trouble you with as much poysonous hypocrisie, desperate fraude, smoothe malice, hidden ambition, and smiling envie, as in any living person could be harbored. [. . .]

[. . .] Till this sonne of mine (God knowes, woorthie of a more vertuous, and more fortunate father) forgetting my abhominable wrongs, not recking danger, and neglecting the present good way he was in doing himselfe good, came hether to doo this kind office you see him performe towards me, to my unspeakable griefe; not onely because his kindnes is a glasse even to my blind eyes, of my naughtines, but that above all griefes, it greeves me he should desperately adventure the losse of his soul-deserving life for mine, that yet owe more to furtune for my deserts, as if he would cary mudde in a chest of christall. For well I know, he that now raigneth, how much soever (and with good reason) he despiseth me, of all men despised; yet he will not let slippe any advantage to make away him, whose just title (ennobled by courage and goodness) may one day shake the seate of a never secure tyrannie. And for this cause I craved of him to leade me to the toppe of this rocke, indeede I must confesse, with meaning to free him from so Serpentine a companion as I am. But he finding what I purposed, onely therein since he was borne, shewed himselfe disobedient unto me. And now Gentlemen, you have the true storie, which I pray you publish to the world, that my mischievous proceedinges may be the glorie of his filiall pietie, the onely reward now left for so great a merite. And if it may be, let me obtaine that of you, which my sonne denies me: for never was there more pity in saving any, then in ending me; both because therein my agonies shall ende, and so shall you preserve this excellent young man, who els wilfully folowes his owne ruine. [. . .]

The two princes help Leonatus to defeat Plexirtus (Edmund in King Lear*) in a series of battles and restore his father to the throne.*

In which season the blind King (having in the chief cittie of his Realme, set the crowne upon his sonne *Leonatus* head) with many teares (both of joy and sorrow) setting forth to the whole people, his owne fault and his sonnes vertue, after he had kist him, and forst his sonne to accept honour of him (as of his newe-become subject) even in a moment died, as it should seeme: his hart broken with unkindnes and affliction, stretched so farre beyond his limits with this excesse of comfort, as it was able no longer to keep safe his roial spirits. But the new King (having no lesse lovingly performed all duties to him dead, then alive) pursued on the siege of his unnatural brother, asmuch for the revenge of his father, as for the establishing of his owne quiet. In which siege truly I cannot but acknowledge the prowesse of those two brothers, then whom the Princes never found in all their travell two men of greater habilitie to performe, nor of habler skill for conduct. [. . .]

The State

"Love cools, friendship falls off, brothers divide; in cities, mutinies; in countries, discord; in palaces, treason; and the bond cracked 'twixt son and father." (Gloucester to Edmund, 1.2.99–101)

Shakespeare's sources include not only narratives of the plot but also ideas, identities, and languages of early seventeenth-century England. This and the following sections provide examples of different strains of thought that surrounded Shakespeare's artistic choices and perhaps informed his original audience's understanding of them.

As Gloucester apprehends, the dissolution of an entire world impends in *King Lear*. The gravity and scope of Shakespeare's portrait of loss can be measured in part by contrasting it with the social ideals of Tudor-Stuart political culture. The world of these ideals and ideologies was, at least in theory, one in which the divisions of kingdoms or families went against both God and nature. With the accession of King James VI of Scotland to the English throne in 1603 (he became James I), Britain achieved a political unity not experienced since mythic times (if then). Divinely ordered and sanctioned, hierarchical and homologous (so that the organization of the family was thought to resemble that of kingdom, and both, heavenly order), Tudor-Stuart society was described by its official imaginations in ways meant to ward off precisely the kinds of destruction that *King Lear* details.

While our own world offers many examples of powerful rule, royalty is no longer the dominant form or even a vital one. One of the hardest things for a modern audience to comprehend about Renaissance kingship is its sacred nature. When King Lear says, "they told me I was everything" (4.6.104), he really means it: Renaissance kings were God's deputies on earth, beings of a semi-divine nature, ordained by God to govern his people, even as the father was for his family. King James I of England continued the practice of "touching" for the "king's evil," a ceremony in which the touch of a king's hand was thought to hold miraculous power over disease. A king was not merely a leader or a powerful politician but a near god. His mere humanity was a scandal even in a Christian culture accustomed to the idea of a god made flesh. We should experience Lear's sovereignty, no matter how extreme its exercise, as that of one not only accustomed to being obeyed but also ordained to be so. Furthermore, while it is difficult for audiences of a democratic age to imagine monarchic hierarchy as a form of solace or security (rather than oppression or exploitation), such was indeed the case for the early modern world. Hence the keenness in the play and the culture to differentiate righteous power from tyranny. King Lear himself cries, "Take physic, pomp; / Expose thyself to feel what wretches feel, / That thou mayst shake the superflux to them / And show the heavens more just" (3.4.33–36). Lear's fall from power, albeit initiated and exacerbated by his own actions, signals the unmaking of a world.

The geographical integrity of Britain was further proof to English minds of the divinely sanctioned nature of their political integrity. One of the most famous passages in Shakespeare's *Richard II* elegizes the island as "This other Eden, demi-paradise, / This fortress built by Nature for herself / Against infection and the hand of war. . . . this little world / This precious stone set in the silver sea" (2.1.42–46). It is significant that these idealizing words were written in 1596, when the isle of Britain was composed of *two* kingdoms, England and Scotland (Wales had been annexed to the English crown in 1284). For a society that feared civil division as a harbinger of dissolution, King James's arrival from Scotland brought a welcome literality to the images of national unity founded in geographic (which was to say divine) authority. Ironically, the king's ambitions for the legal and economic union of the two countries met with great resistance from the English parliament. (Members heard in James's ambitions a disturbing tendency to augment royal sovereignty at the expense of the Commons and the constitution.) The conflict revealed fault lines of culture and tradition forebodingly reminiscent of Lear's own fractured kingdom. Unlike the island paradise of *Richard II*, the geography of Lear's Britain is hardly Edenic, and its weather, at best, a sign of divine displeasure or, worse, indifference.

King Lear creates a craving for human decencies that tends to obscure political measurement. An English audience could hope fervently that Cordelia's forces will triumph, even though they constitute a foreign invasion of Britain. When Cornwall deems Gloucester's aid to Lear as punishable treason, he is technically correct, but no audience would cheer for him. It is a testimony to the play's power that Shakespeare succeeds in dwarfing such concerns of state, given how pressing they were in his own culture. The materials selected in this section give some sense of these concerns.

Homily on Obedience (1570; 1623)

> *This selection is from the "Homily" written in the wake of the 1569 Northern Rebellion. Homilies were prescripted sermons designated by the government for preachers to read in churches (so as to avoid the dangers inherent in sermons the preachers might compose themselves). This homily gives a sense of what Shakespeare's culture both admired in political order and feared in its absence, even if homily visions addressed ideals rather than practical realities. Note the links between divine, social, familial, and natural orders—all in crisis in* King Lear. *The selection that follows is a Jacobean printing (1623).*

from *An Exhortation Concerning Good Order and Obedience to Rulers and Magistrates* (Anonymous, London 1570; 1623)

Almighty GOD hath created and appointed all things in heaven, e a rth, and waters in a most excellent and perfect order. In Heaven,

hee hath appointed distinct and severall orders and states of
Archangels and Angels. In earth hee hath assigned and appointed
Kings, Princes, with other governours under them, in all good and
necessary order. The water above is kept, and rayneth downe in
due time and season. The Sun, Moone, Starres, Rainebow, Thunder, Lightning, Clouds, and all Birdes of the ayre, doe keepe their
order. The Earth, Trees, Seedes, Plantes, Hearbes, Corne, Grasse,
and all maner of Beasts keepe themselves in order: all the parts of
the whole yeare, as Winter, Summer, Moneths, Nights, and Dayes,
continue in their order: all kindes of Fishes in the Sea, Rivers, and
Waters, with all Fountaines, Springs, yea, the Seas themselves
keepe their comely course and order: and man himselfe also hath
all his parts both within and without, as soule, heart, minde, memory, understanding, reason, speech, with all and singular corporall
members of his body in a profitable, necessarie, and pleasant
order: every degree of people in their vocation, calling and office,
hath appointed to them their duty and order: some are in high
degree, some in low, some Kings and Princes, some inferiours and
subjects, Priests, and lay men, masters and servants, fathers, and
children, husbands, and wives, rich and poore, and every one have
neede of other, so that in all things is to bee lauded and praised the
goodly order of GOD, without the which no house, no Citie, no
Commonwealth can continue and endure, or last. For where there
is no right order, there reigneth all abuse, carnall liberty, enormitie,
sinne, and Babylonicall confusion. Take away Kings, Princes,
Rulers, Magistrates, Judges, and such estates of GODS order, no
man shall ride or goe by the high way unrobed, no man shall sleepe
in his owne house or bedde unkilled, no man shall keepe his wife,
children, and possession in quietnesse, all things shall be common,
and there must needes follow all mischiefe, and utter destruction
both of soules, bodies, goodes, and common wealthes. But blessed
bee GOD, that wee in this Realme of England, feele not the horrible calamities, miseries, and wretchednesse, which all they
undoubtedly feele and suffer, that lacke this godly order, and
praysed bee GOD, that wee know the great excellent benefit of
God shewed towards us in this behalfe, GOD hath sent us his high
gift, our most deare Soveraigne Lord King JAMES, with a godly,
wise, and honourable Counsell, with other superiors and inferiours, in a beautifull order, and godly.

Charles Merbury (fl. 1581)

Charles Merbury was the son of a dependent of the Duke and Duchess of Suffolk; he held a minor post in the household of the Lord Chamberlain in the 1570s and 1580s. Merbury's comparative discussion of kingship considers the alternatives and varieties of sovereignty only to conclude that absolute monarchy (especially English absolute monarchy), while not the only form of government, is the best form. He emphasizes the source of royal power in divinity and its difference from simple tyranny; a good king is attentive to the happiness of his subjects—a recognition Lear arrives at in 3.4. He also exhibits the common horror of a nonlineal succession of the throne.

from *A Brief Discourse of Royal Monarchie, as of the Best Common Weale* (London, 1581); sig. B3v–F3v passim

Between a good King and a Tyrant there is this difference. The one is courteous, merciful, endowed with all virtue: the other is haughty, and cruel, defiled with all vice. The one embraceth equity, and justice: the other treadeth both Gods law, and mans law under his feet. The one hath his mind, and all his care upon the health, and wealth of his subjects: the other esteemeth his own pleasure more than their profit, his own wealth, more than their good wills [. . .] the one looketh for everlasting joy: the other can hardly escape everlasting pain. [. . .]

Seeing therefore that Lineal Succession is so sure a foundation, as all good kingdoms both do, and may boldly build upon: And contrarily Election so weak a sand or rather so dangerous a Sea, as it is able to sink the tallest ship of City, or Country that saileth therein [. . .] the best, and most royal Prince is not to receive his Scepter by any such hap, or hazard of Fortune [. . .] it is not sufficient that so royall a prince be descended lineally, and lawfully into his kingdom: But he must also possess, and exercise such royal and princely power therein, as is most fit for his worthiness, and for his subjects happiness: neither in so extreme a manner, as to make a God of himself (as Alexander the great would have done,) and slaves of his vassals (as the Great Turk at this daye doth): Neither in yet so slender sort, as to have the sword carried after him, and to be but a little better than a cipher, or a shadow of a Prince.

He is to have therefore (by the grace, and permission of Almighty God) that power which the Latines [call] *maiestatem*: [. . .] that is, Power full and perpetual over all his subjects in general and over every one in particular [. . .] his Power shall last (by Gods grace) perpetually: first during his own life in himself, and then after his death in his sons, and successors [. . .] . Our prince, who is the Image of God on Earth, [. . .] is not to acknowledge any greater than himself: nor any authority greater than his own [. . .] . Though some do maintain that a Prince ought to be subject unto the states and peers of his realm [. . .] . An opinion (if it be not well tempered, and conveniently limited) most prejudicial unto the estate of a Monarchy [. . .] much less is he subject in anything unto the Multitude of the common people, who as they have more authority are for the most part more insolent, and more disposed unto rebellion.

Sir Thomas Smith (1513–1577)

> *Elizabethan scholar and diplomat Sir Thomas Smith describes the history and traditions of the English commonweal in the selection presented here. He is unusually specific for this period about the distribution of English sovereignty among locations other than the monarchy, such as parliament. But he is nevertheless unstinting about the honor and glory due an English monarch and the signs and symbols of monarchy. Smith helps us understand how what might seem like peripheral slights or insults to Lear's authority (e.g., Regan putting Caius in the stocks, or Regan and Cornwall not greeting Lear upon his arrival) are more than mere failures of etiquette.*

from *De Republica Anglorum* (London, 1583)[1]

To be short the prince is the life, the head, and the authoritie of all thinges that be doone in the realme of England. And to no prince is doone more honor and reverence than to the King and Queene of Englande, no man speaketh to the prince nor serveth at the table but in adoration and kneeling, all persons of the realme be bareheaded before him: insomuch that in the chamber of presence where the cloath of estate is set, no man dare walke, yea though the prince be not there, no man dare tarrie there but bareheaded. This

[1]Ed. Mary Dewar (Cambridge University Press, 1982), p. 88.

is understood of them of the realme: For all strangers be suffered there and in all places to use the maner of their countrie, such is the civilitie of our nation.

James VI of Scotland (1566–1625)

James published The Trew Law *when he was king of Scotland, four years before he ascended to the English throne. The Scottish monarchy was a comparatively weaker institution and was often pressed to assert its prerogatives over and against strong feudal magnates, which perhaps accounts for James's insistence here on the rights, origins, and sanctities of his rule—an insistence that may have sounded rather high-handed to an English ear more accustomed to Elizabeth I's dulcet rhetoric of the interdependence of Crown and commonwealth. To make his case, James takes pains to compare royal authority to paternal authority. As in* King Lear, *kingly and fatherly identities and powers, high-handedness and deep affection, are compounded.*

from *The Trew Law of Free Monarchies* (Edinburgh, 1599); sig. A2r–v

Kings are called Gods[1] by the propheticall King *David*, because they sit upon GOD his Throne in the earth, and have the count of their administration to give unto him. Their office is, *To minister justice and judgement to the people*,[2] as the same *David* saith: *To advance the good, and punish the evill*,[3] as he likewise saith: *To establish good Lawes to his people, and procure obedience to the same* as divers good Kings of *Judah* did:[4] *To procure the peace of*

---

[1]Psalms 82.6: "I have said, ye are gods; and all of you are children of the earth."

[2]Psalms 101.1, 8: "I will sing of mercy and judgement: unto thee, O Lord, will I sing . . . I will early destroy all the wicked on the land, that I may cut off all wicked doers from the city of the Lord."

[3]Psalm 101.6–7: "Whoso privily slandereth his neighbour, him shall I cut off: him that hath an high look and a proud heart will I not suffer. He that worketh deceit shall not dwell within my house: he that telleth lies shall not tarry in my sight."

[4]Kings 18.2: "And he did that which was right in the sight of the Lord." For accounts of godly kings, see 2 Chronicles 29, 34, and 35; 2 Kings 22 and 23.2.

the people, as the same *David* saith:[5] *To decide all controversies that can arise among them,* as *Salomon* did: *To be the Minister of God for the weale of them that doe well, and as the minister of God, to take vengeance upon them that doe evill,*[6] as S. *Paul* saith. And finally, *As a good Pastour, to goe out and in before his people*[7] as is said in the first of *Samuel: That through the Princes prosperitie, the peoples peace may be procured,*[8] as *Jeremie* saith.

And therefore in the Coronation of our owne Kings, as well as of every Christian *Monarche,* they give their Oath, first to maintaine the Religion presently professed within their countrie, according to their lawes, whereby it is established, and to punish all those that should presse to alter, or disturbe the profession thereof; And nex to maintaine all the lowable and good Lawes made by their predecessours to see them put in execution, and the breakers and violaters thereof, to be punished, according to the tenour of the same: And lastly, to maintaine the whole countrey, and every state therein, in all their ancient Priviledges and Liberties, as well against all forreine enemies, as among themselves: And shortly to procure the weale and flourishing of his people, not onely in maintaining and putting to execution the olde lowable lawes of the countrey, and by establishing of new (as necessitie and evill maners will require) but by all other meanes possible to fore-see and prevent all dangers, that are likely to fall upon them, and to maintaine concord, wealth, and civilitie among them, as a loving Father, and careful watchman, caring for them more then for himselfe, knowing himselfe to be ordained for them, and they not for him; and therefore countable to that great God, who placed him as his lieutenant over them, upon the perill of his soule to procure the weale of both soules and bodies, as farre as in him lieth, of all them that are committed to his charge. [. . .]

---

[5] Psalms 72.2: "He shall judge thy people with righteousness, and thy poor with judgment."

[6] 1 Kings 3.9: "Give therefore thy servant an understanding heart to judge thy people, that I may discern between good and bad: for who is able to judge this thy so great a people?"

[7] Romans 13.4: "For [a king] is minister of God to thee for good. But if thou do that which is evil, be afraid, for he beareth not the sword in vain: for he is the minister of God, a revenger to execute wrath upon him that doeth evil."

[8] Jeremiah 29.7: "Seek the peace of the city whither I have caused you to be carried away captives, and pray unto the Lord for it, for in the peace thereof shall ye have peace."

By the Law of Nature the King becomes a naturall Father to all his Lieges at his Coronation: And as the Father of his fatherly duty is bound to care for the nourishing, education, and vertuous government of his children; even so is the king bound to care for all his subjects. As all the toile and paine that the father can take for his children, will be thought light and well bestowed by him, so that the effect thereof redound to their profite and weale; so ought the Prince to doe towards his people. As the kindly father ought to foresee all inconvenients and dangers that may arise towards his children, and though with the hazard of his owne person presse to prevent the same; so ought the King towards his people. As the fathers wrath and correction upon any of his children that offendeth, ought to be by a fatherly chastisement seasoned with pitie, as long as there is any hope of amendment in them; so ought the King towards any of his Lieges that offend in that measure. And shortly, as the Fathers chiefe joy ought to be in procuring his childrens welfare, rejoycing at their weale, sorrowing and pitying at their evill, to hazard for their safetie, travell for their rest, wake for their sleepe; and in a word, to thinke that his earthly felicitie and life standeth and liveth more in them, nor in himselfe; so ought a good Prince thinke of his people. [. . .]

[. . .] The King towards his people is rightly compared to a father of children, and to a head of a body composed of diuers members: For as fathers, the good Princes, and Magistrates of the people of God acknowledged themselves to their subjects. And for all other well ruled Common-wealths, the stile of *Pater patrice* was ever, and is commonly used to Kings. And the proper office of a King towards his Subjects, agrees very well with the office of the head towards the body, and all members thereof: For from the head, being the seate of Judgement, proceedeth the care and foresight of guiding, and preventing all evill that may come to the body or any part thereof. The head cares for the body, so doeth the King for his people. As the discourse and direction flowes from the head, and the execution according thereunto belongs to the rest of the members, every one according to their office: so is it betwixt a wise Prince, and his people. [. . .]

And now first for the fathers part (whose naturall love to his children I described in the first part of this my discourse, speaking of the dutie that Kings owe to their Subjects) consider, I pray you what duetie his children owe to him, & whether upon any pretext whatsoever, it wil not be thought monstrous and unnaturall to his sons, to rise up against him, to control him at their appetite, and when they thinke good to sley him, or cut him off, and adopt to themselves any other they please in his roome: Or can any pretence of wickednes or rigor on his part be a just excuse for his children to put hand into him? And although wee see by the course of nature, that love useth to descend more then to ascend, in case it were trew, that the father hated and wronged the children never so much, will any man, endued with the least sponke of reason, thinke it lawfull for them to meet him with the line? Yea, suppose the father were furiously following his sonnes with a drawen sword, is it lawfull for them to turne and strike againe, or make any resistance but by flight?[9] I thinke surely, if there were not more but the example of bruit beasts & unreasonable creatures, it may serve well enough to qualifie and prove this my argument. We reade often the pietie that the Storkes have to their olde and decayed parents: And generally wee know, that there are many sorts of beasts and fowles, that with violence and many bloody strokes will beat and banish their yong ones from them, how soone they perceive them to be able to fend themselves; but wee never read or heard of any resistance on their part, except among the vipers;[10] which prooves such persons, as ought to be reasonable creatures, and yet unnaturally follow this example, to be endued with their viperous nature.

And for the similitude of the head and the body, it may very well fall out that the head will be forced to garre cut off some rotten member (as I have already said) to keepe the rest of the body in integritie: but what state the body can be in, if the head, for any infirmitie that can fall to it, be cut off, I leave it to the readers judgement.

James I of England (1566–1625)

James's first speech to parliament was to its upper house only—the House of Lords. He put forth his idea for the legal and institutional union of Scotland and England. The English would resist this idea for

[9]Compare this with Edgar's choice in *King Lear* 2.1.

[10]Compare this with 2.4.155–157: "She hath abated me of half my train, / Looked black upon me, struck me with her tongue / Most serpentlike upon the very heart."

more than a century to come, fearing an encroachment on English legal traditions and customs as well as the imagined predations of the Scots. Emphasizing union over division and framing the integrity of the British kingdom as a matter of organic necessity, James's rhetoric casts into relief the horrific and potentially blasphemous civil disorder and international invasion depicted in King Lear.

from *A Speech [. . .] delivered in the Upper House of Parliament on Monday the 19 March 1604, being the first day of the first Parliament* (London, 1604)

And here I must crave your patiences for a little space, to give me leave to discourse more particularly of the benefits that doe arise of that Union which is made in my blood, being a matter that most properly belongeth to me to speake of, as the head wherein that great Body[1] is united. And first, if we were to looke no higher than to naturall and Physicall reasons, we may easily be per-swaded of the great benefits that by that Union do redound to the whole Island: for if twentie thousand men by a strong Armie, is not the double thereof, fourtie thousand, a double the stronger Armie? If a Baron enricheth himselfe with double as many lands as hee had before, is he not double the greater? [. . .] Do we not yet remember, that this Kingdome was divided into seven little Kingdomes, besides Wales?[2] And is it not now the stronger by their union? And hath not the union of Wales to England added a greater strength thereto? Which though it was a great Principali-tie, was nothing comparable in greatnesse and power to the ancient and famous Kingdome of Scotland. But what should we sticke[3] upon any naturall appearance, when it is manifest that God by his Almightie providence hath preordained it so to be? Hath not God first united these two Kingdomes both in Lan-guage, Religion, and similitude of maners? Yea, hath hee not made us all in one Island, compassed with one Sea, and of it selfe by nature so indivisible, as almost those that were borderers themselves on the late Borders,[4] cannot distinguish, nor know, or

[1] Of the kingdom.
[2] Of the Saxon heptarchy, united under King Alfred.
[3] Rest with.
[4] The "badlands" between England and Scotland.

discerne their owne limits? These two Countries being separated neither by Sea, nor great River, Mountaine, nor other strength of nature, but onely by little small brookes, or demolished little walles, so as rather they were divided in apprehension, then in effect; And now in the end and fulnesse of time united, the right and title of both in my Person, alike lineally descended of both the Crownes, whereby it is now become like a little World within it selfe, being intrenched and fortified round about with a naturall, and yet admirable strong pond or ditch, whereby all the former feares of this Nation are now quite cut off. [. . .] What God hath conjoyned then, let no man separate. I am the Husband, and all the whole Isle is my lawfull Wife; I am the Head, and it is my Body; I am the Shepherd, and it is my flocke.

Thomas Sackville (1536–1608) and Thomas Norton (1532–1584)

Thomas Sackville and Thomas Norton were lawyers, and their play Gorboduc *was written for the 1561–1562 Christmas festivities at the Inner Temple, the center of the legal profession in London. As humanists and aspiring politicians, it is not surprising that they depict a familiar theme of Tudor-Stuart political discourse: the disasters that follow a king's absolutist failure to heed the advice of councilors. (While Tudor-Stuart culture venerated monarchy, it also advised the give-and-take provided by sage, humanist-trained statesmen.) The prospect of the kingdom's division was a particular anxiety—ironically so since Britain was still composed of two kingdoms that had a history of mutual aggression. In 1562, with a young unmarried Queen Elizabeth on the throne for just a few years, the implicit issue of advice was the duty to marry and provide an heir (so that Gorboduc-like divisions of the kingdom would be averted). The play was reprinted in 1590, when the aging and childless Elizabeth I's persistent refusal to follow advice to name her own successor was becoming a matter of pressing national concern.*

The excerpt here gives the plea of Eubulus, councilor to the king, not to divide the kingdom between his two sons; he cites the precedents of British history and the infirmities of human nature. Gorboduc *replies in a more measured manner than Lear to Kent, but with as much intransigence.*

from *Gorboduc* (London, 1562)

EUBULUS. Your wonted true regard of faithful hearts
   Makes me, O King, the bolder to presume
   To speak what I conceive within my breast,
   Although the same do not agree at all
   With that which other here my lords have said,   5
   Nor which yourself have seemèd best to like.
   Pardon I crave, and that my words be deemed
   To flow from hearty zeal unto your grace
   And to the safety of your common weal.
   To part your realm unto my lords, your sons,   10
   I think not good for you, ne yet for them,
   But worst of all for this our native land.
   Within one land one single rule is best.
   Divided reigns do make divided hearts,
   But peace preserves the country and the prince.   15
   Such is in man the greedy mind to reign,
   So great is his desire to climb aloft,
   In worldly stage the stateliest parts to bear,
   That faith and justice and all kindly love
   Do yield unto desire of sovereignty,   20
   Where egal state doth raise an egal hope
   To win the thing that either would attain.
   Your grace rememb'reth how in passèd years
   The mighty Brute, first prince of all this land,
   Possessed the same and ruled it well in one.   25
   He, thinking that the compass[1] did suffice
   For his three sons three kingdoms eke to make,
   Cut it in three, as you would now in twain.
   But how much British blood hath since been spilt
   To join again the sundered unity,   30
   What princes slain before their timely hour,
   What waste of towns and people in the land,
   What treasons heaped on murders and on spoils,
   Whose just revenge even yet is scarcely ceased;
   Ruthful remembrance is yet raw in mind.   35
   The gods forbid the like to chance again.

---

[1]Amount of land.

And you, O King, give not the cause thereof.
My lord Ferrex, your elder son, perhaps,
Whom kind and custom gives a rightful hope
To be your heir and to succeed your reign,   40
Shall think that he doth suffer greater wrong
Than he perchance will bear, if power serve.
Porrex, the younger, so upraised in state,
Perhaps in courage will be raised also.[2]
If flattery then, which fails not to assail   45
The tender minds of yet unskillful youth,
In one shall kindle and increase disdain,
And envy in the other's heart inflame,
This fire shall waste their love, their lives, their land,
And ruthful ruin shall destroy them both.   50
I wish not this, O King, so to befall,
But fear the thing that I do most abhor.
Give no beginning to so dreadful end.
Keep them in order and obedience,
And let them both by now obeying you   55
Learn such behavior as beseems their state:
The elder, mildness in his governance,
The younger, a yielding contentedness.
And keep them near unto your presence still
That they, restrainèd by the awe of you,   60
May live in compass of well tempered stay
And pass the perils of their youthful years.
Your agèd life draws on to feebler time,
Wherein you shall less able be to bear
The travails that in youth you have sustained,   65
Both in your person's and your realm's defense.
If, planting now your sons in further parts,
You send them further from your present reach,
Less shall you know how they themselves demean.
Traitorous corrupters of their pliant youth   70
Shall have, unspied, a much more free access;
And if ambition and inflamed disdain

---

[2]See Gloucester's professed even-handedness in *King Lear* (1.1.18) and its effect on Edmund's ambitions.

Shall arm the one, the other, or them both,
To civil war or to usurping pride,
Late shall you rue that you ne recked³ before.   75
Good is, I grant, of all to hope the best,
But not to live still⁴ dreadless of the worst.
So trust the one that the other be foreseen.
Arm not unskillfulness with princely power.
But you, that long have wisely ruled the reins   80
Of royalty within your noble real,
So hold them while the gods for our avails⁵
Shall stretch the thread of your prolongèd days.
Too soon he clamb into the flaming car
Whose want of skill did set the earth on fire.⁶   85
Time and example of your noble grace
Shall teach your sons both to obey and rule.
When time hath taught them, time shall make them place,
The place that now is full; and so I pray
Long it remain, to comfort of us all.   90
GORBODUC. I take your faithful hearts in thankful part.
But sith I see no cause to draw my mind
To fear the nature of my loving sons,
Or to misdeem that envy or disdain
Can there work hate where nature planteth love.   95
In one self purpose do I still abide,
My love extendeth egally to both;
My land sufficeth for them both also.
Humber shall part the marches⁷ of their realms.
The southern part the elder shall possess;   100
The northern shall Porrex, the younger, rule.
In quiet I will pass mine agèd days,
Free from the travail and the painful cares

³Reckoned, heeded.

⁴Always.

⁵Benefits.

⁶This refers to the son of the classical sun god (Jupiter/Apollo), who stole his father's chariot and, unable to control its horses, crashed to the earth in a fiery blaze; a figure of overweening ambition.

⁷The river Humber shall be the dividing line.

That hasten age upon the worthiest kings.
But, lest the fraud that ye do seem to fear   105
Of flattering tongues corrupt their tender youth
And writhe them to the ways of youthful lust,
To climbing pride, or to revenging hate,
Or to neglecting of their careful charge,
Lewdly to live in wanton recklessness,   110
Or to oppressing of the rightful cause,
Or not to wreak[8] the wrongs done to the poor,
To tread down truth or favor false deceit,
I mean to join to either of my sons
Some one of those whose long approvèd faith   115
And wisdom tried may well assure my heart
That mining[9] fraud shall find no way to creep
Into their fencèd[10] ears with grave advice.
This is the end, and so I pray you all
To bear my sons the love and loyalty   120
That I have found within your faithful breasts.

Samuel Harsnett (1561–1631)

Samuel Harsnett's text is usually cited as Shakespeare's source for the names of the devils recited by Poor Tom in 3.6 and a model of the "exorcism" practiced by Edgar upon his father in 4.1. But critic Stephen Greenblatt has proposed that the influence of this text goes beyond mere names. He argues that Harsnett seeks to cast exorcism itself as a theatrical practice in order to demystify and discredit Roman Catholicism, and thus also provides Shakespeare with a source for the impression that "King Lear is haunted by a sense of ritual and beliefs that are no longer efficacious, that have been emptied out" ("Shakespeare and the Exorcists," 1985, p. 175).

[8]Heed.
[9]Undermining.
[10]Defended.

from *A Declaration of Egregious Popish Impostures, to withdraw the harts of her Majesties Subjects from their alleageance, and from the truth of Christian Religion professed in England, under the pretence of casting out devils* (London, 1603)

Chapter 10: The strange names of their devils.

Now that I have acquainted you with the names of the Master,[1] and his twelve disciples, the names of the places wherein, and the names of the persons upon whom these wonders were shewed: it seemes not incongruent that I relate unto you the names of the devils, whom in this glorious pageant they did dispossesse. [. . .] It may seeme that our vagrant devils here did take theyr fashion of new names from our wandring Jesuits who to dissemble themselves, have always three, or foure odde conceited names in their budget: or els they[2] did so plague the poore devils with theyr holy charmes, and enchaunted geare, and did so intoxicate them with their dreadful fumigations,[3] as they made some so giddy-headed, that they gave themselves giddy names, they wist not what. Or else there is a confederation between our wandring Exorcists, and these walking devils, and they are agreed of certaine uncouth no-significant names, which goe currant amongst themselves, as the Gipsies are of gibridge,[4] which none but themselves can spell without a paire of spectacles. Howsoever it is, it is not amisse that you be acquainted with these extravagant names of devils, least meeting them otherwise by chance, you mistaken them for the names of Tapsters, or Juglers.[5]

First then, to marshall them in as good order, as such disorderly cattell will be brought into, you are to understand, that there were in our possessed 5 Captaines, or Commaunders above the rest. Captain *Pippin*, *Marwoods* devil, Captaine *Philpot*, *Trayfords* devil, Captaine *Maho Saras* devil, Captaine *Modu*, *Maynies* devil,

---

[1]Father Weston, head of the team of exorcists (parodied here as Christ and the apostles).

[2]The exorcists.

[3]Incense used in Roman Catholic rituals.

[4]Gibberish.

[5]Inn-keepers, or magicians.

and Captaine *Soforce, Anne Smiths* devil. [. . .][6] [T]he names of the spirits cast out of Trayford were these, Hilco, Smolkin, Hillio, Hiaclito, and Lustie huffe-cap: this last seems some swaggering punie devil, dropt out of a Tinkers budget.[7] [. . .] Fratteretto, Fliberdigibbet, Hoberdidance, Tocobatto were foure devils of the round, or Morrice,[8] whom Sara in her fits, tuned together, in measure and sweet cadence. And least you should conceive, that the devils had no musicke in hell, especially that they would goe a maying without theyr musicke, the Fidler comes in with his Taber, & Pipe,[9] and a whole Morice after him, with motly visards[10] for theyr better grace. These foure had forty assistants under them, as themselves doe confesse. [. . .] Maho was generall Dictator of hell: and yet for good manners sake, hee was contented of his good nature to make shew, that himselfe was under the check of Modu, the graund devil in MA: Maynie.[11] These were all in poore Sara at a chop, with these the poore soule travailed up and downe full two yeeres together: so as during those two yeeres, it had beene all one to say, one is gone to hell, or he is gone to Sara Williams, for shee poore wench had all hell in her belly. And had had it still to this day for any thing we know, if it had not pleased FA[12] Weston and his twelve holy disciples, to have delivered her of that devil-childe.

---

[6]Marwood, Trayford, Sara, Maynies, and Anne Smith were the names of the possessed persons.

[7]A leather pouch.

[8]The Morris dance, a folk dance.

[9]A tabor was a small drum, which with the whistle (pipe) provided accompaniment for dancing.

[10]Visors, or masks.

[11]Master.

[12]Father.

The Household

The early modern household was organized according to the same dictates as the state. It was a hierarchy in which fathers ruled over all subordinate members: wives, children, and servants. The assumption, as the *Homily on Obedience* shows, is that the family was a version of the realm and vice versa. Children were the property of their parents, to dispose of as the parents saw fit. The obligations of children included above all obedience; if authority were obeyed, all would be well. *King Lear* explores the contradictions between familial and political domains, between love and power, the demands of the heart and those of social order. King Lear's love for Cordelia, for instance, and his desire to "set my rest / On her kind nursery" (1.1.120-121) conflicts with what marriage will require of her. As she, to her loss, points out to her father: "Haply, when I shall wed, / That lord whose hand must take my plight shall carry / Half my love with him, half my care and duty" (1.1.97–99).

A potential source of domestic discord was property, particularly in an aristocratic family. Sons of the lower and middle social orders could apprentice to a trade or be educated for a profession (marrying, ideally, when their training was complete), and daughters hoped for a comfortable marriage. However, high-born sons and daughters, not destined for trades or professions, could depend on their parents well into adulthood, with resentment possible on both sides (a fear Edmund exploits in framing Edgar in 1.2). A real-life instance of such occurred in 1603–1604, when the eldest of Brian Annesley's three daughters tried to have her elderly father declared a lunatic so as to assume control of his affairs. The youngest daughter (Cordell) appealed the case to Sir Robert Cecil and inherited the property after her father's death (see R. A. Foakes, *King Lear,* p. 90).

The reliance of aristocratic power on landed property presented further constraints on autonomous choice. Because the marriage of high-born children was a means of conserving, even increasing real estate, marrying for love alone was beside the point. (The King of France's acceptance of the dowerless Cordelia is either the stuff of fairy tales or Shakespeare's suggestion of an extremely cynical political gamble.)

A further consequence of the landed nature of a noble family's power base, and hence its reliance on patrilineal succession, was that not only was the longevity of a parent a frustration to the children's inheritance but also the entitlements of the eldest son were a source of resentment to the younger siblings. In order to keep the estate consolidated, all or most of the real estate and its revenues went to the eldest son, under a system known as *primogeniture* ("first born").

It is revealing of Edmund's sophistry that while he complains that his lack of legitimacy bars him from property, his resentment of Edgar would have been the same had he been legitimate, given that he is younger than Edgar. *King Lear* writes these issues on the largest of scales, the politics of the family intensified by the royal setting. Michel de Montaigne's essay "Of the Affection of Fathers for Their Children," excerpted in this section, registers the delicate balance of obligations between noble parents and their offspring and provides a context for understanding why the fathers in Shakespeare's play are so ready to believe ill of their children.

If subordinates resent authority, authority fears its subordinates. Renaissance discussions of the patriarchal family are alert to the prospect of rebellion from wives, children, and servants (in the latter category we can locate Lear's knights, Kent's Caius, Cornwall's servants, and Oswald). Women were of particular concern, both in their potential for insubordination in general (Eve is the prototype) and for sexual license in particular (an assertion of control over property belonging to fathers and husbands). Female insubordination is a frequent motif in *King Lear.* Joseph Swetnam's *Arraignment of Lewd [. . .] Women* (1615) and Jane Anger's *Her*

Protection for Women (1589) give opposing caricatures of female identity against which the complexities of Shakespeare's characterizations of Lear's daughters can be measured. Even as Goneril and Regan fulfill the stereotype of insubordinate, lustful women, Shakespeare gives them psychological complexity: aggrieved by their father's clear preference for Cordelia, as long-suffering in their duty to one who has "ever but slenderly known himself"(1.1.291–292). Whether a production stages Lear's knights as actually unruly (as Peter Brooks did) can make a big difference in our perception of his daughters' objections to them. Cordelia, on the other hand, while often celebrated for purity, principle, and loyalty, refuses to flatter her father in a way that may well "have appeared as outrageous to a Jacobean audience" (R. A. Foakes, "Introduction," *King Lear*, p. 39). And, violating gender roles as well as national allegiance, she leads an army against England.

It should be noted that Renaissance understandings of the family were not solely concerned with the conduct of power. The nature of filial and paternal love was also a prime focus. What may be most striking to our own ears is the emphasis on the sheer exorbitance of a parent's love for a child. The fear is not that a parent would be too tyrannical, but rather too loving—or too "kind" a father, as Lear puts it, "whose frank heart gave all" (3.4.20). Love, as James I notes in *The Trew Law of Free Monarchies* (see earlier, p. 161), was thought to "descend" from above and was considered far stronger than a child's love for his or her parents. As intense as Lear's exercise of paternal power (e.g., his cursing of Goneril) is the strength of his fatherly affections. So his demand that his daughters say how much they love him may not be merely rhetorical but a genuine inquiry stemming from an anxious curiosity. Renaissance fatherhood was often imagined as a species of unrequited love—perhaps because in a hierarchical culture it was usually only the powerful who could speak. Children and other subordinates thus appear inscrutable and susceptible to misjudgment, as Lear and Gloucester demonstrate.

The selection from the domestic conduct book by William Gouge gives a sense of the cultural norms Shakespeare would have been working within and against. Another member of Lear's household, the fool, is illuminated by comparison with the selections from Armin and Erasmus.

Shakespeare's plays, more frequently than the more conventional texts of his culture, make matter (and poetry) out of the contradictions, blind spots, and conflicts of that culture. What does *King Lear* have in common with these conventional texts, and where does it leave them behind?

Michel de Montaigne (1533–1592)

The writings of the philosopher and essayist Michel de Montaigne were eagerly received far from his native France. John Florio's translation of Montaigne's Essays *appeared in 1603 and is linked to* King Lear *by instances of vocabulary (see R. A. Foakes,* King Lear, *p. 104) as well as by more thematic issues: the deforming power of property relations between generations; the onerousness of old age for both parent and child; and the potential advantage of distributing wealth to children when they are most in need of it.*

from "Of the Affection of Fathers for Their Children"[1]

If there be any law truly natural, that is to say, any instinct that is seen universally and perpetually imprinted in both beasts and men (which is not without controversy), I can say, that in my opinion, next to the care every animal has of its own preservation, and to avoid that which may hurt him, the affection that the begetter bears to his offspring holds the second place in this rank. And seeing that nature appears to have recommended it to us, having regard to the extension and progression of the successive pieces of this machine of hers, 'tis no wonder if, on the contrary, that of children toward their parents is not so great. [. . .]

[. . .] I, for my part, have a strange disgust for those propensions that are started in us without the mediation and direction of the judgment, as, upon the subject I am speaking of, I cannot entertain that passion of dandling and caressing infants scarcely born, having as yet neither motion of soul nor shape of body distinguishable, by which they can render themselves amiable, and have not willingly

---

[1]From *The Essays of Michel de Montaigne* (trans. Charles Cotton, ed. W. Carew Hazlitt, (London, 1892); ch. LIX, pp. 366–374, passim.

suffered them to be nursed near me.[2] A true and regular affection ought to spring and increase with the knowledge they give us of themselves, and then, if they are worthy of it, the natural propension walking hand in hand with reason, to cherish them with a truly paternal love; and so to judge, also, if they be otherwise, still rendering ourselves to reason, notwithstanding the inclination of nature. 'Tis oft times quite otherwise; and, most commonly, we find ourselves more taken with the running up and down, the games, and puerile simplicities of our children, than we do, afterward, with their most complete actions; as if we had loved them for our sport, like monkeys, and not as men; and some there are, who are very liberal in buying them balls to play withal, who are very close-handed for the least necessary expense when they come to age. Nay, it looks as if the jealousy of seeing them appear in and enjoy the world when we are about to leave it, rendered us more niggardly and stingy toward them; it vexes us that they tread upon our heels, as if to solicit us to go out[3]; if this were to be feared, since the order of things will have it so that they cannot, to speak the truth, be nor live, but at the expense of our being and life, we should never meddle with being fathers at all.

For my part, I think it cruelty and injustice not to receive them into the share and society of our goods, and not to make them partakers in the intelligence of our domestic affairs when they are capable, and not to lessen and contract own expenses to make the more room for theirs, seeing we beget them to that effect. 'Tis unjust that an old fellow, broken and half dead, should alone, in a corner of the chimney, enjoy the money that would suffice for the maintenance and advancement of many children, and suffer them, in the meantime, to lose their best years for want of means to advance themselves in the public service and the knowledge of men. A man by this course drives them to despair, and to seek out by any means, how unjust or dishonorable soever, to provide for their own support; as I have, in my time, seen several young men of good extraction so addicted to stealing that no correction could cure them of it. [. . .]

---

[2]It was common in aristocratic families to wet-nurse children out of the home.

[3]See Edmund's account of Edgar's impatience, and Gloucester's response, at 1.2.45–52.

And if a man should tell me, as a lord of very good understanding once did, that "he hoarded up wealth, not to extract any other fruit and use from his parismony, but to make himself honored and sought after by his relations; and that age having deprived him of all other power, it was the only remaining remedy to maintain his authority in his family, and to keep him from being neglected and despised by all around," in truth, not only old age, but all other imbecility, according to Aristotle,[4] is the promoter of avarice; that is something, but it is physic for a disease that a man should prevent the birth of. A father is very miserable who has no other hold on his children's affection than the need they have of his assistance, if that can be called affection; he must render himself worthy to be respected by his virtue and wisdom, and beloved by his kindness and the sweetness of his manners; even the very ashes of a rich matter have their value; and we are wont to have the bones and relics of worthy men in regard and reverence. No old age can be so decrepit in a man who has passed his life in honor, but it must be venerable, especially to his children, whose soul he must have trained up to their duty by reason, not by necessity and the need they have of him, not by harshness and compulsion. [. . .]

Do we desire to be beloved of our children? Will we remove from them all occasion of wishing our death (though no occasion of so horrid a wish can either be just or excusable, *"Nullum scelus rationem habet"*[5]), let us reasonably accommodate their lives with what is in our power. In order to this, we should not marry so young that our age shall in a manner be confounded with theirs; for this inconvenience plunges us into many very great difficulties, and especially the gentry of the nation, who are of a condition wherein they have little to do, and who live upon their rents only: for elsewhere, with people who live by their labor, the pluralty and company of children is an increase of the common stock; they are so many new tools and instruments wherewith to grow rich. [. . .]

But a father worn out with age and infirmities, and deprived by his weakness and want of health of the common society of men,

---

[4]Aristotle (384–322 BCE) was a Greek philosopher (and student of Plato) whose writings treat matters of logic, metaphysics, the natural world, politics, ethics, and art.

[5]"No wickedness is founded on reason." (From *Ab urbe condita libri* xxviii, by Titus Livius (59 BCE–17 CE). This 142-book history of Rome, from its origins to 9 BCE, is famed for its oratorical style.

wrongs himself and his to rake together a great mass of treasure. He has lived long enough, if he be wise, to have a mind to strip himself to go to bed, not to his very shirt, I confess, but to that, and a good warm dressing-gown; the remaining pomps, of which he has no further use, he ought voluntarily to surrender to those to whom by the order of nature they belong.[6] 'Tis reason he should refer the use of these things to them, seeing that nature has reduced him to such a state that he cannot enjoy them himself; otherwise there is doubtless malice and envy in the case. The greatest act of the Emperor Charles V[7] was that when, in imitation of some of the ancients of his own quality, confessing it but reason to strip ourselves when our clothes encumber and grow too heavy for us, and to lie down when our legs begin to fail us, he resigned his possessions, grandeur, and power to his son, when he found himself failing in vigor and steadiness for the conduct of his affairs suitable with the glory he had therein acquired.

"Solve senescentem mature sanus equum, ne Peccet ad extremum ridendus, et ilia ducat."[8]

This fault of not perceiving betimes and of not being sensible of the feebleness and extreme alteration that age naturally brings both upon body and mind, which, in my opinion, is equal, if indeed the soul has not more than half, has lost the reputation of most of the great men in the world. I have known in my time, and been intimately acquainted with persons of great authority, whom one might easily discern marvelously lapsed from the sufficiency I knew they were once endued with, by the reputation they had acquired in their former years, whom I could heartily, for their own sakes, have wished at home at their ease, discharged of their public or military employments, which were now grown too heavy for their shoulders. [. . .]

I do not mean that a man should so install them [his children] as not to reserve to himself a liberty to retract; I, who am now

---

[6]Compare with Goneril's opinion at 2.4.259–261: "What need you five-and-twenty, ten, or five, / To follow in a house where twice so many / Have a command to tend you?" or Regan, 2.4.198: "I pray you, father, being weak, seem so."

[7]Charles V (1500–1558) Emperor of the Holy Roman Empire 1519–1556.

[8]"Dismiss the old horse in good time, lest, falling in the lists, the spectators laugh." Horace, *Epistles* I book 8. Horace (65–8 BC) was a Latin poet, his *Epistles* treat philosophical questions about how best to lead one's life.

arrived to the age wherein such things are fit to be done, would resign to them the enjoyment of my house and goods, but with a power of revocation if they should give me cause to alter my mind; I would leave to them the use, that being no longer convenient for me; and, of the general authority and power over all, would reserve as much as I thought good to myself: having always held that it must needs be a great satisfaction to an aged father himself to put his children into the way of governing his affairs, and to have power during his own life to control their behavior, supplying them with instruction and advice from his own experience, and himself to transfer the ancient honor and order of his house into the hands of those who are to succeed him, and by that means to satisfy himself as to the hopes he may conceive of their future conduct. And in order to this I would not avoid their company; I would observe them near at hand, and partake, according to the condition of my age, of their feasts and jollities. If I did not live absolutely among them, which I could not do without annoying them and their friends, by reason of the morosity of my age and the restlessness of my infirmities, and without violating also the rules and order of living I should then have set down to myself, I would, at least, live near them in some retired part of my house, not the best in show, but the most commodious. [. . .] I would endeavor by pleasant conversation to create in my children a warm and unfeigned friendship and good will toward me, which in well descended natures is not hard to do; for if they be furious brutes, of which this age of ours produces thousands, we are then to hate and avoid them as such. [. . .] And 'tis also folly and injustice to deprive children, when grown up, of familiarity with their father, and to carry a scornful and austere countenance toward them, thinking by that to keep them in awe and obedience; for it is a very idle farce that, instead of producing the effect designed, renders fathers distasteful, and, which is worse, ridiculous to their own children. They have youth and vigor in possession, and consequently the breath and favor of the world; and therefore receive these fierce and tyrannical looks—mere scarecrows—of a man without blood, either in his heart or veins, with mockery and contempt. Though I could make myself feared, I had yet much rather make myself beloved: there are so many sorts of defects in old age, so much imbecility, and it is so liable to contempt, that the best acquisition a man can make is the kindness and affection of his own family; command and fear are no longer his weapons.

William Gouge (1578–1653)

> *As a puritan, minister William Gouge articulates a strand of social thought far removed from the noble family. Puritan "conduct books" were intended to render the family a nursery of spiritual life as well as of the economic prosperity that Protestants took to signify God's favor. Yet even from this perspective, much of Gouge's text describes the obligations and behaviors of the early modern nuclear family in general and codifies identities and affects that were widely familiar. Note his emphasis on the differences between a child's love for his or her parents and a parent's for a child, and compare his description of a servant's behavior with the conduct of the disguised Kent, Oswald, or Cornwall's servants.*

from *Of Domesticall Duties* (London, 1622)

1. *Of children's love to their parents* (pp. 428–430)

I make the fountain[1] of children's duties to be a mixed and compound disposition, in respect of that authority and affection which is mixed together in parents. The authority of parents requireth fear in children, and their affection, love. So entire and so ardent is parents' affection towards their children, as it would make children too bold and insolent if there were not authority mixed therewith to work fear: and so supreme and absolute is their authority over them, as it would make children like slaves to dread their parents, if a fatherly affection were not tempered therewith to breed love. But both these joined together make a very good composition: love like sugar sweetneth fear, and fear like salt seasoneth love: and thus, to join them both together, it is a loving-fear, or a fearing-love, which is the ground of children's duties.

Where Christ forbiddeth an excessive love in children to their parents,[2] he implieth that parents are a fit object for children to love,

---

[1]Source.

[2]Marginal note reads Matthew 10.37: "He that loveth father or mother more than me is not worthy of me: and he that loveth son or daughter more than me is not worthy of me."

so as their love be well moderated: yea he implieth that it is an affection even by nature ingraffed[3] in children to love their parents [. . .]

That love which naturally parents have to their children, ought in equity to breed in children a love to their parents. For love deserveth love: and most unworthy are they to be loved, who cannot love again. The love of parents above all others is to be answered with love on children's part to the uttermost of their power, because it is free, great, and constant.

Besides, there is a necessity of love in children to their parents, lest for want thereof, their subjection (which of all others ought to be most free) should turn into slavish servitude.

This ought children the rather to labour after, because by nature they are nothing so prone to love their parents, as their parents are to love them. Love is weighty, and, as weighty things, it descendeth. Children therefore with conscience of duty must labour to make supply of this defect, and help nature by grace. I deny not but naturally there is in children a greater love to their parents, than to others: yet in comparison the heat of parents love to them, their love to their parents is but cold. Wherefore as the heat of the Sun shining much and long on a stone wall, draweth a reflection of heat from that wall: so the hot beams of parents love, which with fervency and constancy is cast on children, ought to provoke and stir up children to send forth a reflection of love on their parents. [. . .]

3. Of a child's feare of his parent. (pp. 431–432)

To the forenamed duty of love, must feare be added, which is a childes awful respect of his parent.

This awful respect ariseth from an honourable esteem which a child in his judgment and opinion hath of his parent, as he is his parent; and from it proceedeth on the one side, a desire and endeavour in all things to please the parent, and on the other side a loathness[4] to offend him.

In this respect the fear of a child is opposed to the fear of a slave. For a childes fear being mixed with love, hath respect to the offense which a parent may take: but a slaves fear, which is ordinarily mixed

[3]Ingrained.
[4]Reluctance.

with hatred, hath respect to nothing but the punishment which his master may inflict upon him. The forenamed fear is so proper to children, as that awful respect which the Saints bear to God, is called a filial or child-like fear.

This fear in a child is an especial branch of that honour which the law requireth of children to their parents[5] [. . .] this fear keepeth love in compass, and restraineth a children from overmuch sauciness, and malipartness.[6]

And it is a case of a childes reverend and dutiful carriage to his parent. For as the heart is affected the carriage will be ordered. [. . .]

Wherefore to breed and cherish this fear, and to prevent or redress the contrary extreme, let children well inform themselves of their parents place and authority, how they are in Gods stead, and a means under God of their children's being: children have received their very substance from the substance of their parents. In which respect though they should seem contemptible to others, yet not to their children.

4. *Of a childes reverence in refraining speech before his parent, and his hearkening to his parent.* (pp. 434–435)

The outward reverence which children owe to their parents consisteth partly in their speech, partly in their carriage.[7]

Their speech both to and of their parents must savor of reverence. [. . .]

The two branches of silence, in forbearing to speak (especially when parents are speaking, or till parents give leave to their children to speak,) and in breaking off speech, when parents come into the place where children are speaking, are tokens of great reverence. Thus children testify that there are some in place whom they much respect and honour. [. . .] The like may be said of children's patience in enduring their parents speech [. . .] though parents in their speech seem to be long and tedious, yet must children endure it.

And it is very needful that patience be added to silence, because many parents in tender love of their children, and earnest desire of

---

[5]Marginal note reads Exodus 20.12: "Honor thy father and thy mother: that thy days may be long upon the land which the Lord thy God giveth thee."

[6]Back-talking.

[7]Demeanor.

their good, think they can never speak enough in instructing and admonishing them. The many exhortations given in Scripture unto children to *hear, hearken, give ear, give heed, mark*, and *observe* the words of their parents, doe imply the forenamed patience and silence. [. . .]

Contrary to silence is sauciness (as we speak) and overmuch boldness in children. [. . .]

5. Of a childes reverence in framing his speech to his parent.

A childes reverence in well framing his speech to his parents may many waies be manifested, as

1. By giving unto them reverend and honourable titles. [. . .]
2. By using few words before their parents: and those few not without just occasion, being first spoken to by their parents, or having leave of them, or making known to them some needful matter: at least not against their parents liking, so as their parents should be offended thereby. And if they observe their parents to be unwilling to hear them speak any more of such and such a matter, then ought they to lay their hands upon their mouths, as Isaac (Genesis 22.7) and Jacob (Genesis 27.12). This is a token of great respect. [. . .]

6. Of the vices in children contrary to the forenamed reverence in speech.

1. *Pride*: when children scorn to give the title of Father, or Mother, to their parents. This is the mind of many who have gotten more wealth or honour, then ever their parents had. In public especially such children most refuse to give those titles. *Solomon* was not so minded. He being a great king, sitting upon his throne, in sight and hearing of all his people that were about him, called *Bathsheba Mother*.
2. *Loquacity*, and too much importunity, or rather impudence in speech, when children having to do with their parents, can never have done (as we speak) but must needs urge matters to the very uttermost. Many parents are much provoked thereby. It skilleth not that the childe have the right, especially in a matter of no great consequence. For reverence sake the child must forbear, at least for a time. [. . .]

3. *Stoutness*, when children answer their parents as if they were their equals: giving word for word. It doth as ill become children to answer again, as servants (to whom the Apostle hath expressly forbidden it, Tit. 2.9). Both law and nature forbiddeth children to be provoked hereunto, by any thing that their parents say or doe; how great then is their fault who give scornful and stout words to their parents when they are no way provoked. [. . .]

5. *Stubborness*, when children pout, lour, swell, and give no answer at all to their parents. This is too common a fault in children, and many parents are much offended and grieved thereat. We heard before of a childlike silence which was very commendable, and a token of great reverence, but this is worthy of much blame, a token of great undutifulness, and as carefully to be avoided, as that to be practiced.

*   *   *

Duties of Parents

1. *Of that love which parents owe to their children.* (pp. 498–499)

The fountain of parents duties is Love. This is expressly enjoined to them. Many approved examples are recorded hereof: as Abraham's, Isaacs, Rebekah's, and others.[8]

Great reason there is why this affection should be fast fixed in the heart of parents towards their children. For great is the pain, pains, cost, and care, which parents must undergo for their children. But if love be in them, no pain, pains, cost, or care will seem too much. Herein appeareth the wise providence of God, who by nature hath so fast fixed love in the hearts of parents, as if there be any in whom it aboundeth not, he is counted unnatural. If love did not abound in parents, many children would be neglected and lost. For if parents look not to their children, who will? If none look to them, they must needs perish, for they are not able to help themselves. As God by nature hath planted love in all parents, so Christians ought even for conscience sake, to nourish, increase, and blow up this fire of love, that they may thereby be made more forward to do every duty with cheerfulness. The more fervent love is, the more

---

[8]See Genesis 22.2 and 25.8 for these stories of parental devotion.

readily will every duty be performed. [. . .] The extreme contrary to love in the defect is want of natural affection, which is reckoned in the catalogue of notorious sins. Though love of children be by nature engraven in mans heart, yet many clean put it out through covetousness, lust vain-glory, superstition, idolatry, and other vices: whereby it commeth to pass that in stead of the good which they should do for their children, they bring much mischief upon them. [. . .] too high on this ladder of unnaturalness do they climb, who hate their children, and that (which make the sin to be out of measure sinful) for piety and integrity: as many Popish and profane parents, who have children truly religious: and in that respect ought so much the more to be loved.[9]

The extreme in the excess [of loving] is too much doting upon children: as they do who so unmeasurably love them, as they make reckoning of nothing in comparison of children. Even God himself is lightly esteemed, his worship neglected, his word transgressed, all duty to others omitted, their own souls forgotten through care of children. Is not this mere apish kindness? For Apes kill their young ones with hugging. This is not love, but plain dotage. But what may be said of those that are so hellishly enamored of their children as to commit incest or buggery with them?

* * *

Duties of Servants

Of a servants fear of his master (pp. 594–595)

The other part of that fountain, from whence the duties of servants flow, resteth in the affection: and it is in one word Fear: which is an awful dread of a master. An awe in regard of his masters place, a dread in regard of his masters power. An awe is such a reverend esteem of his master, as maketh him *account his master worthy of all honor*: which St. Paul expressly enjoineth servants to do.[10] A dread is such a fear of provoking his master's wrath, as maketh him think and cast every way how to please him. This is it which the

---

[9]Religious difference between parents and children was a potential source of inter-generational conflict in the wake of the Reformation.

[10]Marginal note reads 1 Timothy 6.1: "Let as many servants as are under the yoke count their own masters worthy of all honour, that the name of God and his doctrine be not blasphemous."

Apostle here intimateth under these two words, fear and trembling. In both these respects St. Peter commandeth servants to be subject in all fear.[11]

So proper is this fear to a servant in relation to his master, as where it is wanting, there is a plain denial of his masters place and power, which God intimateth under this expostilation, *If I be a master, where is my feare?*[12] That is you plainly show that you account me not your master, because in your heart there is no fear of me.

This fear will draw servants on, cheerfully to perform all duty: the more it aboundeth, the more desire and endeavor there will be to please, and to give good contentment (and this is a point commanded to servants, *to please well in all things:*[13]) yea it will glad the heart of a servant to see his service prosper well: hereof we have a worthy pattern in Abraham's servant, whose care to do his business, as his master would have it, and prayer for God's assistance therein, and thanks for God's blessing thereon, sheweth an aweful respect which he bare to his master.

Again, on the other side, this fear will keep men from offending their masters [. . .] and in this respect it may prevent many mischiefs which their masters offence and wrath might bring upon them.

One especial means to breed and preserve this fear in servants, is, a due consideration of the ground of their masters place and power: which is God's appointment: God hath placed them in his stead, and in part given them his power: they are the Deputies and Ministers of God, and therefore in Scripture the title "Lord" is after a peculiar manner given to them. What maketh subjects stand in awe of inferior Magistrates? Is it not because they bear the King's person, and have authority and power given unto them of the King?

---

[11]Marginal note reads 1 Peter 2.18: "Servants be subject to your masters with all fear; not only to the good and gentle, but also to the forward."

[12]Malachi 1.6.

[13]Marginal note reads Titus 2.9: "Exhort servants to be obedient unto their own masters, and to please them well in all things, not answering again."

Joseph Swetnam (fl. 1617)

Joseph Swetnam's text launched an early-seventeenth-century skirmish in a pamphlet war that had been waged for centuries.[1] Debate on the relative merits of female virtues and vices had long been the matter of rhetorical training and display, a feature that perhaps accounts for the flamboyant nature of Swetnam's portrait of female weaknesses. Behind every joke lies a truth, however, and this selection can be compared to the fool's recurrent comments on female chastity, Albany's reaction to Goneril, Lear's diatribe against the female sex in 4.6.116–127 (prompted by his recognition of the play's chief adulterer, Gloucester), or the unchaste ambitions of Goneril and Regan for Edmund.

from *The Arraignment of Lewd, Idle, Forward, and Unconstant Women* . . . with a commendation of wise, virtuous, and honest women. Pleasant for Married Men, profitable for Young men, and hurtfull to none. (London, 1615) Ch. 1.

CHAPTER I. This first Chapter showeth to what use Women were made; it also showeth that most of them degenerate from the use they were framed unto by leading a proud, lazy, and idle life, to the great hindrance of their poor Husbands.

Moses[2] describeth a woman thus: "At the first beginning," saith "A woman was made to be a helper unto man." And so they are deed, for she helpeth to spend and consume that which man painfully getteth. He also saith that they were made of the rib of a man, and that their forward nature showeth; for a rib is a crooked thing good for nothing else, and women are crooked by nature, for small occcasion will cause them to be angry.

Again, in a manner she was no sooner made but straightway her mind was set upon mischief, for by her aspiring mind and wanton will she quickly procured man's fall. And therefore ever since they are and have been a woe unto man and follow the line of their first leader.

---

[1]See *Half Humankind, Contexts and Texts of the Controversy about Women in England 1540–1640*, eds. Katherine Usher Henderson and Barbara F. McManus (Urbana, Illinois, 1985); and Linda Woodbridge, *Women and the English Renaissance: Literature and the Nature of Womankind 1540–1620* (Urbana, Illinois, 1986).

[2]See Genesis 2.18.

For I pray you, let us consider the times past with the time present: first, that of David and Solomon,[3] if they had occasion so many hundred years ago to exclaim so bitterly against women. For the one of them said that it was better to be a doorkeeper and better dwell in a den amongst Lions than to be in the house with a froward and wicked woman, and the other said that the climbing up of a sandy hill to an aged man was nothing so wearisome as to be troubled with a froward woman. And further he saith that the malice of a beast is not like the malice of a wicked woman, nor that there is nothing more dangerous than a women in her fury.

The Lion being bitten with hunger, the Bear being robbed of her young ones, the Viper being trod on, all these are nothing so terrible as the fury of a woman. A buck may be enclosed in a Park; a bridle rules a horse; a Wolf may be tied; a Tiger may be tamed; but a froward woman will never be tamed.[4] No spur will make her go, nor no bridle will hold her back, for if a woman hold an opinion, no man can draw her from it. Tell her of her fault, she will not believe that she is in any fault; give her good counsel, but she will not take it. If you do but look after another woman, then she will be jealous; the more thou lovest her, the more she will disdain thee. And if thou threaten her, then she will be angry; flatter her, and then she will be proud. And if thou forbear her,[5] it maketh her bold, and if thou chasten her, then she will turn to a Serpent. At a word, a woman will never forget an injury nor give thanks for a good turn. What wise man then will exchange gold for dross, pleasure for pain, a quiet life for wrangling brawls, from the which the married men are never free?

Solomon saith that women are like unto wine, for that they will make men drunk with their devices.

Again in their love a woman is compared to a pumice stone, for which way soever you turn a pumice stone, it is full of holes; even so are women's hearts, for if love steal in at one hole it steppeth out at another.

---

[3]David and Solomon were ancient Hebrew kings, reputed to have written, respectively, many of the Psalms and the Proverbs.

[4]Compare with the play's many comparisons of women to animals, e.g., in 4.2.41.

[5]Suffer her scolding; compare with Lear's description of Cordelia's voice in 5.3.272–273.

They are also compared unto a painted ship, which seemeth fair outwardly and yet nothing but ballast within her; or as the Idols in Spain which are bravely gilt outwardly and yet nothing but lead within them; or like unto the Sea which at some times is so calm that a cockboat may safely endure her might, but anon again with outrage she is so grown that it overwhelmeth the tallest ship that is.

Jane Anger (fl. 1589)

Like Joseph Swetnam's text, Jane Anger's is a rejoinder in a debate and is the first English defense of women possibly written by a woman. No other information about the author besides the name exists, apart from the title page's notation of her as a "gentlewoman," and it is possible that the name is a pseudonym, perhaps even for a male author, as the rhetorical debate convention in which this text is located (in which authors argued pro *and* contra *female worth) often instanced male authors publishing on both sides of the controversy. Like many of its kind, this text's warrants for female virtue are both scriptural and classical: for every Eve, there is a Mary, and for every Helen, a Lucrece.*

from *Her Protection for Women* (London, 1589), passim.

The creation of man and woman at the first, he being formed *In principio*[1] of dross and filthy clay, did so remain until God saw that in him his workmanship was good, and therefore by the transformation of the dust which was loathsome unto flesh it became purified. Then lacking a help for him, God, making woman of man's flesh that she might be purer than he, doth evidently show how far we women are more excellent than men. Our bodies are fruitful, whereby the world increaseth, and our care wonderful, by which man is preserved. From woman sprang man's salvation. A woman was the first that believed, and a women likewise the first that repented of sin. In women is only true Fidelity; except in her there is [no] constancy, and without her no Housewifery. In the time of their sickness we cannot be wanted,[2] and when they are in health

[1]In the beginning.
[2]Missed.

we for them are most necessary. They are comforted by our means; they [are] nourished by the meats we dress; their bodies [are] freed from diseases by our cleanliness, which otherwise would surfeit unreasonably through their own noisomeness. Without our care they lie in their beds as dogs in litter and go like lost Mackerel swimming in the heat of summer.[3] They love to go handsomely in their apparel and rejoice in the pride thereof, yet who is the cause of it but our carefulness, to see that everything about them be curious?[4] Our virginity makes us virtuous; our conditions, courteous; and our chastity maketh our trueness of love manifest. They confess we are necessary, but they would have us likewise evil. [. . .] That we are liberal they will not deny, since that many of them have (*ex confesso*[5]) received more kindness in one day at our hands than they can repay in a whole year, and some have so glutted themselves with our liberality as they cry "No more."

Fools and Folly

Lear's "all-licensed" fool represents a different species of subordinate from children or servants, and the enigma of his presence warrants special attention. He seems halfway between a child and a servant (and the role was often doubled by the actor, or these days, actress, playing Cordelia). The "court fool" had a long history, although James I's fool, Archie Armstrong, was the first court fool in England in many years.

Royal fools came in two sorts. A "natural" fool was someone either mentally or physically unusual (a dwarf, for instance), perceived as having a kind of simpleton's wisdom; an "artificial" fool was the more professional wit, a species of clown. Although critics have debated what kind of fool Lear's is, both kinds were permitted a proximity to, and irreverence toward, the powerful not allowed

---

[3]Mackerel beached themselves in spawning season.

[4]Well-appointed.

[5]Admittedly (by admission).

to other kinds of followers. A fool's function was thus part truth-teller, part entertainer.

Desiderious Erasmus (1467–1536)

Renaissance humanist Desiderious Erasmus is famed for having rein-troduced irony into Renaissance discourse, in his hugely popular satire against theologians and dignitaries, Enconmium Moriae *(Cologne, 1526), translated into English as* The Praise of Folly *by Thomas Chaloner in 1549. In a later defense of the work to his friend, the theologian Martin Dorp, Erasmus lays out some of the conventions of satirical speech we see in the patterns and riddles of Lear's fool.*

from *A Letter to Martin Dorp* (Antwerp, 1515)

The philosopher Plato, serious-minded though he is, approves of lavish drinking-matches at banquets because he believes that there are certain faults which austerity correct but the gaiety of wine-drinking can dispel. And Horace[1] thinks that joking advice does as much good as serious."What stops a man who can laugh," he said, "from speaking the truth?" This was surely well understood by the famous sages of antiquity who chose to present the most salutary counsel for life in the form of amusing and apparently childish fables, because truth can seem harsh if unadorned, but with something pleasurable to recommend it can penetrate more easily the minds of mortals. No doubt this is the honey which doctors in Lucretius[2] smear on the rim of a cup of wormwood which they pre-scribe for children. And the sort of fools which princes of former times introduced into their courts were there for the express pur-pose of exposing and thereby correcting certain minor faults through their frank speech which offended no one. It would per-haps seem inappropriate to add Christ to this list, but if divine mat-ters are at all comparable with human, his parables have surely

---

[1]Roman poet (65–8 BCE).

[2]Epicurean poet (c. 94–55 or 51 BCE), author of *De Rerum Natura* (*On the Nature of Things*). Wormwood is a bitter herb used as a medicine to kill worms.

some affinity with the fables of the ancients. The truth of the gospel slips more pleasantly into the mind and takes firmer grip there if it is attractively clothed than it would if it were presented undisguised, something which St. Augustine[3] amply confirms in his work *On Christian Doctrine.* [. . .]

[. . .] Make your appeal, says Paul, argue and reprove, in season and out of season. If the apostle wants faults to be attacked in every possible way, do you really want no sore spot to be touched, even when this is done so gently that no one could possibly be hurt unless he deliberately sets out to hurt himself? [. . .] Finally, put everything into the mouth of a comic character so that it will amuse and divert, and the humour of the spoken word will remove any offensiveness. We have all seen how an appropriate and well-timed joke can sometimes influence even grim tyrants. What pleasant or serious speech do you think could have calmed the rage of the great king Pyrrhus[4] as easily as the joke the soldier made? "Why, if only our bottle hadn't given out," he said, "we'd have said far worse things about you." The king laughed and pardoned him. And the two greatest orators, Cicero[5] and Quintilian,[6] had every reason for laying down rules for raising a laugh. Speech which has wit and charm has such power to please that we can enjoy a well-turned phrase even if it is aimed at ourselves, as history relates of Julius Caesar.[7]

Robert Armin (fl. 1610)

Joining Shakespeare's company in 1600, Robert Armin was the actor who played Lear's fool, influencing a shift in Shakespeare's characterizations from the clown (Launcelot Gobbo or Dogberry, played by Will

[3]Early Christian theologian (354–436 CE); his work *On Christian Doctrine* is a vindication of Christianity.

[4]Pyrrhus of Epirus (319–272 BCE) was the most famous of the kings of Molissi, chief architect of a large and powerful state in the northwest area of Greece.

[5]Marcus Tullius Cicero (106–43 BCE), a renowned Roman rhetorician and orator.

[6]Marcus Fabius Quintilian (c. 35–90s CE), a Roman advocate and famous authority on rhetoric.

[7]Julius Caesar (100–44 BCE), a Roman dictator.

Kemp) to a more melancholy court fool (Touchstone or Feste). Armin himself published a book on fools—Foole upon Foole, or Six Sortes of Sottes—*which recounts the (possibly apocryphal) exploits of six contemporary fools. One of the most legendary was Henry VIII's fool Will Sommer (unlike Lear's fool, he was more a jester than a truth-teller).* Foole upon Foole *was very popular and was reprinted in three editions in less than a decade, the last in a pirated text titled* Nest of Ninnies *(1608). This excerpt recounts an incident from Will Sommer's career, here as king's comforter and discomfitor.*

from *Foole upon Foole* (London, 1600); pp. 119–120, 126–128

[5.0] *A description how this merry foole being Will Sommers (the Kings naturall Jester) was as report tels me.*

> Will Sommers borne in Shropshire, as some say,
> Was brought to Greenwich on a holly day:[1]
> Presented to the King, which foole disdain'd   5
> To shake him by the hand, or else asham'd.
> How ere it was, as auncient people say,
> With much a doe was wonne to it that day.
>
> Leane he was, hollow eyde as all report,
> And stoop he did too, yet in all the Court   10
> Few men were more belov'd then was this foole,
> Whose merry prate,[2] kept with the King much rule.
> When he was sad, the King and he would rime,
> Thus Will exiled sadnes many a time.
>
> I could describe him as I did the rest,   15
> But in my minde I doe not thinke it best:
> My reason this, how ere I doe descry him,
> So many knew him that I may belye him.[3]

[1] Holiday.
[2] Prattle.
[3] Misrepresent.

Therefore to please all people one by one,
I holde it best to let that paines alone.   20

Onely thus much, he was a poore mans friend,
And helpt the widdow often in the ende:
The King would ever graunt, what he did crave,
For well he knew, Will no exacting knave,
But wisht the King to doe good deedes great store,   25
Which cause'd the Court to love him more and more.

[. . .]

How this merry foole Will Sommers, to make the King merry asked
him three questions.

How soever these three thinges came in memory, and are for
mirth inserted into Stage playes, I know not, but that Will Sommers
asked them of the King, it is certaine, there are some will affirme it
now living in Greenwich: the King upon a time being extreame
melancholy and full of passion, all that Will Sommers could do,
would not make him merry: Ah says he, this cloude must have a
good showre to clense it, and with that goes behinde the Arras:[4]
Harry says he, Ile goe behinde the Arras and study[5] thee three
questions, and come againe: see therefore you lay aside this melan-
cholye muze, and study to answere mee. I[6] quoth the King, they will
bee wise ones no doubt: at the last out comes William with his wit,
as the foole of the play doth with an anticke looke to please the
beholders. Harry saies he, what is that the lesser it is the more it is
to be feared? The K. muzed at it, but to grace the jest the better (for
he was in that humor to grace good wil, the excellenst Prince of the
earth) the King made answere he knew not: Will made answere it
was a little bridge over a deepe river: at which he smiled, knowing it
was fearfull indeede. What is the next William says the King?
mary[7] this is next, what is the cleanliest trade in the world? mary
sayes the King, I thinke a Comfetmaker,[8] for he deales with nothing

---

[4]Tapestry (after the town in France where produced).

[5]Prepare for you.

[6]Aye.

[7]Marry, indeed.

[8]Apothecary, or maker of preserves and sweetmeets (comfits).

but pure ware, and is attyred cleane in white linnen, when he sels it. No Harry saies Will you are wide,[9] what say you then qu. the King? mary sayes Will I say a durt dauber:[10] out on it sayes the K. that is the foulest, for he is durty up to the elboes. I saies Wil, but then hee washes him cleane againe, and eates his meate cleanly enough. I promise thee Wil saies the K. thou hast a pretty foolish wit: I Harry saies he, it will serve to make a wiser man then you a foole me thinkes: at this the King laught, and demands the third question. Now tel me saies Wil (if you can,) what it is that being borne without life, head, nose, lip or eye, and yet runs terribly roaring throgh the world till it dyes? This is a wonder quoth the King, and no question, and I know it not: Why quoth Will it is a fart. At this the King laught hartily, and was exceeding merry, and bids Will aske any reasonable thing and he would grant it. Thankes Harry saies he, now against I want I know where to finde, for yet I need nothing, but one day I shall for every man sees his latter ende, but knows not his beginning: the King understood his meaning, and so pleasantly departed for that season, and Will layes him downe amongst the Spaniels to sleep.

[9]Off the mark.
[10]A plasterer.

"Good" and "Evil"

King Lear animates a bewildering variety of viewpoints on the supernatural. There are characters who invoke the pagan gods (Lear, 1.4.258); those who doubt the very existence of a deity (Edmund, 1.2.111ff); others convinced, in a rather Old Testament way, of divine vengeance upon human sinfulness (Edgar, 5.3.170–174); and yet others who seem to bear the sufferings and capacity for forgiveness of Christ himself (Cordelia, 4.7.78). In this world of violent, often irrational passions and capricious justice, Shakespeare asks us to confront the question of a human being's ethical nature. Are we subject to a higher law, even if only the good of the community? Are people accountable only to their own, often base, self-interests?

King Lear is nominally set in pre-Christian times (according to Holinshed, 800 BCE). For the audience of Shakespeare's day, such antiquity was regarded as prone to depravity, for which Christianity would prove the remedy and salvation. Shakespeare's early-seventeenth-century audience, moreover, was not just Christian but Protestant, and thus, from their point of view, that much further along to the "promised end" of the apocalypse and the Last Judgment (Roman Catholicism was considered to be superstition). From this vantage point, the confusion and lawlessness that reigns in *King Lear* could have seemed the effect of its remoteness from the Christian era. Yet much of the emotional power of *King Lear* arises from the dramatic and psychological immediacy of its passions and conflicts.

Reformation Christianity, including English Protestantism, was riven with schisms, sects with different views on salvation and on the relationship between church organization and state power. Nor was the Protestant conception of God without difficulties, particularly because salvation was no longer, as in medieval Christianity, a result of works or merit but was the gift of God's mysterious grace extended to the irretrievably unworthy human being. The unpredictability, indeed, the inscrutability, of this God informs *King Lear*. The random indifference of the deity feared by Gloucester, for instance—"As flies to wanton boys are we to th' gods; / They kill us for their sport" (4.1.36–37)—resonates with the God imagined by Calvin, one highly selective in his offers of salvation. The genre of early modern tragedy, as an agon of irrecoverable loss, reflects this shift from an inclusive to a selective deity.

The prospect of a distant, discriminating, or indifferent deity involves a host of questions about human beings. Was a person damned or elect? Out for himself or capable of fellow feeling, including compassion, or the capacity for forgiveness? How could one even know a person's character in a world in which appearances are deceiving? The origin of both Lear's and Gloucester's tragedies in an inability to recognize love belongs with these kinds of problems.

King Lear dramatizes a variety of complex ethical stances. (Even Edmund ends, belatedly, with the thought of doing "Some good . . . / Despite of mine own nature" (5.3.243–244).) Shakespeare's culture contained both anxiety and assurance about the beneficence of God and the human capacity for goodness, as well as evil. The following texts provide glimpses of the varied understandings during the seventeenth century about the relationship of fellow human beings to the heavens and to each other.

William Harrison (1535–1593)

William Harrison was an Elizabethan clergyman. Harrison's description of Celtic Britain (before Christianity) gives a sense of the historical and cultural location of the original Lear story, as well as the suspicion in which this prehistoric period was held by those in Shakespeare's own time. The "Ancient Religion" was associated with idolatry, poly-theism, sacrifice, and great instability; but Harrison also notes resemblances between ancient times and his own late-sixteenth-century English religious polity.

from "Of the Ancient Religion Used in Albion"[1]
An Historical Description of the Island of Britain in Raphael Holinshed, *Chronicles,* book 1 (1587).

Chapt. IX

[. . .] In the beginning this Druiyus[2] did preach unto his hearers, that the soule of man is immortall, that God is omnipotent, mercifull as a father in shewing favor unto the godlie, and just as an upright judge in punishing the wicked; that the secrets of mans hart are not unknowne, and onelie knowne to him; and that as the world and all that is therein had their beginning by him, at his owne will, so shall all things likewise have an end, when he shall see his time. He taught them also with more facilitie, how to observe the courses of the heavens and motions of the planets by arithmeticall industrie, to find out the true quantities of the celestiall bodies by geometricall demonstration, and thereto the compasse of the earth, and hidden natures of things contained in the same by philosophicall contemplation. But alas, this integritie continued not long among his successors, for unto the immortalitie of the soule, they added, that after death it went into another bodie [. . .] the second or succedent, being alwaies either more noble, or more vile than the former, as the partie deserved by his merits, whilest he lived here upon earth [. . .] For said they (of whom Pythagoras,[3] also had, and taught this errour) if the soule apperteined at the first to a king, and he in this estate did not leade his life worthie this calling, it should after his decease be shut up in the bodie of a slave, beggar, cocke,

---

[1]Albion was the ancient name of Britain, either after the white ("alb") cliffs of Dover or after the legendary giant Albion, son of Neptune, reputed to have discovered the country (although later in this selection Albion is a descendent of Cham).

[2]Druiyus was the founder of Druidism. The supremacy of even pre-Christian British religion elaborated here is in keeping with Protestant England's conviction of its own religious pride of place; so too the narrative of degeneration resembled the account in which the practices of Roman Catholicism degraded the purity of the primitive church.

[3]Pythagoras (c. 600s BCE) was said to have introduced the doctrine of transmigration of souls introduced into Greece.

owle, dog, ape, horsse, asse, worme, or monster, there to remaine as in a place of purgation and punishment for a certeine period of time. [. . .] Beside this, it should peradventure sustaine often translation from one bodie unto another, according to the quantitie and quality of his doings here on earth, till it should finallie be purified, and restored againe to an other humane bodie, wherein if it behaved itself more orderlie than at the first: after the next death, it should be preferred, either to the bodie of a king, or other great estate. And thus they made a perpetuall circulation or resolution of our soules, much like unto the continuall motion of the heavens, which never stand still, nor long yeeld one representation and figure. [. . .] They brought in also the worshipping of manie gods, and their severall sacrifices: they honoured likewise the oke,[4] whereon the mistle[5] groweth, and dailie devised infinite other toies[6] (for errour is never assured of hir owne doings) whereof neither Samothes nor Sarron, Magus, nor Druiyus[7] did leave them anie prescription. [. . .]

After the death of Druiyus, Badus his sonne, and fift king of the Celts, succeeded not onelie over the said kingdome, but also in his fathers vertues, whereby it is verie likelie, that the winding and wrapping up of the said religion, after the afore remembred sort into verse, was first devised by him, for he was an excellent poet, and no lesse indued with a singular skill in the practise and speculation of musicke of which two many suppose him to be the verie author and beginner, although unjustly, sith both poetry and song were in use before the flood, as was also the harpe and pipe [. . .] But to proceed, as the cheefe estimation of the Druiydes remained in the end among the Britons onelie, for their knowledge in religion, so did the fame of the Bardes (which were so called of this Bardus for their excellent skill in musicke, poetrie, and secret pointes of their religion). There was little difference also betweene them and the Druiydes, till they so far degenerated from their first institution, that they became to be minstrels at feasts, droonken meetings, and abhominable sacrifices of the idols: where they sang most commonlie

---

[4]The oak was sacred to Druids.
[5]Mistletoe grows on the oak tree as a parasite and was revered by the Druids.
[6]Superstitous innovations.
[7]Samothes, Sarron, Magus, and Druiyus were all originators of Druidism.

no divinitie as before, but the puissant acts of valiant princes, and fabulous narrations of the adulteries of the gods. [. . .]

Thus we see as in a glasse the state of religion, for a time, after the first inhabitation of this island: but how long it continued in such soundnesse, as the originall authors left it, in good sooth I cannot say, yet this is most certeine, that after a time, when Albion arrived here, the religion earst imbraced fell into great decaie. For whereas Japhet & Samothes[8] with their children taught nothing else than such doctrine as they had learned of Noah: Cham[9] the great grandfather of this our Albion, and his disciples utterlie renouncing to follow their steps, gave their minds wholie to seduce and lead their hearers headlong unto all error. Whereby his posteritie not onelie corrupted this our island, with most filthie trades and practises; but also all mankind, generallie where they became, with vicious life, and most ungodlie conversation. [. . .]

Thus we see in generall maner, how idolatrie, honoring of the starres, and brood of inferiour gods were hatched at the first, which folies in processe of time came also into Britaine, as did the names of Saturne & Jupiter, etc: as shall appeare hereafter. [. . .]

After Brute,[10] idolatrie and superstition still increased more and more among us, insomuch that beside the Druiysh and Bardlike ceremonies, and those also that came in with Albion and Brute himselfe: our countriemen either brought hither from abroad, or dailie invented at home new religion and rites, whereby it came to passe that in the stead of the onelie and immortall God (of whom Samothes and his posteritie did preach in times past) now they honored the said Samothes himselfe under the name of Dis and Saturne: also Jupiter, Mars, Minerva, Mercurie, Apollo, Diana; and finallie Hercules, unto whome they dedicated the gates and porches of their temples, entrances into their regions, cities, townes and houses, with their limits and bounds (as the papists did the gates of their cities and ports unto Botulph & Giles[11]) because fortitude and wisedome are the cheefe upholders and bearers up of common-wealths and kingdoms,

[8]Japhet was one of the sons of Noah, Samothes is his son.

[9]Cham was the youngest of Noah's sons, who saw "the nakedness of his father," and father to Canaan, thus cursed to be a "Servant of servants . . . unto his brethren" (Genesis 9:22).

[10]Brute, or Brutus, great-grandson of Aeneas and first king of Britain.

[11]Names of Roman Catholic saints (the analogy is meant to convey idolatrous taint).

both which they ascribed to Hercules[12] (forgetting God) and divers
other idols whose names I now remember not. In lieu moreover of
sheepe and oxen, they offred mankind also unto some of them,
killing their offendors, prisoners, and oft such strangers as came from
farre unto them, by shutting up great numbers of them togither in
huge images made of wicker, reed, haie, or other light matter: and
then setting all on fire togither, they not onelie consumed the miserable creatures to ashes (sometimes adding other beasts unto them)
but also reputed it to be the most acceptable sacrifice that could be
made unto their idols [. . .] But to proceed with our owne gods and
idols, more pertinent to my purpose than the rehersall of forreine
demeanours: I find that huge temples in like sort were builded unto
them, so that in the time of Lucius,[13] when the light of salvation
began stronglie to shine in Britaine, thorough the preaching of the
gospell, the Christians discovered 25 Flamines or idol-churches,
beside three Archflamines, whose preests were then as our Archbish-
ops are now, in that they had superior charge of all the rest, the other
being reputed as inferiours, and subject to their jurisdiction in cases
of religion, and superstitious ceremonies. Hitherto yee have heard of
the time, werein idolatrie reigned and blinded the harts of such as
dwelled in this iland. Now let us see the success of the gospell, after
the death and passion of Jesus Christ our saviour.

Jean Calvin (1509–1564)

*The writings of the reformer Jean Calvin permeated Reformation cul-
ture, though the extremity of his views on predestination was often
tempered by other thinkers (such as Richard Hooker). Calvin's vision
of human sinfulness is a dark one, intended to produce the shame and
self-loathing deemed necessary to true faith. It is especially disturbing
as a portrait of the inevitability of humankind's degenerate nature, as
sin was said to pass from parent to child. (Compare this with the
resemblances between Lear and his daughters on matters of pride or
willfulness.)*

[12]The son of Zeus and Alcmena, renowned for superhuman strength.
[13]Fabled as the first Christian British king.

from *Institutes of the Christian Religion*[1]

1. It was not without reason that the ancient proverb so strongly recommended to man the knowledge of himself. For if it is deemed disgraceful to be ignorant of things pertaining to the business of life, much more disgraceful is self-ignorance, in consequence of which we miserably deceive ourselves in matters of the highest moment, and so walk blindfold. But the more useful the precept is, the more careful we must be not to use it preposterously, as we see certain philosophers have done. For they, when exhorting man to know himself, state the motive to be, that he may not be ignorant of his own excellence and dignity. They wish him to see nothing in himself but what will fill him with vain confidence, and inflate him with pride. But self-knowledge consists in this, *first,* When reflecting on what God gave us at our creation, and still continues graciously to give, we perceive how great the excellence of our nature would have been had its integrity remained, and, at the same time, remember that we have nothing of our own, but depend entirely on God, from whom we hold at pleasure whatever he has seen it meet to bestow; *secondly,* When viewing our miserable condition since Adam's fall, all confidence and boasting are overthrown, we blush for shame, and feel truly humble. For us God at first formed us in his own image, that he might elevate our minds to the pursuit of virtue, and the contemplation of eternal life, so to prevent us from heartlessly burying those noble qualities which distinguish us from the lower animals, it is of importance to know that we were endued with reason and intelligence, in order that we might cultivate a holy and honourable life, and regard a blessed immortality as our destined aim. At the same time, it is impossible to think of our primeval dignity without being immediately reminded of the sad spectacle of our ignominy and corruption, ever since we fell from our original in the person of our first parent. [. . .] In this way, we feel dissatisfied with ourselves, and become truly humble, while we are inflamed with new desires to seek after God, in whom each may regain those good qualities of which all are found to be utterly destitute.

---

[1](Basle, 1536); book 2, ch. 1, "Through the Fall and Revolt of Adam, the whole human race made accursed and degenerate. Of Original Sin."

[. . .] There is nothing more acceptable to the human mind than flattery, and, accordingly, when told that its endowments are of a high order, it is apt to be excessively credulous. Hence it is not strange that the greater part of mankind have erred so egregiously in this matter. Owing to the innate self-love by which all are blinded, we most willingly persuade ourselves that we do not possess a single quality which is deserving of hatred; and hence, independent of any countenance from without, general credit is given to the very foolish idea, that man is perfectly sufficient of himself for all the purposes of a good and happy life. If any are disposed to think more modestly, and concede somewhat to God, that they may not seem to arrogate everything as their own, still, in making the division, they apportion matters so that the chief ground of confidence and boasting always remains with themselves. Then, if a discourse is pronounced which flatters the pride spontaneously springing up in man's inmost heart, nothing seems more delightful. Accordingly, in every age, he who is most forward in extolling the excellence of human nature, is received with the loudest applause. But be this heralding of human excellence what it may, by teaching man to rest in himself, it does nothing more than fascinate by its sweetness, and, at the same time, so delude as to drown in perdition all who assent to it. For what avails it to proceed in vain confidence, to deliberate, resolve, plan, and attempt what we deem pertinent to the purpose, and, at the very outset, prove deficient and destitute both of sound intelligence and true virtue, though we still confidently persist till we rush headlong on destruction? But this is the best that can happen to those who put confidence in their own powers. Whosoever, therefore, gives heed to those teachers who merely employ us in contemplating our good qualities, so far from making progress in self-knowledge, will be plunged into the most pernicious ignorance.

[. . .] But he who tries himself by the standard of divine justice, finds nothing to inspire him with confidence; and hence, the more thorough his self-examination, the greater his despondency. Abandoning all dependence on himself, he feels that he is utterly incapable of duly regulating his conduct. It is not the will of God, however, that we should forget the primeval dignity which he bestowed on our first parents—a dignity which may well stimulate us to the pursuit of goodness and justice. It is impossible for us to think of our first original, or the end for which we were created, without being urged to meditate on immortality, and to seek the kingdom of God. But such meditation, so far from raising our spirits, rather casts them down, and makes us humble. For what is our original? One from which we have fallen. What the end of our creation? One from which we have altogether strayed, so that, weary of our miserable lot, we groan, and groaning sigh for a dignity now lost. When we say that man should see nothing in himself which can raise his spirits, our meaning is, that he possesss nothing on which he can proudly plume himself. [. . .]

[. . .] Therefore, since through man's fault a curse has extended above and below, over all the regions of the world, there is nothing unreasonable in its extending to all his offspring. After the heavenly image in man was effaced, he not only was himself punished by a withdrawal of the ornaments in which he had been arrayed—viz. wisdom, virtue, justice, truth, and holiness, and by the substitution in their place of those dire pests, blindness, impotence, vanity, impurity, and unrighteousness, but he involved his posterity also, and plunged them in the same wretchedness. This is the hereditary corruption to which early Christian writers gave the name of Original Sin, meaning by the term the depravation of a nature formerly good and pure. [. . .]

6. We thus see that the impurity of parents is transmitted to their children, so that all, without exception, are originally depraved. The commencement of this depravity will not be found until we ascend to the first parent of all as the fountain head. We must, therefore, hold it for certain that, in regard to human nature, Adam was not merely a progenitor, but, as it were, a root, and that accordingly, by his corruption, the whole human race was deservedly vitiated. [. . .]

[. . .] Children come not by spiritual regeneration but carnal descent. Accordingly, as Augustine[2] says, "Both the condemned unbeliever and the acquitted believer beget offspring not acquitted but condemned, because the nature which begets is corrupt." Moreover, though godly parents do in some measure contribute to the holiness of their offspring, this is by the blessing of God; a blessing, however, which does not prevent the primary and universal

[2]St. Augustine (354–436 CE) was an early Christian theologian.

curse of the whole race from previously taking effect. Guit is from nature, whereas sanctification is from supernatural grace.

[. . .] Original sin, then, may be defined a hereditary corruption and depravity of our nature, extending to all the parts of the soul, which first makes us obnoxious to the wrath of God, and then produces in us works which in Scripture are termed works of the flesh. This corruption is repeatedly designated by Paul by the term sin (Gal. v.19[3]); while the works which proceed from it, such as adultery, fornication, theft, hatred, murder, revellings, he terms, in the same way, the fruits of sin, though in various passages of Scripture, and even by Paul himself, they are also termed sins.

Richard Hooker (1554?–1600)

The Elizabethan theologian Richard Hooker intended his work in part as a defense of the national church, and he does so by tracing its structures to God's design in natural law and human nature. His is a far more optimistic vision of human nature, community, and possibility than Calvin's. Readers who trace a redemptive or compensatory movement in King Lear *might find cultural corroboration in Hooker's philosophy.*

from *Of the Laws of Ecclesiastical Polity* (London, 1593), book 1, ch. 3.2, ch. 8.1–8.3, and ch. 10.2–10.5

[. . .] as it cometh to pass in a kingdom rightly ordered, that after a law is once published, it presently takes effect far and wide, all states framing themselves thereunto; even so let us think it fareth in the natural course of the world: since the time that God did first proclaim the edicts of his law upon it, heaven and earth have hearkened unto his voice, and their labour hath been to do his will: He *made a law for the rain.* He gave his *decree unto the sea, that the waters should not pass his commandment.* Now if nature should intermit her course, and leave altogether, though it were but for a while, the observation of her own laws: if those principal and mother elements of the world, whereof all things in this lower

---

[3]St. Paul, letter to the Galatians, 5.19: "Now the works of the flesh are manifest, which are these: Adultery, fornication, uncleanness, lasciviousness."

world are made, should lose the qualities which now they have, if the frame of that heavenly arch erected over our heads should loosen and dissolve itself: if celestial spheres should forget their wonted motions and by irregular volubility, turn themselves any way as it might happen: if the prince of the lights of heaven which now as a Giant doth run his unwearied course, should as it were through a languishing faintness begin to stand and to rest himself: if the Moon should wander from her beaten way, the times and seasons of the year blend themselves by disordered and confused mixture, the winds breathe out their last gasp, the clouds yield no rain, the earth be defeated of heavenly influence, the fruits of the earth pine away as children at the withered breasts of their mother no longer able to yield them relief, what would become of man himself, whom these things now do all serve? See we not plainly that obedience of creatures unto the law of nature is the stay of the whole world? [. . .] But howsoever these swervings are now and then incident into the course of nature, nevertheless so constantly the laws of nature are by natural agents observed, that no man denieth but those things which nature worketh, are wrought either always or for the most part after one and the same manner. If here it be demanded what that is which keepeth nature in obedience to her own law, we must have recourse to that higher law whereof we have already spoken, and because all other laws do thereon depend, from thence we must borrow so much as shall need for brief resolution in this point. [. . .] Nevertheless, forasmuch as the works of nature are no less exact, than if she did both behold and study how to express some absolute shape or mirror always present before her; yea, such her dexterity and skill appeareth, that no intellectual creature in the world were able by capacity to do that which nature doth without capacity and knowledge; it cannot be, but nature hath some director of infinite knowledge to guide her in all her ways. Who the guide of nature but only the God of nature? *In him we live, move, and are.* Those things which nature is said to do, are by divine art performed, using nature as an instrument: nor is there any such art of knowledge divine in nature herself working, but in the guide of nature's work. [. . .] The manner of this divine efficiency being far above us, we are no more able to conceive by our reason, than creatures unreasonable by their sense are able to apprehend after what manner we dispose and order the course of

our affairs. Only thus much is discerned, that the natural generation and process of all things receiveth order of proceeding from the
settled stability of divine understanding. This appointeth unto them
their kinds of working, the disposition whereof in the purity of
God's own knowledge and will is rightly termed by the name of
Providence. The same being referred unto the things themselves
here disposed by it, was wont by the ancient to be called *natural
destiny*. That law the performance whereof we behold in things natural, is as it were an authentical, or an original draught written in
the bosom of God himself; whose spirit being to execute the same,
useth every particular nature, every mere natural agent only as an
instrument created at the beginning, and ever since the beginning
used to work his own will and pleasure withal. Nature therefore is
nothing else but God's instrument: [. . .]

**Of the natural way of finding out laws by reason
to guide the will unto that which is good.**

[8a] 8. [. . .] Seeing therefore that for the framing of men's actions the
knowledge of good from evil is necessary; it only resteth that we
search how this may be had. Neither must we suppose that there
needeth one rule to know the good, and another the evil by. For he
that knoweth what is straight, doth even thereby discern what is
crooked, because the absence of straightness in bodies capable
thereof is crookedness. Goodness in actions is like unto straightness,
wherefore that which is done well we term right. For as the straight
way is most acceptable to him that traveleth, because by it he cometh
soonest to his journey's end: so in action, that which doth lie the even-
est between us and the end we desire, must needs be the fittest for our
use. Besides which fitness for use there is also in rectitude, beauty; as
contrariwise in obliquity deformity. And that which is good in the
actions of men, doth not only delight as profitable, but as amiable
also. [. . .] And of discerning goodness there are but these two ways;
the one the knowledge of the causes whereby it is made such, the
other the observation of those signs and tokens, which being annexed
always unto goodness, argue that where they are found, there also
goodness is, although we know not the cause by force whereof it is
there. The former of these is the most sure and infallible way, but so
hard that all shun it, and had rather walk as men do in the dark by

haphazard, than tread so long and intricate mazes for knowledge sake. As therefore Physicians are many times forced to leave such methods of curing as themselves know to be the fittest, and being overruled by their patients' impatiency are fain to try the best they can, in taking that way of cure, which the cured will yield unto: in like sort, considering how the case doth stand with this present age full of tongue and weak of brain, behold we yield to the stream thereof; into the causes of goodness we will not make any curious or deep inquiry; to touch them now and then it shall be sufficient, when they are so near at hand that easily they may be conceived without any far removed discourse: that way we are contented to prove, which being the worse in itself, is notwithstanding now by reason of common imbecility the fitter and likelier to be brooked. Signs and tokens to know good by, are of sundry kinds: some more certain and some less. The most certain token of evident goodness is, if the general persuasion of all men do so account it. And therefore a common received error is never utterly overthrown, till such time as we go from signs unto causes, and show some manifest root or fountain thereof common unto all, whereby it may clearly appear how it hath come to pass that so many have been overseen. In which case surmises and slight probabilities will not serve, because the universal consent of men is the perfectest and strongest in this kind which comprehendeth only the signs and tokens of goodness. Things casual do vary, and that which a man doth but chance to think well of, cannot still have the like hap. Wherefore although we know not the cause, yet thus much we may know, that some necessary cause there is, whensoever the judgements of all men generally or for the most part run one and the same way, especially in matters of natural discourse. [. . .] The general and perpetual voice of men is as the sentence of God himself. For that which all men have at all times learned, nature herself must needs have taught; and God being the author of nature, her voice is but his instrument. By her from him we receive whatsoever in such sort we learn. Infinite duties there are, the goodness whereof is by this rule sufficiently manifested, although we had no other warrant besides to approve them. The apostle St. Paul having speech concerning the Heathen saith of them, *They are a law unto themselves.*[1]

---

[1]Romans 2.14: "For when the Gentiles, which have not the law, do by nature the things contained in the law, these, having not the law, are a law unto themselves."

His meaning is, that by force of the light of reason, wherewith God illuminateth everyone which cometh into the world, men being enabled to know truth from falsehood, and good from evil, do thereby learn in many things what the will of God is; which will himself not revealing by any extraordinary means unto them, but they by natural discourse attaining the knowledge thereof, seem the makers of those laws which indeed are his, and they but only the finders of them out. [. . .]

[Chapter 10.2] [. . .] All men desire to lead in this world an happy life. That life is led most happily, wherein all virtue is exercised without impediment or let. The Apostle[2] in exhorting men to contentment, although they have in this world no more than very bare food and raiment, giveth us thereby to understand, that those are even the lowest of things necessary, that if we should be stripped of all those things without which we might possibly be, yet these must be left, that destitution in these is such an impediment, as till it be removed, suffereth not the mind of man to admit any other care. For this cause first God assigned *Adam* maintenance of life, and then appointed him a law to observe. For this cause after men began to grow to a number: the first thing we read they gave themselves unto, was the tilling of the earth, and the feeding of cattle. Having by this mean whereon to live, the principal actions of their life afterward are noted by the exercise of their religion. True it is that the kingdom of God must be the first thing in our purposes and desires. But inasmuch as righteous life presupposeth life, inasmuch as to live virtuously it is impossible except we live, therefore the first impediment, which naturally we endeavour to remove, is penury and want of things without which we cannot live. Unto life many implements are necessary; more, if we seek (as all men naturally do) such a life as hath in it joy, comfort, delight and pleasure. To this end we see how quickly sundry arts Mechanical were found out in the very prime of the world. As things of greatest necessity are always first provided for, so things of greatest dignity are most accounted of by all such as judge rightly. Although therefore riches be a thing which every man wisheth, yet no man of judgement can esteem it better to be rich, than wise, virtuous and religious. If we be both or either of

---

[2] 1 Timothy 6.8: "And having food and raiment let us be therewith content."

these, it is not because we are so born. For into the world we come as empty of the one as of the other, as naked in mind as we are in body. [. . .] But neither that which we learn of ourselves, nor that which others teach us can prevail, where wickedness and malice have taken deep root. If therefore when there was but as yet one only family in the world, no means of instruction human or divine could prevent effusion of blood: how could it be chosen but that when families were multiplied and increased upon earth, after separation each providing for itself, envy, strife, contention and violence must grow amongst them? for hath not nature furnished man with wit and valour, as it were with amour, which may be used as well unto extreme evil as good? yea, were they not used by the rest of the world unto evil; unto the contrary only by *Seth, Enoch,*[3] and those few the rest in that line? We all make complaint of the iniquity of our times: not unjustly; for the days are evil. But compare them with those times, wherein there were no civil societies, with those times wherein there was as yet no manner of public regiment established, with those times wherein there were not above 8 persons righteous living upon the face of the earth: and we have surely good cause to think that God hath blessed us exceedingly, and hath made us behold most happy days. To take away all such mutual grievances, injuries, and wrongs, there was no way, but only by growing unto composition and agreement amongst themselves, by ordaining some kind of government public, and by yielding themselves subject thereunto, that unto whom they granted authority to rule and govern, by them the peace, tranquillity, and happy estate of the rest might be procured. [. . .] therefore that strifes and troubles would be endless, except they gave their common consent all to be ordered by some whom they should agree upon: without which consent, there was no reason, that one man should take upon him to be Lord or Judge over another; because although there be according to the opinion of some very great and judicious men a kind of natural right in the noble, wise, and virtuous, to govern them which are of servile disposition; nevertheless for manifestation of this their right, and men's more peaceable contentment on both sides, the assent of them who are to be governed, seemeth necessary. To fathers

---

[3]Examples of virtuous men willing to defy others in order to serve God's will.

within their private families nature hath given a supreme power, for which cause we see throughout the world even from the first foundation thereof, all men have ever been taken as lords and lawful kings in their own houses. Howbeit over a whole grand multitude having no such dependency upon anyone, and consisting of so many families, as every politic society in the world doth, impossible it is that any should have complete lawful power but by consent of men, or immediate appointment of God; because not having the natural superiority of fathers, their power must needs be either usurped, and then unlawful; or if lawful, then either granted or consented unto by them over whom they exercise the same, or else given extraordinarily from God, unto whom all the world is subject. It is no improbable opinion therefore which the Arch-philosopher[4] was of, that as the chiefest person in every household was always as it were a king, so when numbers of households joined themselves in civil society together, kings were the first kind of governors amongst them. [. . .] So that in a word all public regiment of what kind soever seemeth evidently to have risen from deliberate advice, consultation, and composition between men, judging it convenient and behoveful; there being no impossibility in nature considered by itself, but that men might have lived without any public regiment. Howbeit, the corruption of our nature being presupposed, we may not deny but that the law of nature doth now require of necessity some kind of regiment, so that to bring things unto the first course they were in, and utterly to take away all kind of public government in the world, were apparently to overturn the whole world.

Thomas Hobbes (1588–1679)

Thomas Hobbes's work of political philosophy, like Hooker's, undertakes to describe natural law and its role in shaping human community and institutions. Unlike Hooker, however, his sense of the role of self-interest in human affairs makes his vision of human society far less comfortable. While this text postdates King Lear *by nearly fifty years,*

---

[4]Aristotle (384–322 BCE), author of *Politics*; see books 1 and 4.

it is helpful in framing some of the play's issues. If Edmund had a political theory, it would be Hobbes's.

from *Leviathan* (London, 1651) part 1; ch. 6; ch. 13, passim.

Of Man
Part I, Chap. 13

The Incommodities of such a War   Whatsoever therefore is consequent to a time of Warre, where every man is Enemy to every man; the same is consequent to the time, wherein men live without other security, than what their own strength, and their own invention shall furnish them withall. In such condition, there is no place for Industry; because the fruit thereof is uncertain: and consequently no Culture of the Earth; no Navigation, nor use of the commodities that may be imported by Sea; no commodious Building; no Instruments of moving, and removing such things as require much force; no Knowledge of the face of the Earth; no account of Time; no Arts; no Letters; no Society; and which is worst of all, continuall feare, and danger of violent death; And the life of man, solitary, poore, nasty, brutish, and short.

It may seem strange to some man, that has not well weighed these things; that Nature should thus dissociate, and render men apt to invade, and destroy one another: and he may therefore, not trusting to this Inference, made from the Passions, desire perhaps to have the same confirmed by Experience. Let him therefore consider with himselfe, when taking a journey, he armes himselfe, and seeks to go well accompanied; when going to sleep, he locks his dores; when even in his house he locks his chests; and this when he knows there bee Lawes, and publike Officers, armed, to revenge all injuries shall bee done him; what opinion he has of his fellow subjects, when he rides armed; of his fellow Citizens, when he locks his dores; and of his children, and servants, when he locks his chests. Does he not there as much accuse mankind by his actions, as I do by my words? But neither of us accuse mans nature in it. The Desires, and other Passions of man, are in themselves no Sin. No more are the Actions, that proceed from those Passions, till they know a Law that forbids them: which till Lawes be made they cannot know: nor can any Law be made, till they have agreed upon the Person that shall make it.

[63] It may peradventure be thought, there was never such a time, nor condition of warre as this; and I believe it was never generally so, over all the world: but there are many places, where they live so now. For the savage people in many places of *America*, except the government of small Families, the concord whereof dependeth on naturall lust, have no government at all; and live at this day in that brutish manner, as I said before. Howsoever, it may be perceived what manner of life there would be, where there were no common Power to feare; by the manner of life, which men that have formerly lived under a peacefull government, use to degenerate into, in a civill Warre. [. . .]

CHAP. XIV

Of the first and second NATURALL LAWES, *and of* CONTRACTS

Right of Nature what

The Right Of Nature, which Writers commonly call *Jus Naturale*, is the Liberty each man hath, to use his own power, as he will himselfe, for the preservation of his own Nature; that is to say, of his own Life; and consequently, of doing any thing, which in his own Judgement, and Reason, hee shall conceive to be the aptest means thereunto. [. . .]

Naturally every man has Right to everything

And because the condition of Man, (as hath been declared in the precedent Chapter) is a condition of Warre of every one against every one; in which case every one is governed by his own Reason; and there is nothing he can make use of, that may not be a help unto him, in preserving his life against his enemyes; It followeth, that in such a condition, every man has a Right to every thing; even to one anothers body. And therefore, as long as this naturall Right of every man to every thing endureth, there can be no security to any man, (how strong or wise soever he be,) of living out the time, which Nature ordinarily alloweth men to live. And consequently it

The Fundamentall Law of Nature

is a precept, or generall rule of Reason, *That every man, ought to endeavour Peace, as farre as he has hope of obtaining it; and when he cannot obtain it, that he may seek, and use, all helps, and advantages of Warre.* The first branch of which Rule, containeth the first, and Fundamentall Law of Nature; which is, *to seek Peace, and follow it.* The Second, the summe of the Right of Nature; which is, *By all means we can, to defend our selves.*

St. Augustine (354–430)

In stark contrast to Hobbes, analogues for the notions of compassion and forgiveness, which some critics find animated in Cordelia ("No cause, no cause" (4.7.78)), are legion in this period as both ideal and injunction. The writings of St. Augustine were a pervasive resource for this ethos in early modern theology. This passage from The City of God *provides one model of forgiveness, or at least refusal of vengeance, necessary not only to individual salvation but also to social cohesion.*

from *The City of God* (c. 413–427)

Book XIX[1]

27. That the peace of those who serve God cannot in this mortal life be apprehended in its perfection

But the peace which is peculiar to ourselves we enjoy now with God by faith, and shall hereafter enjoy eternally with Him by sight. But the peace which we enjoy in this life, whether common to all or peculiar to ourselves, is rather the solace of our misery than the positive enjoyment of felicity. Our very righteousness, too, though true in so far as it has respect to the true good, is yet in this life of such a kind that it consists rather in the remission of sins than in the perfecting of virtues. Witness the prayer of the whole city of God in its pilgrim state, for it cries to God by the mouth of all its members, "Forgive us our debts as we forgive our debtors."[2] And this prayer is efficacious not for those whose faith is "without works and dead,"[3] but for those whose faith "worketh by love."[4] For as reason, though subjected to God, is yet "pressed down by the corruptible body,"[5] so long as it is in this mortal condition, it has not perfect authority over vice, and therefore this prayer is needed by

[1] pp. 707–708.

[2] Matthew 6.12.

[3] James 2.17: " Even so faith, if it hath not works, is dead, being alone."

[4] Galatians, 5.6: "For in Jesus Christ neither circumcision availeth any thing, nor uncircumcision, but faith which worketh by love."

[5] Wisdom 9.15.

the righteous. For though it exercises authority, the vices do not submit without a struggle. For however well one maintains the conflict, and however thoroughly he has subdued these enemies, there steals in some evil thing, which, if it do not find ready expression in act, slips out by the lips, or insinuates itself into the thought; and therefore his peace is not full so long as he is at war with his vices. For it is a doubtful conflict he wages with those that resist, and his victory over those that are defeated is not secure, but full of anxiety and effort. Amidst these temptations, therefore, of all which it has been summarily said in the divine oracles, "Is not human life upon earth a temptation?"[6] who but a proud man can presume that he so lives that he has no need to say to God, "Forgive us our debts?" And such a man is not great, but swollen and puffed up with vanity, and is justly resisted by Him who abundantly gives grace to the humble. Whence it is said, "God resisteth the proud, but giveth grace to the humble."[7] In this, then, consists the righteousness of a man, that he submit himself to God, his body to his soul, and his vices even when they rebel, to his reason, which either defeats or at least resists them; and also that he beg from God grace to do his duty, and the pardon of his sins, and that he render to God thanks for all the blessings he receives. But, in that final peace to which all our righteousness has reference, and for the sake of which it is maintained, as our nature shall enjoy a sound immortality and incorruption, and shall have no more vices, and as we shall experience no resistance either from ourselves or from others, it will not be necessary that reason should rule vices which no longer exist, but God shall rule the man, and the soul shall rule the body, with a sweetness and facility suitable to the felicity of a life which is done with bondage. And this condition shall there be eternal, and we shall be assured of its eternity; and thus the peace of this blessedness and the blessedness of this peace shall be the supreme good.

[6]Job 7.1.
[7]James 4.6; 1 Peter 5.5.

Early Readings and Rewritings

It is only recently that *King Lear* has been deemed the greatest of Shakespeare's tragedies (R. A. Foakes, *Hamlet versus Lear*, 1993). This was not always the case, or if so it was only acknowledged askance. Although John Keats and William Hazlitt were impressed with the greatness of *King Lear* in the Romantic era, it was *Hamlet* that was Shakespeare's acknowledged masterpiece. The uncompromising bleakness of *King Lear*—its portrait of human savagery, its resolute refusal of redemption, and the endurance required by its formal design—has made critical and theatrical celebration difficult. The sheer unbearableness of this play was confessed in 1765 by Samuel Johnson, who undertook to edit Shakespeare's works for the reader (as opposed to the stage): "I was many years ago so shocked by Cordelia's death, that I know not whether I ever endured to read again the last scenes of the play till I undertook to revise them as an editor." This is a response that has persisted throughout the centuries. Stephen Booth, one of the twentieth century's most perceptive critics of this play, writes:

> I myself first read the last scenes of King Lear while undergoing a sophomore survey course in which I was taking on a full semester's reading in the twenty-four hours immediately preceding the final examination; it was about three o'clock on a spring afternoon and I sat in a chair on a stuffy afternoon and cried. (*King Lear, Macbeth, Indefinition and Tragedy*, 1983)

The problem of how to assimilate King Lear's panoply of suffering to theatrical and ethical tastes has made its reception history a
relatively unusual one in Shakespeare's canon. Johnson's sentiments
register in the venue of literary criticism what had been a theatrical
truth since 1681, when the Restoration jack-of-all-literary-trades
Nahum Tate presented a revised version of the play in which
Cordelia lives to marry Edgar (a resolution that reversed the losses
not only of Shakespeare's version but of his relatively less tragic
source materials). Tate's version held the stage for the next century
and a half, until William Macready restored Shakespeare's version
in 1838. So for nearly 150 years Shakespeare's *King Lear* was a
play for reading (hence the specificity of Keats's sonnet, "On Sitting
Down to Read King Lear Once Again"). Moreover, with a mentally
deteriorating king on the English throne (George III, 1760–1820), it
was not possible to stage *King Lear. Lear* returned to the stage,
however, at a moment when Shakespeare's reputation as a poet best
apprehended in the imagination of a reader was being reinforced by
Romantic writers. The influence of the novel (a form born in the
eighteenth century), with its studies of character, also contributed
to a focus on Shakespearean portraits of psychology, rather than on
power or plot or even poetic texture. The verisimilar conventions of
the later-nineteenth-century stage, whose vast auditoriums favored
spectacle over language, preferred elaborate realistic scenery (as
opposed to the stock scenery of the eighteenth century or the mini-
mal properties of Shakespeare's own period). Such conditions
helped reinforce this readerly understanding of the play, which,
with its imaginary cliffs and its rapid movement from staterooms to
violent storms, can present a difficult challenge for a stagecraft dedicated to realistic visualizations of its events. Perhaps the greatest
challenge to performance is that much of this play—tellingly, the
blinding of Gloucester—is unbearable to see.

This sense of the unsuitability of *King Lear* for the stage held
sway until the early twentieth century. It informs the sensibility of
the great critic A. C. Bradley, whose work on the four tragedies
(*Lear, Hamlet, Othello,* and *Macbeth*) began to advance the idea of
the play's greatness as consisting precisely in the starkness of its
vision. Bradley's discussion builds on the traditions of his predeces-
sors and sets the terms of much that followed.

The twentieth century saw the advent of professional literary criticism, with its host of approaches (e.g., formalist, historicist, feminist) to the plays. The play's apocalyptic tenor is also expressive of this century's own political catastrophes, a resonance that has made *King Lear* an increasingly desirable candidate for the stage, as well as the subject of several films. The proliferation and variety of these recent versions of the play make them impossible to excerpt here in any representative manner; readers desiring to explore this territory, as well as that of performance history, should consult the "Further Reading" section.

Nahum Tate (1652–1715)

> *Nahum Tate's* King Lear *for much of its stage life (150 years) was seen as an improvement of Shakespeare's play. The most notorious "improvement" is Tate's ending—a match between a still living Cordelia and Edgar. He also simplified the emotional logic, rooting Lear's initial actions in a propensity to rage, making Edmund the culprit in both plots (Edmund's soliloquy opens the play), softening Gloucester's character, and hardening villains' villainy. Tate's prefatory comments, reproduced here, give some sense of the cultural tastes that account for such changes. The excerpts track the Edgar and Cordelia story.*

from *The History of King Lear* (London, 1681)[1]

from Tate's dedication letter to
"My Esteemed FRIEND Thomas Boteler, Esq."

SIR, [. . .] *'Twas my good fortune to light on one Expedient to rectifie what was wanting in the Regularity and Probability of the Tale, which was to run through the whole,* A Love *betwixt* Edgar *and* Cordelia, *that never chang'd word with each other in the Original. This renders* Cordelia's *Indifference and her Father's Passion in the first Scene probable. It likewise gives Countenance to* Edgar's

[1]Reprinted as *Shakespeare Adaptations: The Tempest, The Mock Tempest, and King Lear*, with an Introduction and Notes by Montague Summers (Boston, 1922).

Disguise, making that a generous Design that was before a poor Shift to save his Life. The Distress of the Story is evidently heightned by it; and it particularly gave Occasion of a New Scene or Two, of more Success (perhaps) than Merit. This Method necessarily threw me on making the Tale conclude in a Success to the innocent distrest Persons: Otherwise I must have incumbred the Stage with dead Bodies, which Conduct makes many Tragedies conclude with unseasonable Jests. Yet was I Rackt with no small Fears for so bold a Change, till I found it well receiv'd by my Audience; and if this will not satisfie the Reader, I can produce an Authority that questionless will. Neither is it of so Trivial an Undertaking to make a Tragedy end happily, for 'tis more difficult to Save than 'tis to Kill: The Dagger and Cup of Poyson are alwaies in Readiness; but to bring the Action to the last Extremity, and then by probable Means to recover All, will require the Art and Judgment of a Writer, and cost him many a Pang in the Performance. [. . .]

Your obliged Friend
and humble Servant,
N. *Tate.*

[This exchange concludes the dowry scene of Act 1, Scene 1]

Remain Edgar *and* Cordelia.
EDGAR. Has Heaven then weigh'd the Merit of my Love,
Or is't the Raving of my sickly Thought?
Cou'd *Burgundy* forgo so rich a Prize,
And leave her to despairing *Edgar's* Arms?
Have I thy Hand *Cordelia?* Do I clasp it?
The Hand that was this Minute to have join'd   5
My hated Rival's? Do I kneel before thee,
And offer at thy Feet my panting Heart?
Smile, Princess, and convince me; for as yet
I doubt, and dare not trust the dazling Joy.
CORDELIA. Some Comfort yet, that 'twas no vicious Blot   10
That has depriv'd me of a Father's Grace,
But meerly want of that which makes me Rich
In wanting it; a smooth professing Tongue:
O Sisters! I am loth to call your Fault

As it deserves; but use our Father well, 15
And wrong'd *Cordelia* never shall repine.
    EDGAR. O heav'nly Maid! that art thyself thy Dow'r,
Richer in Vertue than the Stars in Light,
If *Edgar's* humble Fortunes may be grac't
With thy Acceptance, at thy Feet he lays 'em. 20
Ha, my *Cordelia!* dost thou turn away?
What have I done t' offend thee?
    CORDELIA.   Talk't of Love.
    EDGAR. Then I've offended oft, *Cordelia* too
Has oft permitted me so to offend. 25
    CORDELIA. When, *Edgar,* I permitted your Addresses,
I was the darling Daughter of a King,
Nor can I now forget my Royal Birth,
And live dependant on my Lover's Fortune;
I cannot to so low a Fate submit; 30
And therefore study to forget your Passion,
And trouble me upon this Theam no more.
    EDGAR. Thus Majesty takes most State in Distress!
How are we tost on Fortune's fickle Flood!
The Wave that with surprizing Kindness brought 35
The dear Wreck to my Arms, has snatcht it back,
And left me mourning on the barren Shoar.
    CORDELIA. This baseness of th' ignoble *Burgundy,* [*Aside.*
Draws just Suspicion on the Race of Men;
His Love was Int'rest, so may *Edgar's* be, 40
And He, but with more Complement, dissemble;
If so, I shall oblige him by denying:
But if his Love be fixt, such constant Flame
As warms our Breasts, if such I find his Passion,
My Heart as grateful to his Truth shall be, 45
And Cold *Cordelia* prove as kind as He.   *Exit.*

[*from Act 3, Scene 4: Disguised Edgar meets* Cordelia *and her
maid* Arante]
    EDGAR.   O my tumultuous Blood!
By all my trembling Veins *Cordelia's* Voice!
'Tis she her self!——My Senses sure conform
To my wild Garb, and I am Mad indeed.

CORDELIA. Whate're thou art, befriend a wretched Virgin,   5
And if thou canst direct our weary search.

EDGAR. Who relieves poor *Tom*, that sleeps on the Nettle, with
the Hedge-pig for his Pillow.

> Whilst Smug ply'd the Bellows
> She truckt with her Fellows,   10
> The Freckle-fac't Mab
> Was a Blouze and a Drab,

Yet *Swithin* made *Oberon* jealous——Oh! Torture.

ARANTE. Alack, Madam, a poor wandring Lunatick.

CORDELIA. And yet his Language seem'd but now well temper'd. 15
Speak, Friend, to one more wretched than thy self,
And if thou hast one Interval of sense,
Inform us if thou canst where we may find
A poor old Man, who through this Heath has stray'd
The tedious Night——Speak, sawest thou such a One?   20

EDGAR. The King, her Father, whom she's come to seek   [*Aside*.]
Through all the Terrors of this Night. O Gods!
That such amazing Piety, such Tenderness
Shou'd yet to me be Cruel——-
Yes, Fair One, such a One was lately here,   25
And is convey'd by some that came to seek him,
T' a Neighb'ring Cottage; but distinctly where,
I know not.

CORDELIA. Blessings on 'em,
Let's find him out, *Arante*, for thou seest
We are in Heavens Protection.   [*Going off*.]

EDGAR. O *Cordelia*!

CORDELIA.   Ha!——Thou knowst my Name.

EDGAR. As you did once know *Edgar's*.

CORDELIA.   *Edgar!*

EDGAR. The poor Remains of *Edgar*, what your Scorn
Has left him.

CORDELIA. Do we wake, *Arante*?

EDGAR. My Father seeks my Life, which I preserv'd   35
In hopes of some blest Minute to oblidge
Distrest *Cordelia*, and the Gods have giv'n it;
That Thought alone prevail'd with me to take
This Frantick Dress, to make the Earth my Bed,

With these bare Limbs all change of Seasons bide,   40
Noons scorching Heat, and Midnights piercing Cold,
To feed on Offals, and to drink with Herds,
To combat with the Winds, and be the Sport
Of Clowns, or what's more wretched yet, their Pity.
    ARANTE. Was ever Tale so full of Misery!   45
    EDGAR. But such a Fall as this I grant was due
To my aspiring Love, for 'twas presumptuous,
Though not presumptuously persu'd;
For well you know I wore my Flames conceal'd,
And silent as the Lamps that Burn in Tombs,   50
'Till you perceiv'd my Grief, with modest Grace
Drew forth the Secret, and then seal'd my Pardon.
    CORDELIA. You had your Pardon, nor can you Challenge more.
    EDGAR. What do I Challenge more?
Such Vanity agrees not with these Rags;   55
When in my prosp'rous State rich *Gloster's* Heir,
You silenc'd my Pretences, and enjoyn'd me
To trouble you upon that Theam no more;
Then what Reception must Love's Language find
From these bare Limbs and Beggers humble Weeds?   60
    CORDELIA. Such as the Voice of Pardon to a Wretch
Condemn'd; such as the Shouts of succ'ring Forces
To a Town besieg'd.
    EDGAR. Ah! what new Method now of Cruelty?
    CORDELIA. Come to my Arms, thou dearest, best of Men,   65
And take the kindest Vows that e're were spoke
By a protesting Maid.
    EDGAR.   Is't possible?
    CORDELIA. By the dear Vital Stream that baths my Heart,
These hallow'd Rags of Thine, and naked Vertue,
These abject Tassels, these fantastick Shreds,   70
(Ridiculous ev'n to the meanest Clown)
To me are dearer than the richest Pomp
Of purple Monarchs.
    EDGAR.   Generous charming Maid,
The Gods alone that made, can rate thy Worth!
This most amazing Excellence shall be   75
Fame's Triumph, in succeeding Ages, when

Thy bright Example shall adorn the Scene,
And teach the World Perfection.
    CORDELIA.   Cold and weary,
We'll rest a while, *Arante,* on that Straw,
Then forward to find out the poor Old King.   80
    EDGAR. Look I have Flint and Steel, the Implements
Of wandring Lunaticks, I'll strike a Light,
And make a Fire beneath this Shed, to dry
Thy Storm-drencht Garments, e're thou Lie to rest thee;
Then Fierce and Wakefull as th' *Hesperian* Dragon,   85
I'll watch beside thee to protect thy Sleep;
Mean while, the Stars shall dart their kindest Beams,
And Angels Visit my *Cordelia's* Dreams.

                                                  [*Exeunt.*]

[*from Act 5, Scene 5: the play's final scene*]
    ALBANY. Bring in old *Kent;* and *Edgar,* guide you hither
Your Father, whom you said was near,   [*Exit* Edgar.]
He may be an Ear-Witness as the least
Of our Proceedings.   [Kent *brought in here.*]
    LEAR.   Who are you?
My Eyes are none o'th Best, I'll tell you streight;   5
Oh *Albany!* Well, Sir, we are your Captives,
And you are come to see Death pass upon us.
Why this Delay.——Or is't your Highness's Pleasure
To give us first the Torture? Say ye so?
Why here's old *Kent* and I, as tough a Pair   10
As e'er bore Tyrants Stroke.——But my *Cordelia,*
My poor *Cordelia* here, O pity.——
    ALBANY. Take off their Chains.——Thou injur'd Majesty,
The Wheel of Fortune now has made her Circle,
And Blessings yet stand 'twixt thy Grave and thee.   15
    LEAR. Com'st thou inhumane Lord, to sooth us back
To a Fool's Paradise of Hope, to make
Our Doom more wretched? Go to, we are too well
Acquainted with Misfortune to be gull'd
With Lying Hope; no, we will hope no more.   20
    ALBANY. I have a Tale, t'unfold so full of Wonder
As cannot meet an easy Faith;

But by that Royal injur'd Head 'tis true.

    KENT. What wou'd your Highness?

    ALBANY. Know, the noble *Edgar*   25

Impeacht Lord *Edmund,* since the Fight, of Treason

And dar'd him for the Proof to single Combat,

In which the Gods confirm'd his Charge by Conquest;

I left ev'n now the Traytor wounded Mortally!

    LEAR. And whether tends this Story?

    ALBANY.   'Ere they fought   30

Lord *Edgar* gave into my Hands this Paper,

A blacker Scrowl of Treason, and of Lust,

Than can be found in the Records of Hell;

There, sacred Sir, behold the Character

Of *Goneril*, the worst of Daughters, but   35

More vicious Wife.

    CORDELIA. Cou'd there be yet Addition to their Guilt?

What will not they that wrong a Father do?

    ALBANY. Since then my Injuries, *Lear*, fall in with thine,

I have resolv'd the same Redress for both.   40

    KENT. What says my Lord?

    CORDELIA.   Speak, for methought I heard

The charming Voice of a descending God.

    ALBANY. The Troops, by *Edmund* rais'd, I have disbanded;

Those that remain are under my Command.

What Comfort may be brought to chear your Age,   45

And heal your savage Wrongs, shall be apply'd,

For to your Majesty we do resign

Your Kingdom, save what Part your self conferr'd

On us in Marriage.

    KENT.   Hear you that, my Liege?

    CORDELIA. Then there are Gods, and Vertue is their Care.   50

    LEAR. Is't Possible?

Let the Spheres stop their Course, the Sun make Hault,

The Winds be husht, the Seas and Fountains rest;

All Nature pause, and listen to the Change.

Where is my *Kent*, my *Cajus?*

    KENT.   Here, my Liege.   55

    LEAR. Why I have News that will recal thy Youth;

Ha! Didst thou hear't, or did th' inspiring Gods

Whisper to me alone? Old *Lear* shall be
A King again.

    KENT. The Prince, that like a God has Pow'r, has said it.   60

    LEAR. *Cordelia* then shall be a Queen, mark that:
Cordelia shall be a Queen; Winds catch the Sound,
And bear it on your rosie Wings to Heav'n.
Cordelia is a Queen.

               Re-enter Edgar *with* Gloster.

    ALBANY. Look, Sir, where pious *Edgar* comes,   65
Leading his Eye-less Father. O my Liege!
His wond'rous Story will deserve your Leisure;
What he has done and suffer'd for your Sake,
What for the fair *Cordelia's*.

    GLOSTER. Where's my Liege? Conduct me to his Knees, to hail 70
His second Birth of Empire; my dear *Edgar*
Has, with himself, reveal'd the King's blest Restauration

    LEAR. My poor dark *Gloster*.

    GLOSTER. O let me kiss that once more sceptred Hand!

    LEAR. Hold, thou mistak'st the Majesty, kneel here;   75
Cordelia has our Pow'r, *Cordelia's* Queen.
Speak, is not that the noble Suff'ring *Edgar?*

    GLOSTER. My pious Son, more dear than my lost Eyes.

    LEAR. I wrong'd him too, but here's the fair Amends.

    EDGAR. Your Leave, my Liege, for an unwelcome Message. 80
Edmund (but that's a Trifle) is expir'd;
What more will touch you, your imperious Daughters,
Goneril and haughty *Regan,* both are dead,
Each by the other poison'd at a Banquet;
This, Dying, they confest.   85

    CORDELIA. O fatal Period of ill govern'd Life!

    LEAR. Ingratefull as they were, my Heart feels yet
A Pang of Nature for their wretched Fall;——
But, *Edgar,* I defer thy Joys too long:
Thou serv'dst distrest *Cordelia;* take her Crown'd; 90
Th' imperial Grace fresh blooming on her Brow;
Nay, *Gloster,* thou hast here a Father's Right,
Thy helping Hand t'heap Blessings on their Heads.

    KENT. Old *Kent* throws in his hearty Wishes too.

    EDGAR. The Gods and you too largely Recompence 95

What I have done; the Gift strikes Merit dumb.
    CORDELIA. Nor do I blush to own my Self o'er-paid
For all my Suff'rings past.
    GLOSTER. Now, gentle Gods, give *Gloster* his Discharge.
    LEAR. No, *Gloster*, thou hast Business yet for Life;   100
Thou, *Kent*, and I, retir'd to some cool Cell
Will gently pass our short Reserves of Time
In calm Reflections on our Fortunes past,
Cheer'd with Relation of the prosperous Reign
Of this celestial Pair; thus our Remains   105
Shall in an even Course of Thoughts be past,
Enjoy the present Hour, nor fear the last.
    EDGAR. Our drooping Country now erects her Head,
Peace spreads her balmy Wings, and Plenty blooms.
Divine *Cordelia*, all the Gods can witness   110
How much thy Love to Empire I prefer!
Thy bright Example shall convince the World
(Whatever Storms of Fortune are decreed)
That Truth and Vertue shall at last succeed.

                                 [Exeunt Omnes.]

Lewis Theobald (1688–1744)

> *Lewis Theobald was a poet, dramatist, translator, and editor of Shake-*
> *speare. His comments on Shakespeare's treatment of early sources*
> *reveal Theobald's sense of the author's moral purpose and its influence*
> *on the design of Shakespeare's characters' psychology.*

from *The Censor* (London, 1715)

I come now to speak of those Incidents which are struck out of the
Story, and introduc'd as subservient to the *Tragick* Action. To examine their Force and Propriety I must first consult the Poet's Aim in the
Play. He introduces a fond Father who, almost worn out with Age
and Infirmity, is for transferring his Cares on his Children, who disap-
point the Trust of his Love and, possess'd of the Staff in their own
Hands, condemn and abuse the Affection which bestow'd it. Hence

arise two practical Morals: the first a Caution against Rash and Unwary Bounty, the second against the base Returns and Ingratitude of Children to an Aged Parent. The Error of the first is to be painted in such Colours as are adapted to Compassion, the Baseness of the latter set out in such a Light as is proper to Detestation. To impart a proper Distress to *Lear's* Sufferings *Shakespeare* has given him two Friends, *Kent* and *Gloucester;* the one is made a disguis'd Companion of his Afflictions, the other loses his Eyes by the Command of the Savage Sisters only for interceeding with them for a Father, and acting in his Favour. The good old King is, by the Barbarity of his Daughters, forc'd to relinquish their Roof at Night, and in a Storm. Never was a Description wrought up with a more Masterly Hand than the Poet has here done on the Inclemency of the Season. Nor could Pity be well mov'd from a better Incident than by introducing a poor injur'd old Monarch, bareheaded in the midst of the Tempest, and tortur'd even to Distraction with his Daughters Ingratitude. How exquisitely fine are his Expostulations with the Heavens that seem to take part against him with his Children, and how artful, yet natural, are his Sentiments on this Occasion! [3.2.16–24] [. . .]

What admirable Thoughts of Morality and Instruction has he put in *Lear's* Mouth on the Growling of the Thunder and Flashes of the Lightning! [3.2.48 ff] [. . .]

Now when the Poet has once work'd up the Minds of his Audience to a full Compassion of the King's Misfortunes, to give a finishing stroke to that Passion he makes his Sorrows to have turn'd his Brain. In which Madness, I may venture to say, *Shakespeare* has wrought with such Spirit and so true a Knowledge of Nature that he has never yet nor ever will be equall'd in it by any succeeding Poet. It may be worth observing that there is one peculiar Beauty in this Play, which is, that throughout the whole the same Incidents which force us to pity *Lear* are Incentives to our Hatred against his Daughters.

The two Episodes of *Edgar* and *Edmund* are little dependant on the Fable (could we pretend to pin down *Shakespeare* to a Regularity of Plot), but that the Latter is made an Instrument of encreasing the Vicious Characters of the Daughters, and the Former is to punish him for the adulterous Passion as well as his Treachery and

Misusage to *Gloucester;* and indeed in the last Instance the Moral has some Connection to the main Scope of the Play. That the Daughters are propos'd as Examples of Divine Vengeance against unnatural Children, and as Objects of *Odium*, we have the Poet's own Words to demonstrate; for when their dead Bodies are pro-duc'd on the Stage *Albany* says

> *This Judgement of the Heav'ns, that makes us tremble,*
> *Touches us not with Pity.*——[5.3.231–232]

As to the General Absurdities of *Shakespeare* in this and all his other Tragedies, I have nothing to say. They were owing to his Igno-rance of *Mechanical* Rules and the Constitution of his Story, so can-not come under the Lash of Criticism; yet if they did I could without Regret pardon a Number of them for being so admirably lost in Excellencies. Yet there is one which without the Knowledge of Rules he might have corrected, and that is in the *Catastrophe*[1] of this Piece. *Cordelia* and *Lear* ought to have surviv'd, as Mr. *Tate* has made them in his Alteration of this Tragedy: Virtue ought to be rewarded as well as Vice punish'd; but in their Deaths this Moral is broke through. *Shakespeare* has done the same in his *Hamlet,* but permit me to make one Observation in his Defence there, that *Hamlet* having the Blood of his Uncle on his Hands *Blood will have Blood,* as the Poet has himself express'd it in *Macbeth.*

I must conclude with some short Remarks on the third thing propos'd, which is the Artful Preservation of *Lear's* Character. Had *Shakespeare* read all that *Aristotle, Horace,* and the Criticks have wrote on this Score he could not have wrought more happily. He proposes to represent an Old Man, o'er-gone with Infirmities as well as Years; one who was fond of Flattery and being fair spoken, of a hot and impetuous Temper, and impatient of Controul or Con-tradiction.

His Fondness of Flattery is sufficiently evidenc'd in the par-celling out his Dominions, and immediate discarding of *Cordelia* for not striking in with this Frailty of his. His Impatience of being contradicted appears in his Wrath to *Kent,* who would have diss-waded him from so rash an Action. [1.1.120–125] [. . .]

---

[1]The part of a drama following the climax and leading to the conclusion.

The same Artful Breaking out of his Temper is evident on *Goneril's* first Affront to him in retrenching the Number of his Followers. There is a Grace that cannot be conceiv'd in the sudden Starts of his Passion on being controul'd, and which best shews it self in forcing Us to admire it. [1.4.294–301] [. . .]

I cannot sufficiently admire his Struggles with his Testy Humour; his seeming Desire of restraining it, and the Force with which it resists his Endeavours and flies out into Rage and Imprecations. To quote Instances of half these Beauties were to copy Speeches out of every Scene where *Lear* either is with his Daughters or discoursing of them. The Charms of the *Sentiments*, and *Diction*, are too numerous to come under the Observation of a single Paper and will better be commended when introduc'd occasionally and least expected.

Samuel Johnson (1709–1784)

Samuel Johnson is still among the most influential of Shakespeare's critics. While much of his thinking takes place in notes on individual lines and words, he also expounds at some length on Lear's character. We can see his attempt to counter criticism of Shakespeare's characterization by considering his historical location and his sense of Shakespeare's moral purpose and design.

from "Notes on King Lear"
The Plays of William Shakespeare (London, 1765); 6.158–159

The tragedy of Lear is deservedly celebrated among the dramas of Shakespeare. There is perhaps no play which keeps the attention so strongly fixed; which so much agitates our passions and interests our curiosity. The artful involutions of distinct interests, the striking opposition of contrary characters, the sudden changes of fortune, and the quick succession of events, fill the mind with a perpetual tumult of indignation, pity, and hope. There is no scene which does not contribute to the aggravation of the distress or conduct of the action, and scarce a line which does not conduce to the progress of the scene. So powerful is the current of the poet's imagination, that the mind, which once ventures within it, is hurried irresistibly along.

On the seeming improbability of Lear's conduct it may be observed, that he is represented according to histories at that time vulgarly[1] received as true. And perhaps if we turn our thoughts upon the barbarity and ignorance of the age to which this story is referred, it will appear not so unlikely as while we estimate Lear's manners by our own. Such preference of one daughter to another, or resignation of dominion on such conditions, would be yet credible, if told of a petty prince of Guinea or Madagascar. Shakespeare, indeed, by the mention of his earls and dukes, has given us the idea of times more civilised, and of life regulated by softer manners; and the truth is, that though he so nicely discriminates, and so minutely describes the characters of men, he commonly neglects and confounds the characters of ages, by mingling customs ancient and modern, English and foreign.

My learned friend Mr. Warton, who has in the *Adventurer*[2] very minutely criticised this play, remarks, that the instances of cruelty are too savage and shocking, and that the intervention of Edmund destroys the simplicity of the story. These objections may, I think, be answered, by repeating, that the cruelty of the daughters is an historical fact, to which the poet has added little, having only drawn it into a series by dialogue and action. But I am not able to apologise with equal plausibility for the extrusion of Gloucester's eyes, which seems an act too horrid to be endured in dramatick exhibition, and such as must always compel the mind to relieve its distress by incredulity. Yet let it be remembered that our authour well knew what would please the audience for which he wrote.

The injury done by Edmund to the simplicity of the action is abundantly recompensed by the addition of variety, by the art with which he is made to co-operate with the chief design, and the opportunity which he gives the poet of combining perfidy with perfidy, and connecting the wicked son with the wicked daughters, to impress this important moral, that villany is never at a stop, that crimes lead to crimes, and at last terminate in ruin.

---

[1]Commonly believed to be.

[2]Critic Joseph Warton (1722–1800). His comments appear in nos. 113, 116, and 122 of this periodical.

But though this moral be incidentally enforced, Shakespeare has suffered the virtue of Cordelia to perish in a just cause, contrary to the natural ideas of justice, to the hope of the reader, and, what is yet more strange, to the faith of chronicles. Yet this conduct is justified by *The Spectator*, who blames Tate for giving Cordelia success and happiness in his alteration, and declares, that, in his opinion, "the tragedy has lost half its beauty."[3] [. . .] A play in which the wicked prosper, and the virtuous miscarry, may doubtless be good, because it is a just representation of the common events of human life: but since all reasonable beings naturally love justice, I cannot easily be persuaded, that the observation of justice makes a play worse; or, that if other excellencies are equal, the audience will not always rise better pleased from the final triumph of persecuted virtue.

In the present case the publick has decided. Cordelia, from the time of Tate, has always retired with victory and felicity. And, if my sensations could add any thing to the general suffrage, I might relate, that I was many years ago so shocked by Cordelia's death, that I know not whether I ever endured to read again the last scenes of the play till I undertook to revise them as an editor.

There is another controversy among the criticks concerning this play. It is disputed whether the predominant image in Lear's disordered mind be the loss of his kingdom or the cruelty of his daughters. Mr. Murphy,[4] a very judicious critick, has evinced by induction of particular passages, that the cruelty of his daughters is the primary source of his distress, and that the loss of royalty affects him only as a secondary and subordinate evil; he observes with great justness, that Lear would move our compassion but little, did we not rather consider the injured father than the degraded king.

[3]*The Spectator* was another periodical, published daily by Sir Richard Steele (1672–1729) and Joseph Addison (1672–1719) from March 1711 to December 1712, and revived by Addison in 1714; the critic Addison's comments appear in no. 40.

[4]The critic Arthur Murphy, who wrote about the play in the literary periodical *Gray's Inn Journal*, nos. 16 and 17 (1754 edition).

Mr. GARRICK in the Character of KING LEAR.
Act ỳ 3ᵗ Scene ỳ 1ˢᵗ

Printed for R. Sayer No. 53 Fleet Street & J. Smith No. 35 Cheapside Octᵗ 10. 1760 . 6

Charles Spencer's engraving of the seventeenth-century actor David Garrick (1717–1779) as King Lear in 3.1 (the storm scene), after the 1761 painting by Benjamin Wilson. The production was in 1761 at the Drury Lane Theatre. The ermine-trimmed cloak emphasizes Lear's royalty.

George Colman (1732–1794)

George Colman was a theater manager, popular playwright, and translator who adapted Shakespeare for the eighteenth-century stage. Even though Colman's version was a rare (and commercially unsuccessful) dissent from the favored Tate's version, Colman's Preface gives a rare contemporary objection to Tate's choices. He begins by quoting Tate's account of his purpose in introducing a love relationship between Edgar and Cordelia.

from the Preface to *The History of King Lear*[1]

Now this very expedient of *a love* betwixt Edgar and Cordelia, on which Tate felicitates himself, seemed to me to be one of the capital objections to his alteration. For even supposing that it rendered Cordelia's indifference to her father more probable (an indifference which Shakespeare has no where implied), it assigns a very poor motive for it; so that what Edgar gains on the side of romantick generosity Cordelia loses on that of real virtue. The distress of the story is so far from being heightened by it that it has diffused a languor and insipidity over all the scenes of the play from which Lear is absent, for which I appeal to the sensations of the numerous audiences with which the play has been honoured. And had the scenes been affectingly written they would at least have divided our feelings, which Shakespeare has attached almost entirely to Lear and Cordelia in their parental and filial capacities; thereby producing passages infinitely more tragick than the embraces of Cordelia and the ragged Edgar, which would have appeared too ridiculous for representation had they not been mixed and incorporated with some of the finest scenes of Shakespeare.

Tate, in whose days *love* was the soul of Tragedy as well as Comedy, was, however, so devoted to intrigue that he has not only given Edmund a passion for Cordelia but has injudiciously amplified on his criminal commerce with Goneril and Regan, which is the most disgusting part of the original. The Rev. Dr. Warton has doubted 'whether the cruelty of the daughters is not painted with circumstances too savage and unnatural,'[2] even by Shakespeare. Still, however, in Shakespeare some motives for their conduct are assigned; but as Tate has conducted that part of the fable they are equally cruel and unnatural, without the poet's assigning any motive at all.

[1] George Colman, *The History of King Lear. As it is performed at the Theatre Royal in Covent Garden* [1768] (London, 1768).

[2] Joseph Warton, in *The Adventurer*, no. 132.

In all these circumstances it is generally agreed that Tate's alteration is for the worse, and his *King Lear* would probably have quit-
ted the stage long ago had not the poet made 'the tale conclude in a
success to the innocent distressed persons.' [. . .]

'The utter improbability of Gloucester's imagining, though
blind, that he had leaped down Dover Cliff,' has been justly censured
by Dr. Warton; and in the representation it is still more liable to
objection than in print. I have therefore without scruple omitted it,
preserving, however, at the same time that celebrated description of
the Cliff in the mouth of Edgar. The putting out Gloucester's eyes is
also so unpleasing a circumstance that I would have altered it, if possible; but upon examination it appeared to be so closely interwoven
with the fable that I durst not venture to change it. I had once some
idea of retaining the character of *the fool*, but though Dr. Warton
has very truly observed that the poet 'has so well conducted even the
natural jargon of the beggar and the jestings of the fool, which in
other hands must have sunk into burlesque, that they contribute to
heighten the pathetick;' yet after the most serious consideration I
was convinced that such a scene 'would sink into burlesque' in the
representation, and would not be endured on the modern stage.

Charles Lamb (1775–1834)

*Critic, poet, and essayist Charles Lamb gave force in his writings to the
consideration of Shakespeare's characters as subjects independent of a
stage identity or existence in the play. With his sister Mary he wrote*
Tales from Shakespear *(1807), intended to make the plays accessible to
a juvenile audience. Lamb initiates the prejudice against the actual performance of this and other tragedies (sometimes called the "anti-the-
atrical prejudice") that, in the case of* Lear, *held sway until the
powerful stagings of* King Lear *during the twentieth century. The over-
all objection to stage representation had as much to do with the legitimate theaters of Lamb's day—huge amphitheaters, seating thousands,
and therefore favoring spectacles and special effects over subtlety of
language and characterization—as with the sense that the tragedies
were most truly brought to powerful imaginative life in the meditative
introspections of reading.*

from "On the Tragedies of Shakspeare, considered with reference to their fitness for stage representation" (1810)[1]

Never let me be so ungrateful as to forget the very high degree of satisfaction which I received some years back from seeing for the first time a tragedy of Shakspeare performed, in which these two great performers[2] sustained the principal parts. It seemed to embody and realize conceptions which had hitherto assumed no distinct shape. But dearly do we pay all our life afterwards for this juvenile pleasure, this sense of distinctness. When the novelty is past, we find to our cost that, instead of realizing an idea, we have only materialized and brought down a fine vision to the standard of flesh and blood. We have let go a dream, in quest of an unattainable substance.

How cruelly this operates upon the mind, to have its free conceptions thus cramped and pressed down to the measure of a straitlacing actuality, may be judged from that delightful sensation of freshness with which we turn to those plays of Shakspeare which have escaped being performed, and to those passages in the acting plays of the same writer which have happily been left out in the performance. How far the very custom of hearing anything *spouted,* withers and blows upon a fine passage, may be seen in those speeches from "Henry the Fifth," etc., which are current in the mouths of schoolboys. [. . .] I confess myself utterly unable to appreciate that celebrated soliloquy in "Hamlet," beginning "To be, or not to be," or to tell whether it be good, bad, or indifferent, it has been so handled and pawed about by declamatory boys and men, and torn so inhumanly from its living place and principle of continuity in the play, till it is become to me a perfect dead member.

It may seem a paradox, but I cannot help being of opinion that the plays of Shakspeare are less calculated for performance on a stage than those of almost any other dramatist whatever. Their distinguished excellence is a reason that they should be so; there is so much in them which comes not under the province of acting, with which eye and tone and gesture have nothing to do. [. . .]

---

[1]From *The Dramatic Essays of Charles Lamb*, ed. Brander Matthews (New York, 1891); pp. 166–187 passim.

[2]John Phillip Kemble (1757–1823) and his sister Sarah Siddons (1755–1831). Lady Macbeth was one of her celebrated roles.

So to see Lear acted,—to see an old man tottering about the stage with a walking-stick, turned out of doors by his daughters in a rainy night, has nothing in it but what is painful and disgusting. We want to take him into shelter and relieve him,—that is all the feeling which the acting of Lear ever produced in me. But the Lear of Shakespeare cannot be acted. The contemptible machinery, by which they mimic the storm which he goes out in, is not more inadequate to represent the horrors of the real elements than any actor can be to represent Lear; they might more easily propose to personate the Satan of Milton upon a stage, or one of Michael Angelo's terrible figures. The greatness of Lear is not in corporal dimension, but in intellectual; the explosions of his passion are terrible as a volcano,—they are storms turning up and disclosing to the bottom that sea, his mind, with all its vast riches. It is his mind which is laid bare. This case of flesh and blood seems too insignificant to be thought on, even as he himself neglects it. On the stage we see nothing but corporal infirmities and weakness, the impotence of rage; while we read it, we see not Lear, but we are Lear,—we are in his mind, we are sustained by a grandeur which baffles the malice of daughters and storms. In the aberrations of his reason we discover a mighty, irregular power of reasoning, immethodized from the ordinary purposes of life, but exerting its powers, as the wind blows where it listeth, at will upon the corruptions and abuses of mankind. What have looks or tones to do with that sublime identification of his age with that of the *heavens themselves*, when in his reproaches to them for conniving at the injustice of his children he reminds them that "they themselves are old"? What gestures shall we appropriate to this? What has the voice or the eye to do with such things? But the play is beyond all art, as the tamperings with it show; it is too hard and stony,—it must have love-scenes, and a happy ending. It is not enough that Cordelia is a daughter, she must shine as a lover too. Tate has put his hook in the nostrils of this Leviathan, for Garrick and his followers, the showmen of scene, to draw the mighty beast about more easily. A happy ending!—as if the living matyrdom that Lear had gone through, the flaying of his feelings alive, did not make a fair dismissal from the stage of life the only decorous thing for him. If he is to live and be happy after, if he could sustain this world's burden after, why all this pudder and preparation, why torment us with all this unnecessary sympathy?

As if the childish pleasure of getting his gilt robes and sceptre again could tempt him to act over again his misused station; as if at his years, and with his experience, anything was left but to die!

"Lear" is essentially impossible to be represented on a stage.

from *Tales from Shakespear* (London, 1807)

This popular retelling of Shakespeare's plays for "the young reader" (as the Preface designates the audience) has never been out of print since its first publication almost two hundred years ago. Although the Lambs omit the Gloucester/Edgar/Edmund plot (mentioning Edmund only in relation to Goneril and Regan), they do insist on the fidelity to Shakespeare's tragedy enough to include the death of Cordelia, not only a bold decision in an age when Nahum Tate's revision held the stage but also a rigorous introduction for young readers to Shakespeare's stark tragedy. The following excerpts are from the beginning and the end of the tale.

from "King Lear" (pp. 123–140, passim)

Lear, king of Britain, had three daughters; Goneril, wife to the duke of Albany; Regan, wife to the duke of Cornwall; and Cordelia, a young maid, for whose love the king of France and duke of Burgundy were joint suitors, and were at this time making stay for that purpose in the court of Lear.

The old king, worn out with age and the fatigues of government, he being more than fourscore years old, determined to take no further part in state affairs, but to leave the management to younger strengths, that he might have time to prepare for death, which must at no long period ensue. With this intent he called his three daughters to him, to know from their own lips which of them loved him best, that he might part his kingdom among them in such proportions as their affection for him should seem to deserve.

Goneril, the eldest, declared that she loved her father more than words could give out, that he was dearer to her than the light of her own eyes, dearer than life and liberty, with a deal of such professing stuff, which is easy to counterfeit where there is no real love, only a few fine words delivered with confidence being wanted in that case.

The king, delighted to hear from her own mouth this assurance of her love, and thinking truly that her heart went with it, in a fit of fatherly fondness bestowed upon her and her husband one-third of his ample kingdom.

Then calling to him his second daughter, he demanded what she had to say. Regan, who was made of the same hollow metal as her sister, was not a whit behind in her profession, but rather declared that what her sister had spoken came short of the love which she professed to bear for his highness; insomuch that she found all other joys dead, in comparison with the pleasure which she took in the love of her dear king and father.

Lear blessed himself in having such loving children, as he thought; and could do no less, after the handsome assurances which Regan had made, than bestow a third of his kingdom upon her and her husband, equal in size to that which he had already given away to Goneril.

Then turning to his youngest daughter Cordelia, whom he called his joy, he asked what she had to say, thinking no doubt that she would glad his ears with the same loving speeches which her sisters had uttered, or rather that her expressions would be so much stronger than theirs, as she had always been his darling, and favoured by him above either of them. But Cordelia, disgusted with the flattery of her sisters, whose hearts she knew were far from their lips, and seeing that all their coaxing speeches were only intended to wheedle the old king out of his dominions, that they and their husbands might reign in his lifetime, made no other reply but this,—that she loved his majesty according to her duty, neither more nor less.

The king, shocked with this appearance of ingratitude in his favourite child, desired her to consider her words, and to mend her speech, lest it should mar her fortunes.

Cordelia then told her father, that he was her father, that he had given her breeding, and loved her; that she returned those duties back as was most fit, and did obey him, love him, and most honour him. But that she could not frame her mouth to such large speeches as her sisters had done, or promise to love nothing else in the world. Why had her sisters husbands, if (as they said) they had no love for anything but their father? If she should ever wed, she was sure the lord to whom she gave her hand would want half her love, half of her care and duty; she should never marry like her sisters, to love her father all.

Cordelia, who in earnest loved her old father even almost as extravagantly as her sisters pretended to do, would have plainly told him so at any other time, in more daughter-like and loving terms, and without these qualifications, which did indeed sound a little ungracious; but after the crafty flattering speeches of her sisters, which she had seen drawn such extravagant rewards, she thought the handsomest thing she could do was to love and be silent. This put her affection out of suspicion of mercenary ends, and showed that she loved, but not for gain; and that her professions, the less ostentatious they were, had so much the more of truth and sincerity than her sisters'.

This plainness of speech, which Lear called pride, so enraged the old monarch—who in his best of times always showed much of spleen and rashness, and in whom the dotage incident to old age had so clouded over his reason, that he could not discern truth from flattery, nor a gay painted speech from words that came from the heart—that in a fury of resentment he retracted the third part of his kingdom, which yet remained, and which he had reserved for Cordelia, and gave it away from her, sharing it equally between her two sisters and their husbands, the dukes of Albany and Cornwall; whom he now called to him, and in presence of all his courtiers bestowing a coronet between them, invested them jointly with all the power, revenue, and execution of government, only retaining to himself the name of king; all the rest of royalty he resigned; with this reservation, that himself, with a hundred knights for his attendants, was to be maintained by monthly course in each of his daughters' palaces in turn.

So preposterous a disposal of his kingdom, so little guided by reason, and so much by passion, filled all his courtiers with astonishment and sorrow; but none of them had the courage to interpose between this incensed king and his wrath, except the earl of Kent, who was beginning to speak a good word for Cordelia, when the passionate Lear on pain of death commanded him to desist; but the good Kent was not so to be repelled. He had been ever loyal to Lear, whom he had honoured as a king, loved as a father, followed as a master; and he had never esteemed his life further than as a pawn to wage against his royal master's enemies, nor feared to lose it when

Lear's safety was the motive; not now that Lear was most his own enemy, did this faithful servant of the king forget his old principles, but manfully opposed Lear, to do Lear good; and was unmannerly only because Lear was mad. He had been a most faithful counsellor in times past to the king, and he besought him now, that he would see with his eyes (as he had done in many weighty matters), and go by his advice still; and in his best consideration recall this hideous rashness: for he would answer with his life, his judgment that Lear's youngest daughter did not love him least, nor were those empty-hearted whose low sound gave no token of hollowness. When power bowed to flattery, honour was bound to plainness. For Lear's threats, what could he do to him, whose life was already at his service? That should not hinder duty from speaking.

The honest freedom of this good earl of Kent only stirred up the king's wrath the more, and like a frantic patient who kills his physician, and loves his mortal disease, he banished this true servant, and allotted him but five days to make his preparations for departure; but if on the sixth his hated person was found within the realm of Britain, that moment was to be his death. And Kent bade farewell to the king, and said, that since he chose to show himself in such fashion, it was but banishment to stay there; and before he went, he recommended Cordelia to the protection of the gods, the maid who had so rightly thought, and so discreetly spoken; and only wished that her sisters' large speeches might be answered with deeds of love; and then he went, as he said, to shape his old course to a new country.

The king of France and duke of Burgundy were now called in to hear the determination of Lear about his youngest daughter, and to know whether they would persist in their courtship to Cordelia, now that she was under her father's displeasure, and had no fortune but her own person to recommend her: and the duke of Burgundy declined the match, and would not take her to wife upon such conditions; but the king of France, understanding what the nature of the fault had been which had lost her the love of her father, that it was only a tardiness of speech, and the not being able to frame her tongue to flattery like her sisters, took this young maid by the hand, and saying that her virtues were a dowry above a kingdom, bade Cordelia to take farewell of her sisters and of her father, though he had been unkind, and she should go with him, and be queen of him and of fair France, and reign over fairer possessions than her sisters;

and he called the duke of Burgundy in contempt a waterish duke, because his love for this young maid had in a moment run all away like water.

Then Cordelia with weeping eyes took leave of her sisters, and besought them to love their father well, and make good their professions: and they sullenly told her not to prescribe to them, for they knew their duty; but to strive to content her husband, who had taken her (as they tauntingly expressed it) as Fortune's alms. And Cordelia with a heavy heart departed, for she knew the cunning of her sisters, and she wished her father in better hands than she was about to leave him in. [. . .]

A tender sight it was to see the meeting between this father and daughter; to see the struggles between the joy of this poor old king at beholding again his once darling child, and the shame at receiving such filial kindness from her whom he had cast off for so small a fault in his displeasure; both these passions struggling with the remains of his malady, which in his half-crazed brain sometimes made him that he scarce remembered where he was, or who it was that so kindly kissed him and spoke to him; and then he would beg the standersby not to laugh at him, if he were mistaken in thinking this lady to be his daughter Cordelia! And then to see him fall on his knees to beg pardon of his child; and she, good lady, kneeling all the while to ask a blessing of him, and telling him that it did not become him to kneel, but it was her duty, for she was his child, his true and very child Cordelia! And she kissed him (as she said) to kiss away all her sisters' unkindness, and said that they might be ashamed of themselves, to turn their old kind father with his white beard out into the cold air, when her enemy's dog, though it had bit her (as she prettily expressed it), should have stayed by her fire such a night as that, and warmed himself. And she told her father how she had come from France with purpose to being him assistance; and he said that she must forget and forgive, for he was old and foolish, and did not know what he did; but that to be sure she had great cause not to love him, but her sisters had none. And Cordelia said that she had no cause, no more than they had.

So we will leave this old king in the protection of his dutiful and loving child, where, by the help of sleep and medicine, she and her physicians at length succeeded in winding up the untuned and jarring senses which the cruelty of his other daughters had so violently shaken. Let us return to say a word or two about those cruel daughters.

These monsters of ingratitude, who had been so false to their old father, could not be expected to prove more faithful to their own husbands. They soon grew tired of paying even the appearance of duty and affection, and in an open way showed they had fixed their loves upon another. It happened that the object of their guilty loves was the same. It was Edmund, a natural son of the late earl of Gloucester, who by his treacheries had succeeded in disinheriting his brother Edgar, the lawful heir, from his earldom, and by his wicked practices was now earl himself; a wicked man, and a fit object for the love of such wicked creatures as Goneril and Regan. It falling out about this time that the duke of Cornwall, Regan's husband, died, Regan immediately declared her intention of wedding this earl of Gloucesster, which rousing the jealousy of her sister, to whom as well as to Regan this wicked earl had at sundry times professed love, Goneril found means to make away with her sister by poison; but being detected in her practices, and imprisoned by her husband, the duke of Albany, for this deed, and for her guilty passion for the earl which had come to his ears, she, in a fit of disappointed love and rage, shortly put an end to her own life. Thus the justice of Heaven at last overtook these wicked daughters.

While the eyes of all men were upon this event, admiring the justice displayed in their deserved deaths, the same eyes were suddenly taken off from this sight to admire at the mysterious ways of the same power in the melancholy fate of the young and virtuous daughter, the lady Cordelia, whose good deeds did seem to deserve a more fortunate conclusion: but it is an awful truth, that innocence and piety are not always successful in this world. The forces which Goneril and Regan had sent out under the command of the bad earl of Gloucester were victorious, and Cordelia, by the practices of this wicked earl, who did not like that any should stand between him and the throne, ended her life in prison. Thus, Heaven took this innocent lady to itself in her young years, after showing her to the world an illustrious example of filial duty. Lear did not long survive this kind child.

Before he died, the good earl of Kent, who had still attended his old master's steps from the first of his daughters' ill usage to this sad period of his decay, tried to make him understand that it was he who had followed him under the name of Caius; but Lear's care-crazed brain at that time could not comprehend how that could be, or how Kent and Caius could be the same person: so Kent thought it needless to trouble him with explanations at such a time; and Lear soon after expiring, this faithful servant to the king, between age and grief for his old master's vexations, soon followed him to the grave.

How the judgment of Heaven overtook the bad earl of Gloucester, whose treasons were discovered, and himself slain in single combat with his brother, the lawful earl; and how Goneril's husband, the duke of Albany, who was innocent of the death of Cordelia, and had never encouraged his lady in her wicked proceedings against her father, ascended the throne of Britain after the death of Lear, is needless here to narrate; Lear and his Three Daughters being dead, whose adventures alone concern our story.

William Hazlitt (1778–1830)

William Hazlitt was part of the same literary circle as Lamb and Coleridge and one of the first writers to make a living from his literary journalism. He too found King Lear *a subject for the contemplation of human character rather than theatrical realization, and he admired Lamb's essay on its unsuitability for the stage. Hazlitt's lectures on Shakespeare's plays were widely attended (by Keats, among others) and were a chief public forum for the consideration of taste and art. The lectures were published in 1818. His words on* King Lear *launch the conceit of the inexpressibility of the play's effect. Hazlitt has a refreshing take on Edmund, a rare attention to the fool, and a sense of the play's rhythms, considered as a portrait of passion itself.*

from *The Characters of Shakespear's Plays* (London, 1818)[1]

We wish that we could pass this play over, and say nothing about it. All that we can say must fall far short of the subject; or even of what we ourselves conceive of it. To attempt to give a description of

[1]From *The Collected Works of William Hazlitt*, ed. A. R. Waller and Arnold Glover (London, 1902); pp. 257–260 passim.

An engraving by Henry Fuseli of Lear's entrance at 5.3.256. Fuseli (1741–1825) was an illustrator and translator, an admirer of Michelangelo, and a chief contributor to Boydell's Shakespeare Gallery, *an exhibition of paintings devoted to Shakespeare's works, which opened in London in June 1789. His engraving of Lear bearing Cordelia's body casts the two figures in a classical light and emphasizes Lear's still-powerful paternity.*

the play itself or of its effect upon the mind, is mere impertinence: yet we must say something.—It is then the best of all Shakespear's plays, for it is the one in which he was the most in earnest. He was here fairly caught in the web of his own imagination. The passion which he has taken as his subject is that which strikes its root deepest into the human heart; of which the bond is the hardest to be unloosed; and the cancelling and tearing to pieces of which gives the greatest revulsion to the frame. This depth of nature, this force of passion, this tug and war of the elements of our being, this firm faith in filial piety, and the giddy anarchy and whirling tumult of the thoughts at finding this prop failing it, the contrast between the fixed, immoveable basis of natural affection, and the rapid, irregular stars of imagination, suddenly wrenched from all its accustomed holds and resting-places in the soul, this is what Shakespear has given, and what nobody else but he could give. So we believe.—The mind of Lear, staggering between the weight of attachment and the hurried movements of passion, is like a tall ship driven about by the winds, buffeted by the furious waves, but that still rides above the storm, having its anchor fixed in the bottom of the sea; or it is like the sharp rock circled by the eddying whirlpool that foams and beats against it, or like the solid promontory pushed from its basis by the force of an earthquake.

The character of Lear itself is very finely conceived for the purpose. It is the only ground on which such a story could be built with the greatest truth and effect. It is his rash haste, his violent impetuosity, his blindness to every thing but the dictates of his passions or affections, that produces all his misfortunes, that aggravates his impatience of them, that enforces our pity for him. The part which Cordelia bears in the scene is extremely beautiful: the story is almost told in the first words she utters. We see at once the precipice on which the poor old king stands from his own extravagant and credulous importunity, the indiscreet simplicity of her love (which, to be sure, has a little of her father's obstinacy in it) and the hollowness of her sisters' pretensions. Almost the first burst of that noble tide of passion, which runs through the play, is in the remonstrance of Kent to his royal master on the injustice of his sentence against his youngest daughter—"Be Kent unmannerly, when Lear is mad." (1.1.143–144) This manly plainness, which draws down on him the displeasure of the unadvised king, is worthy of the fidelity with which he adheres to his fallen fortunes. The true character of the two eldest daughters, Regan and Gonerill (they are so thoroughly hateful that we do not even like to repeat their names) breaks out in their answer to Cordelia who desires them to treat their father well—"Prescribe not us our duties" (1.1.277) [sic] he gets 'duties' for 'duty'—their hatred of advice being in proportion to their determination to do wrong, and to their hypocritical pretensions to do right. Their deliberate hypocrisy adds the last finishing to the odiousness of their characters. It is the absence of this detestable quality that is the only relief in the character of Edmund the Bastard, and that at times reconciles us to him. We are not tempted to exaggerate the guilt of his conduct, when he himself gives it up as a bad business, and writes himself down 'plain villain.' Nothing more can be said about it. His religious honesty in this respect is admirable. One speech of his is worth a million. [. . .]

It has been said, and we think justly, that the third act of *Othello*[2] and the three first acts of LEAR, are Shakespear's great master-pieces in the logic of passion: that they contain the highest examples not only of the force of individual passion, but of its dramatic vicissitudes and striking effects arising from the different circumstances and characters of the persons speaking. We see the ebb and flow of the feeling, its pauses and feverish starts, its impatience of opposition, its accumulating force when it has time to recollect itself, the manner in which it avails itself of every passing word or gesture, its haste to repel insinuation, the alternate contraction and dilatation of the soul, and all "the dazzling fence of controversy" in this mortal combat with poisoned weapons, aimed at the heart, where each wound is fatal. We have seen in *Othello*, how the unsuspecting frankness and impetuous passions of the Moor are played upon and exasperated by the artful dexterity of Iago. In the present play, that which aggravates the sense of sympathy in the reader, and of uncontroulable anguish in the swoln heart of Lear, is the petrifying indifference, the cold, calculating, obdurate selfishness of his daughters. His keen passions seem whetted on their stony hearts. The contrast would be too painful, the shock too great, but for the intervention of the Fool, whose

[2]When Othello's faith in Desdemona shifts to fatal jealousy.

well-timed levity comes in to break the continuity of feeling when it can no longer be borne, and to bring into play again the fibres of the heart just as they are growing rigid from over-strained excitement. The imagination is glad to take refuge in the half-comic, half-serious comments of the Fool, just as the mind under the extreme anguish of a surgical operation vents itself in sallies of wit. The character was also a grotesque ornament of the barbarous times, in which alone the tragic ground-work of the story could be laid. In another point of view it is indispensable, inasmuch as while it is a diversion to the too great intensity of our disgust, it carries the pathos to the highest pitch of which it is capable, by shewing the pitiable weakness of the old king's conduct and its irretrievable consequences in the most familiar point of view. Lear may well "beat at the gate which let [his] folly in," (1.4.254–255) after, as the Fool says, "he has made his daughters his mothers." (1.4.163–164) The character is dropped in the third act to make room for the entrance of Edgar as Mad Tom, which well accords with the increasing bustle and wildness of the incidents; and nothing can be more complete than the distinction between Lear's real and Edgar's assumed madness, while the resemblance in the cause of their distresses, from the severing of the nearest ties of natural affection, keeps up a unity of interest. Shakespear's mastery over his subject, if it was not art, was owing to a knowledge of the connecting links of the passions, and their effect upon the mind, still more wonderful than any systematic adherence to rules, and that anticipated and outdid all the efforts of the most refined art, not inspired and rendered instinctive by genius. [. . .]

Samuel Taylor Coleridge (1772–1834)

Poet, critic, and essayist Samuel Taylor Coleridge began lecturing on Shakespeare in 1811. This lecture on King Lear *(1818) was one of a series of character studies. It is attentive to the play's rhythms, construction, and, above all, psychology. Like Hazlitt, Coleridge is drawn to the figure of Edmund, whose rebelliousness against social strictures resonated with the temper of the Romantic age.*

from *Lectures on Shakespeare* (1818)[1]

Of all Shakespeare's plays Macbeth is the most rapid, Hamlet the slowest, in movement. Lear combines length with rapidity,—like the hurricane and the whirlpool, absorbing while it advances. It begins as a stormy day in summer, with brightness; but that brightness is lurid, and anticipates the tempest.

It was not without forethought, nor is it without its due significance, that the division of Lear's kingdom is in the first six lines of the play stated as a thing already determined in all its particulars, previously to the trial of professions, as the relative rewards of which the daughters were to be made to consider their several portions. The strange, yet by no means unnatural, mixture of selfishness, sensibility, and habit of feeling derived from, and fostered by, the particular rank and usages of the individual;—the intense desire of being intensely beloved,—selfish, and yet characteristic of the selfishness of a loving and kindly nature alone;—the self-supportless leaning for all pleasure on another's breast;—the craving after sympathy with a prodigal disinterestedness, frustrated by its own ostentation, and the mode and nature of its claims;—the anxiety, the distrust, the jealousy, which more or less accompany all selfish affections, and are amongst the surest contra-distinctions of mere fondness from true love, and which originate Lear's eager wish to enjoy his daughter's violent professions, whilst the inveterate habits of sovereignty convert the wish into claim and positive right, and an incompliance with it into crime and treason;—these facts, these passions, these moral verities, on which the whole tragedy is founded, are all prepared for, and will to the retrospect be found implied, in these first four or five lines of the play. They let us know that the trial is but a trick; and that the grossness of the old king's rage is in part the natural result of a silly trick suddenly and most unexpectedly baffled and disappointed.

[. . .] The accidental is nowhere the groundwork of the passions, but that which is catholic, which in all ages has been, and ever will be, close and native to the heart of man,—parental anguish from filial ingratitude, the genuineness of worth, though confined in bluntness, and the execrable vileness of a smooth iniquity. [. . .]

---

[1]From *Notes of Lectures on Shakespeare and Other Poets and Dramatists*, ed. Ernest Rhys (London, 1907); pp. 124–129 passim.

[. . .] Having thus in the fewest words, and in a natural reply to as natural a question,—which yet answers the secondary purpose of attracting our attention to the difference or diversity between the characters of Cornwall and Albany,—provided the premises and *data*, as it were, for our after insight into the mind and mood of the person, whose character, passions, and sufferings are the main subject-matter of the play;—from Lear the *persona patiens*[2] of his drama, Shakespeare passes without delay to the second in importance, the chief agent and prime mover, and introduces Edmund to our acquaintance, preparing us with the same felicity of judgment, and in the same easy and natural way, for his character in the seemingly casual communication of its origin and occasion. From the first drawing up of the curtain Edmund has stood before us in the united strength and beauty of earliest manhood. Our eyes have been questioning him. Gifted as he is with high advantages of person, and further endowed by nature with a powerful intellect and a strong energetic will, even without any concurrence of circumstances and accident, pride will necessarily be the sin that most easily besets him. But Edmund is also the known and acknowledged son of the princely Gloster: he, therefore, has both the germ of pride, and the conditions best fitted to evolve and ripen it into a predominant feeling. Yet hitherto no reason appears why it should be other than the not unusual pride of person, talent, and birth,—a pride auxiliary, if not akin, to many virtues, and the natural ally of honourable impulses. But alas! in his own presence his own father takes shame to himself for the frank avowal that he is his father,—he has 'blushed so often to acknowledge him that he is now brazed to it!' (1.1.8–9) Edmund hears the circumstances of his birth spoken of with a most degrading and licentious levity,—his mother described as a wanton by her own paramour, and the remembrance of the animal sting, the low criminal gratifications connected with her wantonness and prostituted beauty, assigned as the reason why 'the whoreson must be acknowledged!' (1.1.21) This, and the consciousness of its notoriety; the gnawing conviction that every show of respect is an effort of courtesy, which recalls, while it represses, a contrary feeling;—this is the ever trickling flow of wormwood and gall into the wounds of pride,—the corrosive *virus* which inoculates

[2]Suffering protagonist.

pride with a venom not its own, with envy, hatred, and a lust for that power which in its blaze of radiance would hide the dark spots on his disc,—with pangs of shame personally undeserved, and therefore felt as wrongs, and with a blind ferment of vindictive working towards the occasions and causes, especially towards a brother, whose stainless birth and lawful honours were the constant remembrancers of his own debasement, and were ever in the way to prevent all chance of its being unknown, or overlooked and forgotten. Add to this, that with excellent judgment, and provident for the claims of the moral sense,—for that which, relatively to the drama, is called poetic justice, and as the fittest means for reconciling the feelings of the spectators to the horrors of Gloster's after sufferings,—at least, of rendering them somewhat less unendurable;— (for I will not disguise my conviction, that in this one point the tragic in this play has been urged beyond the outermost mark and *ne plus ultra*[3] of the dramatic)—Shakespeare has precluded all excuse and palliation of the guilt incurred by both the parents of the base-born Edmund, by Gloster's confession that he was at the time a married man, and already blest with a lawful heir of his fortunes. [. . .] Need it be said how heavy an aggravation, in such a case, the stain of bastardy must have been, were it only that the younger brother was liable to hear his own dishonour and his mother's infamy related by his father with an excusing shrug of the shoulders, and in a tone betwixt waggery and shame!

John Keats (1796–1821)

John Keats's sonnet of January 22, 1818 encapsulates the romantic response to Shakespeare's play as an object for the mind's eye (to be read, rather than seen), as well as its status as a stringent antidote to much contemporary imaginative writing. Keats died at 25 in 1821; the sonnet (originally penned in his copy of Shakespeare's plays and then copied in a letter to his brother and sister-in-law) was first published in 1838. In the letter, January 24, 1818, Keats introduces the sonnet thus: "Nothing is finer for the purposes of great productions, than a very

---

[3]The highest or deepest point capable of being obtained.

gradual ripening of the intellectual powers—As an instance of this— observe—I sat down yesterday to read King Lear once again the thing appeared to demand the prologue of a Sonnet. I wrote it & began to read— ." Just after writing out the sonnet, Keats said, "So you see I am getting at it, with a sort of determination and strength."[1] The text reproduced here is from the version in Keats's copy of Shakespeare.

On Sitting Down to Read King Lear Once Again[2]

O golden-tongued Romance, with serene lute!
    Fair plumed Syren,[3] Queen of far-away!
    Leave melodizing on this wintry day,
Shut up thine olden pages, and be mute.
Adieu! for, once again, the fierce dispute
    Betwixt damnation and impassion'd clay
    Must I burn through; once more humbly assay
The bitter-sweet of this Shaksperean fruit:
Chief Poet! and ye clouds of Albion,
    Begetters of our deep eternal theme!
When through the old oak Forest I am gone,
    Let me not wander in a barren dream,
But, when I am consumed in the fire,
Give me new Phœnix[4] wings to fly at my desire.

A. C. Bradley (1851–1935)

A. C. Bradley was a professor at Oxford University and a literary critic of wide-ranging interests, best remembered for his writings on Shakespeare. His book on the tragedies remains among the most influential critical treatments. While he finds King Lear *a flawed play, he was among the first to argue for its preeminence in the canon.*

[1]*The Letters of John Keats 1814–1821*, 2 vols., ed. Hyder Edward Rollins (Cambridge, Harvard University Press, 1958).
[2]Text from 1.214, in *Poems of John Keats*, ed. G. Thorn Drury (London, 1904); p. 179.
[3]A female creature of Greek mythology whose song lured sailors to their destruction.
[4]Legendary bird reputed to rise anew from a fiery death.

from *Shakespearean Tragedy: Lectures on Hamlet, Othello, King Lear and Macbeth* (London, 1904), pp. 247–249

The stage is the test of strictly dramatic quality, and *King Lear* is too huge for the stage. Of course, I am not denying that it is a great stage-play. It has scenes immensely effective in the theatre; three of them—the two between Lear and Goneril and between Lear, Goneril and Regan, and the ineffably beautiful scene in the Fourth Act between Lear and Cordelia—lose in the theatre very little of the spell they have for imagination; and the gradual interweaving of the two plots is almost as masterly as in *Much Ado*. But (not to speak of defects due to mere carelessness) that which makes the *peculiar* greatness of King Lear,—the immense scope of the work; the mass and variety of intense experience which it contains; the interpenetration of sublime imagination, piercing pathos, and humour almost as moving as the pathos; the vastness of the convulsion both of nature and of human passion; the vagueness of the scene where the action takes place, and of the movements of the figures which cross this scene; the strange atmosphere, cold and dark, which strikes on us as we enter this scene, enfolding these figures and magnifying their dim outlines like a winter mist; the half-realised suggestions of vast universal powers working in the world of individual fates and passions,—all this interferes with dramatic clearness even when the play is read, and in the theatre not only refuses to reveal itself fully through the senses but seems to be almost in contradiction with their reports. But *King Lear*, as a whole, is imperfectly dramatic, and there is something in its very essence which is at war with the senses, and demands a purely imaginative realisation. It is therefore Shakespeare's greatest work, but it is not what Hazlitt called it, the best of his plays; and its comparative unpopularity is due, not merely to the extreme painfulness of the catastrophe, but in part to its dramatic defects, and in part to a failure in many readers to catch the peculiar effects to which I have referred,—a failure which is natural because the appeal is made not so much to dramatic perception as to a rarer and more strictly poetic kind of imagination. [. . .]

2

How is it, now, that this defective drama so overpowers us that we are either unconscious of its blemishes or regard them as almost irrelevant? As soon as we turn to this question we recognise, not merely that *King Lear* possesses purely dramatic qualities which far outweigh its defects, but that its greatness consists partly in imaginative effects of a wider kind. And, looking for the sources of these effects, we find among them some of those very things which appeared to us dramatically faulty or injurious. Thus, to take at once two of the simplest examples of this, that very vagueness in the sense of locality which we have just considered, and again that excess in the bulk of the material and the number of figures, events and movements, while they interfere with the clearness of vision, have at the same time a positive value for imagination. They give the feeling of vastness, the feeling not of a scene or particular place, but of a world; or, to speak more accurately, of a particular place which is also a world. This world is dim to us, partly from its immensity, and partly because it is filled with gloom; and in the gloom shapes approach and recede, whose half-seen faces and motions touch us with dread, horror, or the most painful pity,— sympathies and antipathies which we seem to be feeling not only for them but for the whole race.

Consider next the double action. It has certain strictly dramatic advantages, and may well have had its origin in purely dramatic considerations. To go no further, the secondary plot fills out a story which would by itself have been somewhat thin, and it provides a most effective contrast between its personages and those of the main plot, the tragic strength and stature of the latter being heightened by comparison with the slighter build of the former. But its chief value lies elsewhere, and is not merely dramatic. It lies in the fact—in Shakespeare without a parallel—that the sub-plot simply repeats the theme of the main story. Here, as there, we see an old man 'with a white beard.' He, like Lear, is affectionate, unsuspicious, foolish, and self-willed. He, too, wrongs deeply a child who loves him not less for the wrong. He, too, meets with monstrous ingratitude from the child whom he favours, and is tortured and driven to death. This repetition does not simply double the pain with which the tragedy is witnessed: it startles and terrifies by suggesting that the folly of Lear and the ingratitude of his daughters are no accidents or merely individual aberrations, but that in that dark cold world some fateful malignant influence is abroad, turning the hearts of the fathers against their children and of the children against their fathers, smiting the earth with a curse, so that the brother gives the brother to death and the father the son, blinding the eyes, maddening the brain, freezing the springs of pity, numbing all powers except the nerves of anguish and the dull lust of life.

Hence too, as well as from other sources, comes that feeling which haunts us in *King Lear,* as though we were witnessing something universal,—a conflict not so much of particular persons as of the powers of good and evil in the world. And the treatment of many of the characters confirms this feeling. Considered simply as psychological studies few of them, surely, are of the highest interest. Fine and subtle touches could not be absent from a work of Shakespeare's maturity; but, with the possible exception of Lear himself, no one of the characters strikes us as psychologically a *wonderful* creation, like Hamlet or Iago or even Macbeth; one or two seem even to be somewhat faint and thin. And, what is more significant, it is not quite natural to us to regard them from this point of view at all. Rather we observe a most unusual circumstance. If Lear, Gloster and Albany are set apart, the rest fall into two distinct groups, which are strongly, even violently, contrasted: Cordelia, Kent, Edgar, the Fool on one side, Goneril, Regan, Edmund, Cornwall, Oswald on the other. These characters are in various degrees individualised, most of them completely so; but still in each group there is a quality common to all the members, or one spirit breathing through them all. Here we have unselfish and devoted love, there hard self-seeking. On both sides, further, the common quality takes an extreme form; the love is incapable of being chilled by injury, the selfishness of being softened by pity; and, it may be added, this tendency to extremes is found again in the characters of Lear and Gloster, and is the main source of the accusations of improbability directed against their conduct at certain points. Hence the members of each group tend to appear, at least in part, as varieties of one species; the radical differences of the two species are emphasized in broad hard strokes; and the two are set in conflict, almost as if Shakespeare, like Empedocles,[1] were regarding Love and Hate as the two ultimate forces of the universe. [. . .]

---

[1] A Roman philosopher (c. 492–432 BCE) who argued that the history of the cosmos was governed by a cyclical alternation between love and strife.

Adaptations of King Lear

Poets, novelists, playwrights, and filmmakers have found in *King Lear* both inspiration and argument. Below is a chronological list of some works based on the play.

Nahum Tate, *The History of King Lear* (London, 1681). See pp. 220–228 earlier in this book.

Amelia Opie, *Father and Daughter* (London, 1806). In this sentimental version of a father and daughter separation and reconciliation, a daughter seduced by a cad breaks her father's heart. She is later reunited with her father when he is mad from grief, and she nurses him on his deathbed. He dies on the day he recovers his senses.

Charles Lamb and Mary Lamb, "King Lear" in *Tales from Shakespeare* (London, 1807). See pp. 239–245 earlier in this book.

William Moncrieff, *The Lear of Private Life* (London, 1828). This play is based on Opie's 1806 novel.

Honore de Balzac, *Le Père Goriot* (Paris, 1834). Goriot is an impoverished Parisian vermicelli merchant beggaring himself to keep his daughters in the style to which he has accustomed them.

Ivan Turgenev, *A King Lear of the Steppes* (St. Petersburg, 1870). A giant, having had a portent of his own death, gives his property to his two daughters, who eventually turn him out. In revenge, he tears down his house and is slain by the falling roof beam.

Emile Zola, *La Terre* (Paris, 1888). Zola translates the story to a harsh French countryside and a rapacious peasantry with a bloodlust for their land.

Gordon Bottomley, *King Lear's Wife* (London, 1915). Lear's wife is on her deathbed, Lear has a mistress, and Goneril avenges her mother.

Joseph Mankiewicz, director, *House of Strangers* (1949). Film. A banker rules over his three sons.

————, *Broken Lance* (1954). A cattle baron is the protagonist in this western film.

————, *The Big Show* (1961). This film portrays the death of a circus owner and its effect on his sons.

Robin Maugham, *Mister Lear* (1956). In this play (a comedy), Lear (Walter Crane) is a writer, his youngest daughter's fiancé has poorly reviewed his books, his two elder daughters remodel his house, and the Cordelia figure finishes by falling in love with her father's loyal secretary.

Grigori Kozintsev, *King Lear* (1970). In this stark black-and-white Russian film, Yuri Yarkvet plays Lear. The emphasis falls on the political conditions of the kingdom's decay.

Peter Brook, *King Lear* (1970). Paul Scofield plays a dictatorial Lear in Celtic Britain (filmed in black and white).

Edward Bond, *Lear* (1971). This play provides a dramatic study in the interrelation of violence and pity. The Cordelia figure (not Lear's daughter here) is raped and witnesses the butchering of her first husband, but she rebuilds a state as repressive as that which it replaces. The blind and aged Lear is shot.

Jonathan Miller, director, *BBC's King Lear* (1982). In a seventeenth-century setting, Michael Hordern plays Lear.

Michael Elliot, director, *King Lear* (1983). In this movie for Granada Television, Laurence Olivier plays Lear, and John Hurt plays the fool. The action is placed in Celtic Britain with a Stonehenge set.

Akira Kurosawa, director, *Ran* (1985). Set in feudal Japan, this film presents a variation of *King Lear* with sons instead of daughters.

Howard Barker, *Seven Lears* (1990). A play in which Lear has a mistress in his mother-in-law; both mother and grandmother are loathed by the daughters.

Jane Smiley, *A Thousand Acres* (1991). Goneril (called Ginny) is the narrator in this novel. Three daughters of a tyrannical Midwestern farmer struggle against the elements and the farming economy after their father cedes his land to them. The youngest daughter seeks to restore the land to her father, and the older two suffer variously from the effects of incest and repressed memory.

Richard Eyre, director, *King Lear* (1998, BBC2 film of the 1997 Royal National Theatre production). Ian Holm plays the title role.

Further Reading

Texts (Individual Volumes)

Foakes, R. A., ed. *King Lear*, ed. R. A. Foakes. Arden 3rd series. Walton-on-Thames: Thomas Nelson and Sons, 1997. (The scholarly edition with the highest ratio of notes to text; offers a conflated text that marks F and Q variants with superscript characters.)

Halio, Jay, ed. *The First Quarto of King Lear*. Cambridge: Cambridge University Press, 1994. (An edition based on the 1608 Quarto.)

King Lear. Cambridge: Cambridge University Press, 1994. (An edition based on the 1623 Folio.)

Orgel, Stephen, ed. *King Lear: The 1608 Quarto and 1623 Folio Texts*. New York: Pelican Shakespeare, 2000. (Two editions based on the 1623 Folio and the 1608 Quarto, in one volume.)

Warren, Michael, ed. *The Parallel King Lear, 1608–1623*. Berkeley: University of California Press, 1989. (The 1608 Quarto and 1623 Folio texts printed as facing-page texts, plus unedited facsimile photographs of Quarto 1, Quarto 2, amd Folio texts.)

Criticism
Textual Studies

Blayney, Peter, W. M. *The Texts of 'King Lear' and Their Origins*. Cambridge: Cambridge University Press, 1982.

Carson, Christie, and Jackie Bratton, eds. *The Cambridge King Lear CD-Rom: Texts and Performance Archive*. Cambridge: Cambridge University Press, 2000. (Q1, F1, a conflated text, and Tate's text, as well as an archive of illustrations and photos of three centuries of productions.)

Greg, W. W. *The Shakespeare First Folio: Its Bibliographical and Textual History.* Oxford: Clarendon Press, 1955.

Taylor, Gary, and Michael Warren, eds. *The Division of the Kingdoms.* Oxford: Clarendon, 1983.

Urkowicz, Stephen. *Shakespeare's Revision of King Lear.* Princeton: Princeton University Press, 1980.

Warren, Michael J. "Quarto and Folio *King Lear* and the Interpretation of Albany and Edgar." In *Shakespeare: Pattern of Excelling Nature,* ed. David Bevington and Jay Halio. Newark: University of Delaware Press, 1978; pp. 95–107.

———, "Shakespearean Tragedy Printed and Performed." In *The Cambridge Companion to Shakespearean Tragedy,* ed. Claire McEachern. Cambridge: Cambridge University Press, 2003; pp. 69–85.

Sources and Backgrounds

Brownlow, F. W. *Shakespeare, Harsnett, and the Devils of Denham.* Newark: University of Delaware Press, 1993.

Bullough, Geoffrey. *Narrative and Dramatic Sources of Shakespeare,* vol. 7. London: Routledge and Kegan Paul, 1973.

Danby, John F. *Shakespeare's Doctrine of Nature: A Study of King Lear.* London: Faber and Faber, 1949.

Greenblatt, Stephen. "Shakespeare and the Exorcists." In *Shakespeare and the Question of Theory,* ed. Patricia Parker and Geoffrey Hartmann. London: Methuen, 1985; pp. 163–187.

Murphy, John L. *Darkness and Devils: Exorcism and "King Lear."* Athens, OH: Ohio University Press, 1984.

Welsford, Enid. *The Fool: His Social and Literary History.* London: Faber and Faber, 1935.

Readings

Adelman, Janet. *Suffocating Mothers: Fantasies of Maternal Origin in Shakespeare's Plays, 'Hamlet' to 'The Tempest.'* London: Routledge, 1992.

Alpers, Paul J. "*King Lear* and the Theory of the Sight Pattern." In *A Defense of Reading: A Reader's Approach to Literary Criticism,* ed. Reuben A. Brower and Richard Poirier. New York: E.P. Dutton, 1962.

Booth, Stephen. *King Lear, Macbeth, Indefinition and Tragedy.* New Haven: Yale University Press, 1983.

Bradley, A. C. *Shakespearean Tragedy.* London: Macmillan, 1904.

Cavell, Stanley. *Disowning Knowledge in Six Plays of Shakespeare.* Cambridge: Cambridge University Press, 1987.

Dollimore, Jonathan. *Radical Tragedy: Religion, Ideology and Power in the Drama of Shakespeare and His Contemporaries.* Chicago: University of Chicago Press, 1984.

Elton, William. *King Lear and The Gods.* San Marino, CA: Huntington Library Press, 1966.

Empson, William. "The Praise of Folly" and "Fool in Lear." Both in *The Structure of Complex Words.* London: Chatto and Windus, 1951; pp. 105–157. (3rd edition, 1977.)

Greenblatt, Stephen. "The Cultivation of Anxiety: *King Lear* and His Heirs." *Raritan* 2 (1982): 92–114. Reprinted in *Learning to Curse: Essays on Early Modern Culture* (London: Routledge, 1990): 80–99.

———. "Shakespeare and the Exorcists." In *Shakespearean Representations: The Circulation of Social Energy in Renaissance England.* Berkeley: University of California Press, 1988; pp. 94–128.

Heilman, Robert Bechtold. *This Great Stage: Image and Structure in King Lear.* Baton Rouge: Louisiana State University Press, 1948.

Heinemann, Margot. "Demystifying the Mystery of State: *King Lear* and the World Upside Down." *Shakespeare Survey* 44 (1992): 75–84.

Kahn, Coppelia. "The Absent Mother in *King Lear*." In *Rewriting the Renaissance, The Discourses of Sexual Difference in Early Modern Europe,* ed. Margaret W. Ferguson, Maureen Quilligan, and Nancy J. Vickers. Chicago: University of Chicago Press, 1986; pp. 33–49.

McKluskie, Kathleen. "The Patriarchal Bard: Feminist Criticism and Shakespeare: *King Lear* and *Measure for Measure*." In *Political Shakespeare: Essays in Cultural Materialism,* ed. Jonathan Dollimore and Alan Sinfield. Manchester: Manchester University Press, 1985; pp. 88–108.

Patterson, Annabel. *Censorship and Interpretation: The Conditions of Writing and Reading in Early Modern England.* Madison: University of Wisconsin Press, 1984.

Strier, Richard. "Faithful Servants: Shakespeare's Praise of Disobedience." In *The Historical Renaissance: New Essays on Tudor and Stuart Literature and Culture*, ed. Heather Dubrow and Richard Strier. Chicago: University of Chicago Press, 1988; pp. 104–133.

Wittreich, Joseph. *Image of That Horror: History, Prophecy, and the Apocalypse in "King Lear."* San Marino, CA: Huntington Library, 1984.

Zitner, Sheldon P. *"King Lear* and Its Language." In *Some Facets of King Lear: Essays in Prismatic Criticism*, ed. Rosalie Colie. Toronto: University of Toronto Press, 1974; pp. 3–22.

Performance and Reception Histories

Bratton, J. S. "The Lear of Private Life: Interpretations of *King Lear* in the Nineteenth Century." In *Shakespeare and the Victorian Stage*, ed. Richard Foulkes. Cambridge: Cambridge University Press, 1986; pp. 124–137.

Brooke, Nicholas. *Shakespeare: King Lear*. Great Neck, NY: Barrons, 1963.

Cox, Brian. *The Lear Diaries: The Story of the Royal National Theatre's Production of Shakespeare's "Richard III" and "King Lear."* London: Methuen, 1992.

Foakes, R. A. *"Hamlet" versus "Lear": Cultural Politics and Shakespeare's Art*. Cambridge: Cambridge University Press, 1993.

Holland, Peter, ed. "King Lear." *Shakespeare Studies* 55 (2002). (The entire volume of this periodical is devoted to the play.)

Leggatt, Alexander. *Shakespeare in Performance: 'King Lear.'* Manchester: Manchester University Press, 1991.

Mack, Maynard. *King Lear in Our Time*. Berkeley: University of California Press, 1965.

Rosenberg, Marvin. *The Masks of King Lear*. London: Associated University Presses, 1972.

Stone, G. Winchester, Jr. "Garrick's Production of *King Lear*: A Study of the Temper of the Eighteenth Century Mind." *Studies in Philology* 45 (1948): 89–103.